Oliver Karras

Supporting Requirements Communication for Shared Understanding by Applying Vision Videos in Requirements Engineering

Logos Verlag Berlin

λογος

Bibliografische Information der Deutschen Nationalbibliothek

Die Deutsche Nationalbibliothek verzeichnet diese Publikation in der
Deutschen Nationalbibliografie; detaillierte bibliografische Daten sind
im Internet über http://dnb.d-nb.de abrufbar.

ISBN 978-3-8325-5297-8

Logos Verlag Berlin GmbH
Georg-Knorr-Str. 4, Geb. 10,
D-12681 Berlin
Germany

Tel.:   +49 (0)30 / 42 85 10 90
Fax: +49 (0)30 / 42 85 10 92
http://www.logos-verlag.de

Supporting Requirements Communication for Shared Understanding by Applying Vision Videos in Requirements Engineering

Von der Fakultät für Elektrotechnik und Informatik
der Gottfried Wilhelm Leibniz Universität Hannover
zur Erlangung des akademischen Grades

Doktor rerum naturalium

(abgekürzt: Dr. rer. nat.)

genehmigte Dissertation

von Herrn
Oliver Karras, M. Sc.
geboren am 27.10.1987
in Celle, Deutschland

2021

1. Referent: Prof. Dr. Kurt Schneider
2. Referent: Prof. Dr. Martin Glinz
3. Referent: Prof. Dr. Michael Rohs

Tag der Promotion: 03. März 2021

Even if there are moments when you doubt yourself,
know that there are always people who believe in you.

For my family.

Abstract

[Context.] Requirements engineering is the starting point of every software development project with the overall goal of establishing the vision of the system in its relevant context. The establishment of the vision requires that all parties involved disclose, discuss, and align their mental models of the system by explicitly communicating their objectives, ideas, needs, and expectations. This process serves to develop and negotiate shared understanding and is called requirements communication. Stakeholders and the development team can communicate more effectively if they use practices that enable synchronous, proximate, and proportionate interaction for proactive information exchange. However, requirements engineering practices mainly rely on the use of written documentation, including textual and pictorial representations. This documentation option is in conflict with the required type of interaction among the parties involved since it reinforces asynchronous and distant communication that is often disproportionate to develop and negotiate shared understanding. Although videos are known as a documentation option for rich and effective communication, software professionals neglect this medium as a documentation option for effective requirements communication. Videos that are used to support requirements communication for shared understanding are called vision videos. [Objective.] In the context of this thesis, I analyze the application of videos as a documentation option in requirements engineering for integrating them into requirements engineering practices to support effective requirements communication for shared understanding. [Method & Results.] I apply the technology transfer process to develop a candidate solution for the objective of this thesis. First, I use a survey to investigate why software professionals neglect videos as a documentation option. The insights of this survey substantiate three main issues that impede the production and use of videos as a communication mechanism in requirements engineering by software professionals: (1) An alleged high effort, (2) a lack of knowledge and skills, and (3) a lack of videos with sufficient quality. Based on the issues found, I develop the candidate solution consisting of the two concepts *video as a by-product* and *awareness and guidance*. The concept *video as a by-product* supports the revision of requirements engineering practices by integrating video production and use to obtain videos as a by-product with low effort and in sufficient quality. The concept *awareness and guidance* guides software professionals when they produce and use videos by creating awareness regarding video quality and providing guidance with a condensed guideline for video production and use. I first validate each concept in academia to ensure the fundamental relevance of the candidate solution before validating the entire candidate solution using a case study in the industry. [Conclusion.] The findings in academia and industry indicate that the developed candidate solution helps software professionals to obtain the required awareness, knowledge, and ability to produce and use vision videos at moderate costs and with sufficient quality. These vision videos are suitable for their intended purpose of supporting requirements communication for shared understanding. I am confident that the current version of the candidate solution is a viable and stable basis for future extensions and refinements to extend the application of videos to support effective requirements communication for shared understanding in requirements engineering and beyond.

Keywords: Requirements communication, shared understanding, vision video, video production, by-product, quality model for videos, video production guideline

Zusammenfassung

[**Kontext.**] Requirements Engineering ist der Ausgangspunkt jedes Softwareentwicklungsprojekts mit dem übergeordneten Ziel, die Vision des Systems in seinem relevanten Kontext zu etablieren. Die Etablierung der Vision erfordert, dass alle beteiligten Parteien ihre mentalen Modelle des Systems offenlegen, diskutieren und aufeinander abstimmen, indem sie ihre Ziele, Ideen, Bedürfnisse und Erwartungen explizit kommunizieren. Dieser Prozess dient der Entwicklung und Aushandlung eines gemeinsamen Verständnisses und wird als Anforderungskommunikation bezeichnet. Stakeholder und das Entwicklungsteam können effektiver kommunizieren, wenn sie Praktiken anwenden, die eine synchrone, unmittelbare und angemessene Interaktion für einen proaktiven Informationsaustausch ermöglichen. Allerdings beruhen die Requirements Engineering Praktiken hauptsächlich auf der Verwendung schriftlicher Dokumentation, einschließlich textueller und bildlicher Darstellungen. Diese Dokumentationsoption steht im Konflikt mit der geforderten Art der Interaktion zwischen den beteiligten Parteien, da sie eine asynchrone und distanzierte Kommunikation verstärkt, die oft unverhältnismäßig ist, um ein gemeinsames Verständnis zu entwickeln und auszuhandeln. Obwohl Videos als eine Dokumentationsoption für eine reichhaltige und effektive Kommunikation bekannt sind, vernachlässigen Software-Fachleute dieses Medium als Dokumentationsoption für eine effektive Anforderungskommunikation. Videos, die zur Unterstützung der Anforderungskommunikation für das gemeinsame Verständnis eingesetzt werden, werden als Vision Videos bezeichnet. [**Ziel.**] Im Rahmen dieser Arbeit analysiere ich die Anwendung von Videos als Dokumentationsoption im Requirements Engineering, um sie in Requirements Engineering Praktiken zu integrieren und eine effektive Anforderungskommunikation für gemeinsames Verständnis zu unterstützen. [**Methode & Ergebnisse.**] Ich wende den Technologietransferprozess an, um einen Lösungskandidaten für das Ziel dieser Arbeit zu entwickeln. Zunächst untersuche ich anhand einer Umfrage, warum Software-Fachleute Videos als Dokumentationsoption vernachlässigen. Die Erkenntnisse dieser Umfrage untermauern drei Hauptprobleme, die die Produktion und Verwendung von Videos als Kommunikationsmechanismus im Requirements Engineering durch Software-Fachleute behindern: (1) Ein angeblich hoher Aufwand, (2) ein Mangel an Wissen und Fähigkeiten und (3) ein Mangel an Videos mit ausreichender Qualität. Basierend auf den gefundenen Problemen entwickle ich die Kandidatenlösung, die aus den beiden Konzepten *Video als Nebenprodukt* und *Bewusstsein und Anleitung* besteht. Das Konzept *Video als Nebenprodukt* unterstützt die Überarbeitung von Requirements Engineering Praktiken, indem es die Videoproduktion und -nutzung integriert, um mit geringem Aufwand und in ausreichender Qualität Videos als Nebenprodukt zu erhalten. Das Konzept *Bewusstsein und Anleitung* leitet Software-Fachleute bei der Produktion und Nutzung von Videos an, indem es ein Bewusstsein für die Videoqualität schafft und mit einer komprimierten Richtlinie für die Videoproduktion und -nutzung Anleitung gibt. Ich validiere zunächst jedes Konzept im akademischen Bereich, um die grundlegende Relevanz der Kandidatenlösung sicherzustellen, bevor ich die gesamte Kandidatenlösung anhand einer Fallstudie in der Industrie validiere. [**Fazit.**] Die Ergebnisse aus Wissenschaft und Industrie deuten darauf hin, dass die entwickelte Kandidatenlösung Software-Fachleuten hilft, das erforderliche Bewusstsein, Wissen und die Fähigkeit zu erlangen, Vision Videos zu moderaten Kosten und in ausreichender Qualität zu produzieren und zu verwenden. Diese Vision Videos eignen sich für ihren beabsichtigten

Zweck, die Anforderungskommunikation für ein gemeinsames Verständnis zu unterstützen. Ich bin zuversichtlich, dass die aktuelle Version der Kandidatenlösung eine tragfähige und stabile Basis für zukünftige Erweiterungen und Verfeinerungen ist, um die Anwendung von Videos zur Unterstützung einer effektiven Anforderungskommunikation für ein gemeinsames Verständnis im Requirements Engineering und darüber hinaus auszubauen.

Keywords: Anforderungskommunikation, gemeinsames Verständnis, Vision Video, Videoproduktion, Nebenprodukt, Qualitätsmodell für Videos, Richtlinie zur Videoproduktion

Contents

List of Figures

List of Tables

List of Definitions

1

Introduction

Requirements engineering (RE) is a systematic and disciplined approach to specify and manage requirements to deliver a system that satisfies the stakeholders' needs and thus provides value [196]. Besides a process- and value-oriented facet, requirements engineering focuses on the stakeholders with their needs [58,91]. One central task of requirements engineering is to understand, document, and convey these needs among all parties involved [41,196]. These needs are the basis for system development [208]. One primary measure for project success and the quality of a software-based system is the degree to which the system satisfies the stated and implied needs of its various stakeholders [112,182].

The process of coordinating and communicating the needs of stakeholders so that a development team can implement a solution that the stakeholders accept is called *requirements communication*[1] [80]. Requirements communication involves developing and negotiating a *shared understanding*[2] of the goals, plans, status, and context of a project among all project partners [11,86]. Shared understanding requires all parties involved to disclose, discuss, and align their *mental models*[3] of the future system, i.e., their *visions*[4], by explicitly stating their objectives, ideas, needs, and expectations [11,58]. A common vision can accelerate software development and increase the likelihood of developing a successful system [92,161]. *"Only when they all [stakeholders and development team] share a common vision, scope, and desired outcome is the project likely to be successful"* [38, p. 1]. Therefore, shared understanding is one of the most important objectives in requirements engineering [84]. Shared understanding enables the stakeholders and the development team to assess and agree on what the relevant requirements are [58,85] and what the meaning of these requirements is regarding the future system [82,202].

---

[1]For the definition of the term "requirements communication" used in this thesis, see section 2.1.3, Definition 2.5.
[2]For the definition of the term "shared understanding" used in this thesis, see section 2.2.1, Definition 2.6.
[3]For the definition of the term "mental model" used in this thesis, see section 2.2.1, Definition 2.7.
[4]For the definition of the term "vision" used in this thesis, see section 2.2.3, Definition 2.10.

Effective requirements communication is a central problem of requirements engineering [58, 82, 189]. The effective coordination and communication of stakeholders' needs is difficult due to (1) an overwhelming amount of information to parse, (2) the need for tacit, complex, and specialized knowledge, and (3) the exploratory and creative nature of software projects [11]. In requirements engineering activities such as elicitation and validation effective requirements communication cannot be reliably achieved due to the three previously mentioned reasons [82, 210, 259]. As a consequence, the establishment of a common vision is a challenging task in requirements engineering [25, 60, 193], regardless of whether stakeholders meet in person [154, 184] or not [8,81]. In such situations, effective requirements communication depends on the use of suitable communication mechanisms [11, 92, 154]. Stakeholders and the development team can achieve a shared understanding more easily if they use practices for a proactive information exchange which support synchronous, proximate, and proportionate interaction [11, 210].

Requirements engineering practices rely mainly on the use of written specifications, which may also include images, for communication [124, 248]. However, this documentation option often conflicts with the required type of interaction since textual documentation is an asynchronous, distant, and disproportionate communication mechanism [11]. This conflict is discussed in more detail below to clarify the considered problem statement of this thesis.

1.1 Problem Statement

Although written specifications are suggested by standards, e.g., ISO/IEC/IEEE 29148:2011 [113], their use for communication is cumbersome [139]. Textual and pictorial representations, including digital versions, have low communication richness and effectiveness [8]. Fricker and Glinz [81] investigated the practice of handing over a written specification to a development team. Their results show that the supposedly simple handover insufficiently supports the rich knowledge transfer which is necessary to develop an acceptable system [81]. The readers of the specification were not able to build a consistent mental model of the system. Thus, the readers did not understand the impact of the requirements on the design well enough to assess the suitability of tentative designs [81].

Textual artifacts attempt to communicate and establish a body of knowledge that specifies the important information of which all stakeholders and the development team need to be aware of and whose understanding all of them need to share [11]. However, textual documentation cannot fully meet these goals due to different issues [11]. First, the sender of a document often tacitly equates the handover with the fact that the recipient read and understood the corresponding content. Different studies [157, 220] showed that this assumption is not correct. Recipients often do not read the obtained documents completely since they perceive the documents as too complex, untrustworthy, out of date, and poorly written [79, 157]. Second, documents are written primarily in natural language [84, 172]. This notation impedes effective communication due to its inherent restrictions [5], such as ambiguity [208, 229] and abstraction [32, 75, 132]. These restrictions increase the likelihood of undetected misunderstandings that limit shared understanding [75, 92, 154]. Third, a document cannot capture all necessary information that is relevant to the stakeholders and the development team [11]. A lot of relevant information is tacit and thus requires other communication mechanisms [85, 210, 219].

In consideration of these issues, text-based communication can be subject to a variety of noises that impede the achievement of shared understanding [224]. The communication partners may counteract these noises by conferring directly with each other [208, 210]. However, the use of textual artifacts for requirements communication leads to an increased temporal and spatial distance between the communication partners [8, 11]. Thus, this documentation option reinforces an asynchronous and distant communication which is often disproportionate to develop and negotiate shared understanding [11]. Several studies [2, 5, 48, 84, 157] investigated requirements engineering practices in terms of documentation and communication over the years. All of them indicated a still-existing need for improving documentation for requirements communication which exceeds pictorial representations in textual artifacts. In accordance with each other, the corresponding researchers suggested supplementing specifications, for example with multimedia documentation such as videos, to turn them into an effective means of communication [2, 5, 48]. They concluded the necessity to focus on power and simplicity to increase the relevance of documentation for effective requirements communication [84, 157].

At first, a video is just another documentation option and is therefore associated with similar issues as textual documentation. However, videos offer a better opportunity to achieve effective requirements communication since videos can transfer information more richly and effectively [8, 124]. In contrast to textual artifacts, a video is more concrete due to the required visualization of its content [32, 136, 218, 246]. As a consequence, key concepts such as a vision can be exemplified by videos to detect misunderstanding whose resolving increases the likelihood of shared understanding systematically and significantly [31, 92]. Thus, videos help to bridge the gap between abstraction and detail [31, 165]. Furthermore, a video combines the auditory and visual channel for information transfer. This combination leads to more intensive information processing which, in turn, supports a better understanding of the presented content for a single person as well as a group [208, 238]. While a textual artifact is read by each recipient individually, a video can be viewed together, allowing all viewers to perceive the same image and sound at the same time. This opportunity can facilitate to communicate more closely in terms of time and space. In consideration of power and simplicity, the use of videos may be more proportionate to develop and negotiate a shared understanding. Thus, the use of videos might enable the correspondingly required type of synchronous, proximate, and proportionate interaction for proactive information exchange.

3

Videos are a promising communication mechanism for shared understanding since they require that mental models, i.e., visions of a system, are visualized [259]. The visualization discloses the tacit representation of a future system in the minds of parties involved by externalizing the video producer's mental model and thus making it tangible [92, 158, 238, 246]. A video following this idea is hereinafter referred to as *vision video*[5] [126, 139]. The use of videos in requirements engineering has been discussed in recent years and their contributions have been found to have interesting potential [86, 130, 136, 218]. However, videos are not an established documentation option in requirements engineering [84, 136]. As a consequence, videos are neglected as a means of documentation for effective requirements communication among stakeholders and a development team [124, 136]. In summary, the following problem statement arises which I consider in this thesis:

Problem Statement

While textual artifacts reinforce asynchronous, distant, and disproportionate communication, videos offer a better opportunity for synchronous, close, and proportionate communication. Videos may enable the proactive development and negotiation of shared understanding that is necessary for effective requirements communication.

Despite the known benefits of videos, this medium is neglected as a documentation option for effective requirements communication among stakeholders and a development team. It is necessary to research the issues that prevent the production and use of videos in requirements engineering. When these issues are known, concepts can be developed that overcome them and thus use the potential of videos in requirements engineering.

1.2   Research Objective

Based on the problem statement, this thesis pursues the Research Goal 1.1 to investigate the application of videos as a documentation option for effective requirements communication. I apply the goal definition template [18] to ensure that the scope of this thesis is well-defined.

Research Goal 1.1

Analyze the application of videos as a documentation option
for the purpose of integrating videos into requirements engineering practices
with respect to support effective requirements communication
from the point of view of this researcher
in the context of requirements engineers who coordinate and communicate the stakeholders' needs among stakeholders and a development team to proactively develop and negotiate shared understanding by aligning their mental models of a future system.

---

[5]For the definition of the term "vision video" used in this thesis, see section 2.3, Definition 2.11.

This thesis aims at understanding the reasons that prevent the production and use of videos for requirements communication to develop concepts that overcome these issues to integrate videos into requirements engineering practices. Based on the Research Goal 1.1, I ask the following two research questions.

Research Question 1.1

> *Why are videos neglected as a documentation option for coordinating and communicating stakeholders' needs among stakeholders and a development team in requirements engineering?*

As a first step for integrating videos as a documentation option for communication into requirements engineering practices, it is necessary to understand the reasons why videos are neglected as a communication mechanism. Research Question 1.1 addresses this topic to explain the issues that impede the use of videos in requirements engineering.

Research Question 1.2

> *How can videos be integrated into requirements engineering practices to support the coordination and communication of stakeholders' needs among stakeholders and a development team?*

The answer to Research Question 1.1 provides the basis for answering Research Question 1.2 which focuses on solving the identified issues for using videos in requirements engineering. Based on the insights obtained, concepts for a candidate solution can be developed that overcome these issues so that videos can be more easily integrated into requirements engineering practices to support effective requirements communication.

1.3 Scientific Approach

This section explains the selected scientific approach of this thesis to find answers to the research questions to reach the Research Goal 1.1. For a better understanding of the selected scientific approach, it is important to be explicit about the philosophical stance of this thesis. According to Easterbrook et al.,"*the stance you adopt affects which methods you believe lead to acceptable evidence in response to your research question(s)*" [69, p. 290]. Understanding the adopted stance helps to understand the reasons for selecting the scientific approach.

This thesis is based on the assumption of *postpositivism* and *pragmatism* [62]. Knowledge results from the interpretation of actual, sensible, and verifiable findings (*postpositivism*). These findings originate from "*careful observation and measurement of the objective reality that exists 'out there' in the world*" [62, p. 7], i.e., from empirical science. However, knowledge must also be judged by how useful it is for solving practical problems (*pragmatism*) [69]. Therefore, *pragmatism* values practical knowledge over abstract knowledge which means adopting an engineering approach to research [69]. Under the assumption of *postpositivism* and *pragmatism*, empirical science is part of a knowledge transfer between academia and industry [257]. As Wohlin et al. stated: *"Software engineering is an applied research area, and hence to perform research on industrially relevant problems is expected. It is in many cases insufficient to just do academic research on, for example, requirements engineering [...]"* [257, p. 30].

Following the statement of Wohlin et al. [257], I decided to apply an empirically-based technology transfer model as the scientific approach for this thesis. The technology transfer process demands the transfer of knowledge acquired in academia to the industry as part of the research process [93]. An empirically-based technology transfer model is one possible instantiation of the technology transfer process. Such a model focuses on the use of empirical methods to develop a candidate solution to an industrial problem. This candidate solution must be initially validated in academia before it is transferred to the industry. Figure 1.1 presents the technology transfer model applied in this thesis which consists of the following six steps:

1. **Problem**: Identification of a problem in the industry
2. **Problem statement**: Formulation of the identified problem as a problem statement, including the specification of research questions
3. **Study of practice and science**: Investigation of practice and science regarding the problem statement
4. **Candidate solution**: Development of a solution for the considered problem statement
5. **Validation in academia**: Initial validation of the candidate solution to ensure its fundamental relevance, validity, and soundness before it is presented to the industry
6. **Validation in industry**: Validation of the candidate solution with industry representatives in a real project context

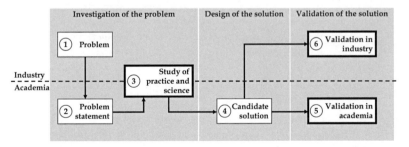

Figure 1.1: Scientific approach: Empirically-based technology transfer model

Based on the previously described central problem of effective requirements communication in requirements engineering (Figure 1.1, (1)), I formulated the problem statement (see section 1.1; Figure 1.1, ②) and research questions (see section 1.2). The study of practice and science (Figure 1.1, ③) investigates the problem statement more closely to find an answer to the Research Question 1.1. Based on the insights obtained, I develop concepts for a candidate solution to integrate videos as a documentation option for requirements communication into requirements engineering practices and thus answer Research Question 1.2 (Figure 1.1, ④). This candidate solution is first validated in academia (Figure 1.1, ⑤) before it is validated in the industry (Figure 1.1, ⑥). In particular, the steps ③, ⑤, and ⑥ (bold-framed) require the selection of suitable empirical methods to examine the problem statement more closely and to validate the developed candidate solution. This selection of suitable methods for the individual steps is done in the respective following chapters.

1.4   Contribution of the Thesis

Based on the scientific approach, this thesis provides a candidate solution consisting of the two concepts *video as a by-product* and *awareness and guidance*. These two concepts address the three main issues for the production and use of videos as a communication mechanism in requirements engineering, that emerged from the study of practice and science.

The three main issues found can be summarized as follows: (1) an alleged high effort for video production and use, (2) a lack of knowledge and skills of software professionals to produce and use videos, and (3) a lack of videos with sufficient quality. The concept *video as a by-product* provides an approach to revise requirements engineering practices for producing and using videos as a by-product at low effort (issue (1)) and with sufficient quality (issue (3)). The concept *awareness and guidance* provides a quality model for videos and a condensed guideline for video production and use to impart software professionals with the knowledge and skills to produce and use videos (issue (2)) with sufficient quality (issue (3)).

This candidate solution is designed to counteract unsafe decisions and actions of software professionals in the production and use of videos as a communication mechanism to support effective requirements communication for shared understanding. Each concept was validated with experiments in academia before the entire candidate solution was transferred to the industry for validation by means of a case study. This thesis offers the following three contributions:

(1) An identification of three main issues why videos are neglected as a documentation option in requirements engineering

(2) An approach to revise requirements engineering practice for producing and using videos as a by-product at moderate cost and sufficient quality

(3) An approach to create awareness regarding video quality and provide guidance of software professionals for producing and using videos at moderate cost and sufficient quality

1.5 Structure of the Thesis

Chapter 2 presents the background of this thesis. The main part of this thesis is structured along the steps of the applied technology transfer model (see Figure 1.2). In chapter 3, I discuss related work that deals with the *support of communication for shared understanding* and the *application of vision videos in requirements engineering*. Chapter 4 presents a survey on *videos as a documentation option in requirements engineering* to investigate the issues that prevent the use videos as a communication mechanism in requirements engineering. Based on the issues found, I develop the candidate solution consisting of the two concepts *video as a by-product* and *awareness and guidance*. In chapter 5, I provide an overview of the candidate solution and the two concepts. Chapter 6 describes the details of the concept *video as a by-product* that offers an approach to revise requirements engineering practice for producing and using videos as a by-product. This approach is applied to the two practices *facilitated meetings* and *prototyping* each of which is validated with experiments in academia. In chapter 7, I present the details of the concept *awareness and guidance*. This concept provides two artifacts to support software professionals when producing and using video: A *quality model for videos* to create awareness regarding video quality and a *condensed guideline for video production and use* to provide guidance. I adapt both artifacts to vision videos due to the specific context of this thesis. While the quality model is validated with an experiment in academia, the guideline is validated with a content validation study. Chapter 8 presents the case study that validates the entire candidate solution in a real project context in the industry. In chapter 9, I conclude this thesis, discuss its limitations, and propose starting points for future work.

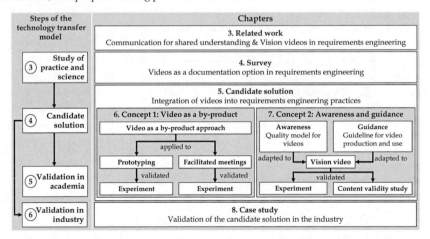

Figure 1.2: Structure of the thesis along the steps of the applied technology transfer model

2

Background

This thesis addresses the integration of videos into requirements engineering practices to support requirements communication for shared understanding. The context of this thesis is defined by the discipline requirements engineering, in particular, the requirements analysis, with its specific objectives. It is also necessary to take a closer look at the application of videos as a documentation option including their production and quality assessment. This chapter provides the necessary information to facilitate the understanding of this thesis.

2.1 Requirements Engineering

There are several definitions, frameworks, and reference models that give an overview of requirements engineering [7,30,66,91,195,196,251]. Although all of them differ slightly from each other, they share the same main goals and activities. This thesis uses the following definition of *requirements engineering* according to Glinz [91], which is also the official definition of the *International Requirements Engineering Board* (IREB).

Definition 2.1 (*Requirements engineering (RE); according to Glinz [91, p. 18]*)

> *Requirements engineering is a systematic and disciplined approach to the specification and management of requirements with the following goals:*
>
> (1) *Knowing the relevant requirements, achieving a consensus among the stakeholders about these requirements, documenting them according to given standards, and managing them systematically,*
>
> (2) *Understanding and documenting the stakeholders' desires and needs;*
>
> (3) *Specifying and managing requirements to minimize the risk of delivering a system that does not meet the stakeholders' desires and needs.*

This definition introduces the two main areas of requirements engineering which are called *requirements analysis* and *requirements management*. These areas include specific *activities* (see Definition 2.2) that focus on particular *practices* (see Definition 2.3) which are implemented through concrete *techniques* (see Definition 2.4).

Definition 2.2 *(Activity; based on Dörr et al. [66, p. 7])*

An activity is the overall classification of a single phase of a typical requirements engineering process.

Definition 2.3 *(Practice; based on Dörr et al. [66, p. 7])*

A practice is an abstract task that in most contexts leads to a qualitative improvement of the requirements engineering process.

Definition 2.4 *(Technique; based on Dörr et al. [66, p. 8])*

A technique is a concrete method that is directly applicable to implement a practice.

Figure 2.1 presents the reference model of Börger et al. [30] which provides an overview of requirements engineering with its two main areas and their respective activities. Below, the activities are briefly described in terms of their practices and goals. The subsequent explanations refer to Börger et al. [30] supplemented by information from Alexander and Stevens [7], Nuseibeh and Easterbrook [182], Pohl [195], Rupp et al. [208], as well as Wiegers and Beatty [251].

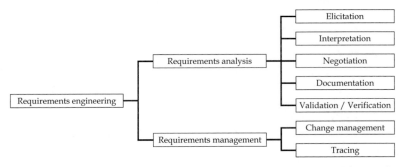

Figure 2.1: Reference model of requirements engineering; based on Börger et al. [30, p. 30]

2.1.1 Requirements Analysis

Requirements analysis is subdivided into elicitation, interpretation, negotiation, validation / verification, and documentation. These five activities encompass all practices involved with exploring, evaluating, documenting, and confirming the requirements for a system.

Elicitation. Elicitation serves to acquire relevant information from the stakeholders such as their needs, goals, tasks, and environments. Further sources such as documents or legacy systems are also identified since they may contribute important information for the future system. The requirements engineer needs to collaborate closely with the stakeholders to obtain and understand this information. Based on the acquired understanding, the requirements engineer defines the boundary of the system. This boundary helps the requirements engineer to elicit the stakeholders' functionality needs and quality expectations that belong to the relevant system context. These needs and expectations are the so-called raw requirements which are initially formulated without considering any quality criteria for requirements.

Interpretation. Interpretation serves to achieve a deeper and more precise understanding of each raw requirement. For this purpose, the elicited information and raw requirements are analyzed to structure and classify them according to, i.a., task goals, functional requirements, quality expectations, business rules, suggested solutions, and other information. Based on the classification, the raw requirements are refined and concretized into well-formulated requirements according to the quality criteria for requirements by decomposing them into a suitable level of detail. Potential gaps, ambiguities, conflicts, and dependencies are identified which need to be clarified in collaboration with the stakeholders.

Negotiation. Negotiation serves to resolve contradictions, conflicts, and dependencies as well as to prioritize the formulated requirements. In close collaboration, the requirements engineer and the stakeholders solve the inconsistencies by finding a compromise that all stakeholders agree with.

Documentation. Documentation serves to represent and store the gathered requirements knowledge in a persistent and well-organized manner. For this purpose, the stakeholders' needs are translated into written requirements and diagrams suitable for comprehension, review, and use by their intended readers, i.a., the development team.

Validation / Verification. Validation and verification serve the substantive and formal examination of the elicited and elaborated requirements. The validation examines whether the requirements coincide with the stakeholders' needs. It is important to ensure that the elaborated requirements enable the development team to implement a solution that satisfies the stakeholders' needs. In contrast, the verification examines whether the elaborated requirements coincide with the elicited raw requirements and related information.

2.1.2 Requirements Management

Requirements management is subdivided into change management and tracing. The two activities encompass the practices for managing elaborated requirements and related information to support change requests and ensure their traceability.

Change Management. Change management serves to anticipate and accommodate the changes of requirements that can always occur to minimize their disruptive impact on a project. Based on an impact analysis, a proposed change request is systematically handled by managing, documenting, and authorizing it. In case of an authorized change, the resulting version of a requirement is maintained and incorporated into the project in a controlled manner.

Tracing. Tracing serves to track connections and dependencies between requirements and assumptions as well as decisions. The goal of tracing is a continuous capture and assignment of this information to document the overall context of a project. Thus, each party involved can trace the history of any relevant information.

This thesis focuses on the requirements analysis with its activities and practices. Before requirements management can happen, it is necessary to understand and document the stakeholders' needs to elicit and elaborate requirements [13, 182]. For this reason, I selected the definition of *requirements engineering* according to Glinz [91] (see Definition 2.1) due to its strong focus on the stakeholders' needs and their meaning for the project success.

2.1.3 Requirements Communication

Any action in the development process requires a sufficient understanding of the stakeholders' needs by all project partners [95, 251]. Before design and implementation, the needs must be coordinated and communicated among all parties involved. This process of conveying needs is referred to as *requirements communication* that is defined as follows:

Definition 2.5 (*Requirements communication; based on Fricker [80]*)

> *Requirements communication is the process of conveying needs from a given customer to a given supplier that enables the supplier to implement a solution that is accepted by the customer.*

In case of software development projects, the *customer* is represented by a set of stakeholders and the *supplier* by the development team [86]. Effective requirements communication includes a shared understanding of the stakeholders' needs among the stakeholders and the development team [86]. Achieving shared understanding minimizes two major risks for project success: (1) The risk of delivering a system that does not meet the stakeholders' needs (cf. Definition 2.1, Goal (3)), and (2) the risk of doing excessive unplanned rework [251]. Therefore, shared understanding is one of the most important requirements engineering objectives [84].

2.2 Requirements Engineering Objectives

In one of the largest requirements engineering surveys, Fricker et al. [84] investigated which objectives are pursued in requirements engineering. According to their results, the three most important requirements engineering objectives are *shared understanding*, good *specification quality*, and a clear *scope*. These three objectives are central to this thesis since they are closely related to each other as well as the need for effective requirements communication.

2.2.1 Shared Understanding

Effective requirements communication involves developing and negotiating a shared understanding of the goals, plans, status, and context of a development project among all project partners [11, 80]. *Shared understanding* is defined as follows:

Definition 2.6 (*Shared understanding; based on Easterbrook [68, p. 193]*)

Two or more persons have a shared understanding of a situation if the elements of their mental models salient to that situation are functionally equivalent. Functional equivalence means that their mental models will provide the same explanations and the same predictions of a situation.

According to Glinz and Fricker [92], shared understanding has two important facets:

(1) Explicit shared understanding is about interpreting explicit, i.e., written, documentation, such as requirements, design documents, and manuals by all persons in the same way.

(2) Implicit shared understanding denotes the common agreement of all persons regarding non-specified knowledge, such as assumptions, opinions, needs, objectives, and values.

In software development projects, relying only on implicit shared understanding does not work since software is too complex for being developed without any explicit documentation [92]. Furthermore, implicit shared understanding goes along with a serious threat that assumptions about its existence or degree might be false. In this case, omitting documentation leads to a system that does not satisfy its stakeholders, resulting in excessive rework for fixing the faults [3, 29, 92]. In contrast, relying only on explicit shared understanding also does not work since the amount of relevant information is potentially infinite. Even if a complete documentation could be created and read, its costs would exceed its benefits, i.e., ensuring that the developed system fulfills the expectations and needs of its stakeholders [3, 92, 189]. Therefore, achieving shared understanding by explicit documentation should be done as far as needed and relying on implicit shared understanding should be done as far as possible [92]. As a consequence, explicit documentation of key concepts, such as a vision, is necessary [92]. However, the optimal amount of explicit documentation is usually unknown why a proper balance between its costs and benefits needs to be determined [92].

Regarding requirements communication, the development of shared understanding requires that the stakeholders and the development team align their mental models, i.e., their visions of the future system, by taking into account their different points of view to achieve functional equivalence. However, *mental models* (see Definition 2.7) are intangible since they

13

are tacit representations in the persons' minds [181,210]. The alignment can be achieved more easily by using practices that use suitable communication mechanisms that support proactive information exchange [11,210]. These communication mechanisms should make the mental models tangible by using external representations that focus on abstraction and summarization [68,238]. Thus, the overall concepts can be established without getting lost in details. An external representation must be actively discussed by all parties involved since it does not embody shared understanding but merely helps to align mental models and thus develop shared understanding [68,92,159]. Mental models are aligned by validating the existence of a common understanding and identifying misunderstanding [68,92,195]. The combination of explicit documentation of the system vision and active interaction of the participants establishes a common context that is based on implicit shared understanding. This context reduces the basic need for documentation and lowers the risk of misunderstandings due to false assumptions [25,92,154]. It is important that the documentation has a sufficient specification quality and is suitable to support the necessary active interaction among all parties involved [136,210].

Definition 2.7 (*Mental model; based on Norman [181, p. 26], Yu and Petter [260]*)

> *A mental model is a conceptual idea in the mind of a person that represents the person's individual understanding of how a system will work. Different persons may hold different mental models of the same system.*

2.2.2 Specification Quality

The general belief is that project success highly depends on the specification quality of the explicit documentation [82]. The quality of documentation should be as good as possible since an incomplete, inaccurate, and inappropriate documentation is one of the main causes of project failures [58]. However, the extent of quality must not impede the development process. While inadequately specified documentation leads to ambiguity and misunderstandings, too much detail and quality delay the development process. In both cases, the costs of a project increase unnecessarily. For this reason, the quality of documentation should be good enough and adapted to the respective situation [82]. Fricker et al. [82,83] identified five criteria that constitute a *good enough specification quality* of documentation:

Definition 2.8 (*Good enough specification quality; based on Fricker et al. [82, p. 73]*)

> *The specification quality of documentation is considered good enough if it is:*
> (1) **Valid** *by being based on the needs of stakeholders,*
> (2) **Consistent** *by containing related information,*
> (3) **Stable** *by not changing for the targeted market release timeframe,*
> (4) **Important** *by being selected for implementation based on priority basis, and*
> (5) **Traceable** *by being related to the stakeholders' needs and the strategy of the company.*

Although these criteria establish some aspects of good enough documentation, documentation quality is a moving target [82]. In case of a change in a project, the quality of documentation may not be good enough anymore. As a consequence, the target has moved and the documentation must be adapted to be good enough again. This moving target of documentation quality can be addressed by replacing the simple handover of a written specification with effective requirements communication supported by good enough documentation [82]. However, as Figure 2.2 shows, not every type of documentation is equally well-suited for communication [8, 158]. While textual and pictorial representations, including digital versions, have low communication richness and effectiveness, videos can enable richer and more effective communication due to the combination of the auditory and visual channels. Besides the criteria mentioned, the suitability of the documentation for communication also affects its quality.

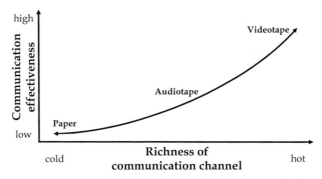

Figure 2.2: Documentation options for communication; based on Ambler [8, p. 84]

Several studies [2,5,48,84,99,120,157,180] investigated industrial requirements engineering practices regarding documentation and communication. All of them indicated that textual and pictorial representations are (1) the most common media used for requirements communication and (2) a crucial challenge due to their low communication richness and effectiveness. All these studies indicate a still-existing need for improving documentation used for supporting requirements communication. Although the strategy of using written specifications to establish shared understanding is, for some purposes, the best available alternative [11], relying only on explicit documentation is insufficient for effective requirements communication [92]. According to Al-Rawas and Easterbrook [5], Carter and Karatsolis [48], as well as Abad et al. [2], written documentation must be supplemented with other media to turn them into an effective means of communication. The use of videos is promising since videos can enable a richer and more effective requirements communication than mere textual and pictorial representations. However, videos also need to exhibit good enough specification quality [157].

15

2.2.3 Clear Scope

Stakeholders and a development team need a clear *scope* (see Definition 2.9) for a project since the scope specifies all required aspects to satisfy the stakeholders' needs [202]. A project without a clear scope impends the risk of failure [251]. Only if all parties involved have a shared understanding of objectives and priorities in advance, they can align their activities and actions to successfully develop a future system [149, 161, 195, 240, 260]. A clear scope ensures that all project partners can quickly assess whether a proposed requirement is in or out of scope [251].

Definition 2.9 (*Scope; based on Pohl and Rupp [196, p. 15], Wiegers and Beatty [251]*)

> *A scope defines which portion of a system vision a project addresses in one release by describing the boundary of a system which indicates which aspects belong to the system and which aspects belong to the context of the system.*

However, the specification of a clear scope requires a common *vision* (see Definition 2.10) which the stakeholders and the development understand, share, and accept [202]. A vision defines the long-term goals of a project and is therefore relatively stable over time [161, 251]. In contrast, a scope is more dynamic since the stakeholders and development team need to adjust the scope for each release within the schedule, budget, resource, and quality constraints [251, 256]. For this reason, the vision always encompasses the scope for each planned release [195, 251]. Hence, a scope is usually a subset of the vision for one release [251]. A common vision serves as a basis for an active communication among all stakeholders and the development team to clearly define the scope of a future system [139]. Pohl summarizes the relationship between vision and scope as follows: *"The* [overall] *goal of the requirements engineering process can be formulated* [. . .] *as 'the establishment of a vision in the relevant system context'"* [195, p. 38].

Definition 2.10 (*Vision; based on Pohl [195, p. 37], Wiegers and Beatty [251, p. 79]*)

> *A vision briefly describes the common essence of the mental models of all stakeholders of an ultimate system that satisfies their needs. A complete vision consists of the problem addressed, the key idea of the solution, and the improvement of the problem by the solution.*

Figure 2.3 summarizes the coherence between the three single objectives and their relation to the overall goal of the requirements engineering process. The overall goal requires a shared understanding (see Figure 2.3, Objective 1) among all parties involved about the aspired vision of the system under development. Stakeholders and the development team can more easily achieve shared understanding by using practices that use explicit documentation with good enough quality that is suited for proactive communication (see Figure 2.3, Objective 2). A common vision is, in turn, necessary to define a clear scope (see Figure 2.3, Objective 3). The vision is the basis for active communication among the stakeholders and the development team to determine the system boundary. As a consequence, achieving all three objectives is necessary to establish the vision of a system in the relevant system context.

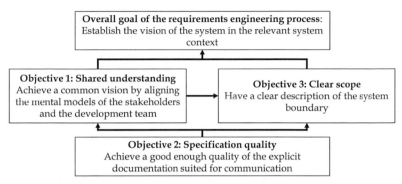

Figure 2.3: Goal tree of the requirements engineering objectives

2.3 Vision Videos as a Documentation Option for Communication

The previous remarks on the objectives of requirements engineering show how important a common vision is. An unclear vision of the overall goals is associated with issues related to company-wide strategy and business objectives [25, 260]. The inability to define a clear vision greatly delays the development process [67, 106] since ambiguous and abstract goals impede effective requirements communication due to speculations and conflicts about what should be developed [46, 96, 154]. For these reasons, a clear and common vision is one of the key concepts in requirements engineering [132,149,195,208] and its establishment is a key challenge in requirements engineering [9,60,184].

The establishment of a vision in its relevant system context demands to fulfill the three underlying requirements engineering objectives which especially require effective requirements communication with proactive information exchange. As stated in section 2.2.2, videos are a promising communication mechanism for effective requirements communication since they require mental models to be visualized. This visualization discloses the mental models by externalizing them and thus making them tangible. Thirty-five years ago, different researchers [36,40,73] already proposed the use of videos to support knowledge transfer in requirements engineering due to the communication richness and effectiveness of videos [129]. According to Carter and Karatsolis [48], short videos of well-expressed key concepts, such as a vision, are an effective and persuasive tool that can produce a significant value as documentation for communication. Creighton et al. support this perspective by emphasizing that a video as a timed medium *"needs to focus on the essentials of the visionary system"* [60, p. 9]. Therefore, videos seem to be adequate to visualize visions and their future impacts. Since 1992, several approaches [36, 60, 140] focused on the use of videos to represent a vision or parts of it (cf. Definition 2.10). A vision and its parts are suitable contents for videos since a vision provides an overview of a project with its overall goals and the total extent of the future system [132, 149, 195]. The concept of videos that represent a vision or its parts is referred to as *vision video* and is defined as follows:

Definition 2.11 (*Vision video; according to Karras [126], Karras et al. [139, p. 2]*)

> *A vision video is a video that represents a vision or parts of it for achieving shared understanding among all parties involved by disclosing, discussing, and aligning their mental models of the future system.*

Vision videos support the development of a common vision, i.e., the common essence of the stakeholders' mental models, which the stakeholders and the development team need to understand, share, and accept [202]. Stakeholders and the development team gain an improved shared understanding of the vision of a project by creating, elaborating, and discussing vision videos [126, 217]. These videos address the underlying cognitive aspects of communication by visualizing the vision of a future system and its use [238, 246, 250]. Thus, the intangible mental models are disclosed by translating them into concrete scenarios and requirements to which individuals can relate to more easily [76, 158, 217, 246]. The overall purpose of these videos is to support coordination and communication among all parties involved at an early stage to enable a proactive exchange of information on the product goals [126, 129, 246]. The explicit representation provides a reference point for the active discussion among the stakeholders and the development team to align their mental models. As a consequence, the desired result of a validated and commonly understood vision can be more easily achieved [61, 126] since critical issues of the mental models are identified, discussed, understood, and, at best, resolved by making them explicit and obvious [29, 126, 246].

As a part of the application of vision videos as a documentation option for communication in requirements engineering, it is necessary to take a closer look at the production (see section 2.3.1) and the quality assessment of videos (see section 2.3.2). These two aspects are elaborated in the following.

2.3.1 Video Production

In contrast to film and television production, video production mainly deals with non-broadcast, low-budget videos most of which are distributed digitally [185]. Nevertheless, video production can range from economically budgeted videos for a specific audience to ambitious presentations for mass distribution [185]. In general, a video is a communication mechanism that enables a video producer to persuasively communicate his ideas and visions to his audience [70, 185]. For this purpose, a video needs to tell a story that attracts and holds its audience [43, 178]. A video has no value unless its intended audience is willing to view the video and understands its message [70, 178]. Although recording a video has become a simple activity due to lighter, smaller, and more powerful equipment such as digital camcorders and smartphones, the video production process has become more complex [178, 185]. The ease of use of modern video equipment cannot replace the necessity of thinking and creativity to produce a good video [43, 178]. Therefore, a video producer needs sufficient knowledge about the video production process to be able to use the benefits of the medium video and to master its restrictions [43, 178, 185].

Figure 2.4 provides an overview of the video production process. The video production process consists of three main steps: *preproduction*, *shooting*, and *postproduction* [70,139,163,178,185]. All three steps in the video production process are equally important and supposed to add value to a video. A poor performance in any of these steps diminishes the final value of a video. Insufficient quality in an early step usually constrains the quality that can be achieved in the later steps. Thus, upstream quality affects downstream quality. In a way, this phenomenon resembles the V-model of a software development lifecycle. Poor performance and misunderstandings in the requirements analysis cannot be compensated by good design. Instead, any early flaw reduces and limits the potential value at the end [139].

Upstream quality affects downstream quality

Preproduction   Shooting   Postproduction

Figure 2.4: Video production process; based on Karras et al. [139, p. 15]

Preproduction. This step lays the foundation for any video based on the time and effort required to plan and prepare the shooting [178]. Preliminaries, preparations, and the organization need to be done before the shooting begins. According to Owens and Millerson, *"ninety percent of the work on a production usually goes into the planning and preparation phase"* [185, p. 37]. The more planning and preparation are done the less time needs to be spent on the actual shooting [163]. Based on a vague idea, a video producer defines the story and single scenes of the video. The relevant contents of the video are specified since each element in a video needs to have a purpose [178].

Shooting. In this step, the video is recorded. A short video clip, a so-called shot, is recorded for each scene of a story [163]. The shots are not filmed in a chronological but a cost-efficient order based on the locations [178]. The single video clips are later combined in the postproduction to the final video [185]. During the recording of each shot, the relevant contents need to be captured aesthetically, avoiding any disrupting and distracting contents such as background noise or irrelevant actions [70].

Postproduction. In this step, the whole video is produced by editing and digitally postprocessing the image and sound of the video. The single shots are connected and arranged to convey the entire planned story [70]. Potential flaws of the shooting, so-called clutter [185], are corrected, e.g., by removing background noises and unnecessary parts of shots [70, 163]. The resulting video needs to communicate the story aesthetically according to the demands of the target audience [70, 178].

2.3.2 Video Quality Assessment

As introduced in section 2.2.2, specification quality is one of the most important requirements engineering objectives. Thus, videos applied in requirements engineering also need to exhibit good enough specification quality suited to support effective requirements communication.

However, there is no established standard for the quality of videos since the concept of *video quality* is rather ill-defined due to numerous factors [247, 252, 254]. There are technical as well as subjective factors that influence the quality of a video [252]. Technical factors include, i.a., video properties (size, resolution, brightness, etc.), record devices, and display devices. Subjective factors include the individual interests, quality expectations, video experiences, and viewing conditions of the viewers [4, 247]. The wide variety and subjectivity of the aforementioned factors substantiate the complexity of video quality and its assessment. This complexity impedes the prediction of how different viewers assess the quality of a video [136, 139]. Video quality can be assessed either subjectively or objectively.

Subjective video quality assessment is the most accurate and reliable practice to determine video quality [4, 247, 252]. Experiments are an established method for subjective video quality assessments since a controlled environment is necessary to avoid potential disruptive factors, e.g., varying viewing conditions [4]. In these experiments, 15 to 30 subjects watch one or more videos and assess the quality of each video directly after the video was completely watched. Each subject assesses his perception of the video quality by assigning a single value on a defined 5- or 7-point scale [4, 222]. For each video, the average of the subjects' assessments is calculated. This value is defined as the Mean Opinion Score (MOS) which indicates the perceived overall quality of a video from the subjects' point o view [4, 252]. The established subjective video quality assessment methods ultimately determine video quality based on the mean opinion score [4]. However, there is inherent variability in the viewers' quality assessment due to their individual interests and expectations [4]. Several recommendations [114–117] provide instructions to conduct subjective assessments of video quality to mitigate this variability.

Although subjective assessments are invaluable for evaluating video quality, their applicability to a larger number of viewers and videos is limited since these methods are time-consuming, cumbersome, and expensive [50]. These restrictions limit the number of videos that can be assessed in a reasonable amount of time. Therefore, large efforts have been made to develop objective video quality assessments. Objective video quality assessments use algorithms that are designed to characterize video quality and to automatically predict the mean opinion score with high accuracy [4, 222, 252]. There are three main types of metrics for objective video quality assessment: *Data metrics*, *picture metrics*, as well as *packet-* and *bitstream-based metrics* [252] (see Figure 2.5). While the first two types are used for the analysis of a decoded video, the third type measures the impact of network losses on the quality of an encoded video.

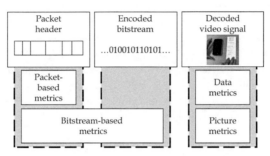

Figure 2.5: The three main types of metrics for objective video quality assessment; based on Winkler and Mohandas [252, p. 662]

Data metrics consider the fidelity of the video signal by comparing byte by byte without any reference to the actual content. The relationship between data metrics and the video quality perceived by the viewers is only approximated so that no data metric is universally reliable [252]. Mean Squared Error (MSE) and Peak Signal-Noise Ratio (PSNR) are two of the most widely used data metrics [247]. *Picture metrics* consider the video data as visual information by quantifying the effects of distortions and structural image contents on the video quality. These metrics are subdivided into vision modeling approaches and engineering approaches. Vision modeling approaches imitate different components of the human visual system, e.g., color perception or contrast sensitivity. Some well-known metrics of the vision modeling approaches are the Visual Differences Predictor (VDP) [63], the Sarnoff JND (Just Noticeable Differences) metric by Lubin and Fibush [160], the Moving Picture Quality Metric (MPQM) by van den Branden Lambrecht and Verscheure [243], and the Perceptual Distortion Metric (PDM) by Winkler [253]. Engineering approaches analyze image contents and distortions, e.g., contours or block artifacts [247]. Two examples of metrics of the engineering approaches are the Structural Similarity index (SSIM) by Wang et al. [249] and the Video Quality Metric (VQM) by Pinson and Wolf [194]. *Packet-* and *bitstream-based metrics* consider the packet header information and the encoded bitstream without fully decoding a video. Some examples of such metrics are the V-Factor by Winkler and Mohandas [252] and the approaches of Verscheure et al. [245] and Kanumuri et al. [121, 122].

Remark. *Further details on all three types of metrics for objective video quality assessment can be found in "Vranješ, M. et al.: Review of Objective Video Quality Metrics and Performance Comparison using Different Databases. Signal Processing: Image Communication 28 (2012), No. 1" [247].*

According to Winkler, *"an important shortcoming of the existing metrics is that they measure image fidelity instead of perceived quality"* [254, p. 151]. All these objective metrics merely attempt to predict the subjective assessment of human viewers but they are not universally reliable due to their limitation on measuring only visual fidelity by mainly focusing on technical factors [4]. Especially, the frequently applied metrics neglect the actual content and emotional impact of a video on its audience [252]. These two dimensions have a strong influence on the perceived quality of a video [188]. The consideration of the content and emotional dimension for objective video quality assessment is an active research area [4, 255]. Different organizations, such as the Video Quality Experts Group[6] (VQEG) or the International Telecommunication Union[7] (ITU), are working on this topic and significant progress has been made [4, 255]. However, there is *"still a long way to video quality metrics that are widely applicable and universally recognized"* [252, p. 667]. The objective metrics are only a support for assessing video quality but cannot replace the subjective assessments by humans [4]. As a consequence, the subjective video quality assessment is the ultimate standard of performance [221].

---

[6]www.vqeg.org
[7]www.itu.int

3

Related Work

This thesis deals with the two topics: *Supporting requirements communication for shared understanding* and *application of vision videos in requirements engineering*. Below, I present related work on these two topics in more detail to explain how this thesis fits into the respective context.

Related Publication. *The related work on the application of vision videos in requirements engineering is based on "Karras, O. et al.: Representing Software Project Vision by Means of Video: A Quality Model for Vision Videos. Journal of Systems and Software 162 (2020)" [139].*

3.1 Supporting Communication for Shared Understanding

The establishment of shared understanding requires effective communication of the stakeholders' needs [11, 80]. According to the theory of shared understanding for software organizations by Aranda [11], software organizations must align their values, structures, and practices to support synchronous, proximate, and proportionate requirements communication to achieve shared understanding. This necessity affects various key concepts in software development, such as *processes, documentation, practices, techniques*, and *tools*, as well as *organizational growth, physical co-location*, and *group cohesion*. This variety of affected key concepts emphasizes the complexity and far-reaching implications of supporting requirements communication for shared understanding. For this reason, a comprehensive overview of related work on supporting requirements communication for shared understanding is difficult. Nevertheless, I provide a brief overview of some approaches that have been published in recent years after Aranda [11] published his extensive theory on shared understanding for software organizations. In this way, I show how this thesis fits into the context of other recently published approaches for supporting requirements communication for shared understanding.

In recent years, several researchers [23, 24, 42, 151] proposed approaches that focus on the support and improvement of requirements communication by identifying communication gaps. These gaps are a significant source of project failures and project overruns, i.a., caused by a lack of shared understanding among the parties involved [25].

Buchan [42] proposed a cognitive model of the development of shared understanding based on empirical data of a case study. The model is a state transition model representing the cognitive tasks of a development team for refining shared understanding. The two main tasks in this model focus on monitoring and addressing potential communications gaps. However, Buchan [42] does not explain how to perform these tasks. Knauss et al. [151] proposed an approach to automatically analyze requirements communication in software projects to detect events that may cause communication gaps and thus require clarification. This approach detects events for clarification by using a classifier that matches the observed communication structures with a catalog of clarification patterns. The classifier and catalog were developed and validated in an industrial case study. According to Knauss et al. [151], researchers can use these patterns to gain a deeper understanding of requirements communication and communication gaps that need clarification to be solved. Bjarnason and Sharp [23] proposed the use of distance measures for localizing gaps in requirements communication and for improving development practices. The distance measures include geographical and cognitive distances between team members as well as semantic distances between requirements and testing artifacts. In a case study, Bjarnason and Sharp [23] showed that the distance measures enabled constructive group reflections on communication gaps and their improvement in development practices. Based on the theory of distances for software engineering, Bjarnason et al. [24] proposed the *Gap Finder* technique to detect potential communications gaps between people and between artifacts as well as to identify practices for mitigating these gaps. In a case study, a development team applied the *Gap Finder* technique that helped the team to reflect and improve their requirements communication.

All the above-mentioned approaches are examples of how requirements communication can be supported and improved by retrospective analysis and reflection of explicit documentation. Sutcliffe and Sawyer [238] as well as Glinz and Fricker [92] have taken a close look at the concept of shared understanding and considered its relationship to established practices and techniques in requirements engineering and software engineering. In coincidence with each other, both pairs of authors concluded that the established practices and techniques are relatively mature to support requirements communication for shared understanding based on the analysis and validation of explicit documentation. However, there is a need for practices and techniques that support social collaboration among stakeholders and a development team to actively develop shared understanding. In particular, researchers must address the handling of implicit shared understanding that is hidden in the minds of the parties involved, thus being

24

potentially known but not explicitly documented [92,238]. Therefore, practices and techniques are needed that make the implicit shared understanding tangible [92,238]. In recent years, some researchers [20,22,110,173] addressed this need by proposing corresponding techniques.

Møller and Tollestrup [173] as well as Hyvönen [110] proposed the use of LEGO blocks as tangible media to create shared understanding among all parties involved in a workshop. The participants use the LEGO blocks to represent key challenges, solutions, and the overall vision for the future system. The use of the LEGO blocks makes it easier for participants to externalize their mental models and thus making them more tangible to other participants. Bittner and Leimeister [22] proposed the *MindMerger* technique which defines a collaboration process for a team to build shared understanding about a target object. The process consists of three phases. First, each team member writes down his description of the target object and reads the description of his partner. Second, the partners reflect on the two descriptions to identify and resolve similarities, differences, and conflicts. Both partners summarize the results of their reflection in a new joint description of the target object. Third, each pair presents its joint description to the entire team. In large-scale action research, Bittner and Leimeister [22] showed that this process improved the shared understanding of the target objects among the members of six different development teams. Beimel and Kedmi-Shahar [20] proposed a technique that they call *conceptual mental model*. This graphical model is a tangible visual representation of the users' conceptual idea about the future system. According to the experimental results, the subjects who created a *conceptual mental model* achieved a better understanding of the future system. This understanding helped them to elicit and elaborate better requirements and use case diagrams compared to the subjects who did not create a *conceptual mental model*.

Like the approaches presented, the candidate solution of this thesis addresses the need for practices and techniques that support social collaboration among stakeholders and a development team to actively develop shared understanding. However, there is a difference in the medium used to make the implicit shared understanding tangible. While the presented approaches use textual and pictorial representations for communication and documentation, this thesis focuses on the application of vision videos since videos are better suited for rich and effective requirements communication (cf. section 2.2.2). For this reason, I subsequently provide an overview of the application of vision videos in requirements engineering to understand how this thesis fits into this context.

3.2 Applying Vision Videos in Requirements Engineering

Several researchers proposed different approaches that focus on the use of videos to represent a vision of parts of it. In Figure 3.1, I illustrate the use of vision videos in requirements engineering using examples of different approaches that I explain in detail below.

(a) System for interactive window shopping by Creighton et al. [60]
(b) System for checking in at an airport by Brill et al. [32]
(c) System for recycling ink and paper in a printer by Bojic et al. [28]

(d) System for borrowing books at a library by Pham et al. [192]
(e) System for handling energy consumption by Rodden et al. [204]
(f) System for buying products online by Karras et al. [140]

(g) System for supporting dementia care by Darby et al. [64]
(h) System for ordering products by Schneider et al. [217]
(i) System for delivering products by Busch et al. [45]

(j) System for handling VIPs at an airport by Xu et al. [258]
(k) System for planing trips and vacations by Xu et al. [259]
(l) System for managing pharmacy supply chains Fricker et al. [86]

Figure 3.1: Examples of vision videos produced with different approaches

Creighton et al. [60] employed videos to describe as-is and visionary scenarios of a system for users, customers, and requirements engineers. While the as-is scenarios illustrate current problems in work practice, the visionary scenario videos show how the envisioned system may look, work, or be used (see Figure 3.1a). Creighton et al. [60] introduced the role of a video producer that can be fulfilled by either a member of the development team or an external video professional. This approach combines the produced videos with Unified Modeling Language (UML) diagrams to trace videos and requirements in later development phases.

Brill et al. [32] used low-effort, ad-hoc videos produced by requirements engineers to represent use cases of a future system to elicit and clarify requirements with customers (see Figure 3.1b). Their experimental results yielded that such videos help to avoid misunderstandings and clarify requirements better than textual use cases.

Bojic et al. [28] examined the effect of the visual refinement of videos presenting a prototype on users' feedback. They used two videos produced by designers, one with low and one with high fidelity (see Figure 3.1c). Based on their results, there was no significant effect of the visual refinement of the videos on the number or type of feedback. Thus, Bojic et al. [28] concluded that their results support the validity of using videos with a low fidelity for prototyping.

Pham et al. [192] proposed an interactive storyboard to support requirements engineers to elicit, validate, and document requirements and visions of stakeholders. The interactive storyboard enables the production of a special kind of video that is enhanced by multimedia technologies such as overlays of hand-drawn sketches (see Figure 3.1d).

Rodden et al. [204] used videos of animated sketches to convey the vision of a future smart energy infrastructure to users (see Figure 3.1e). They presented the videos to users in structured focus groups to stimulate an interactive dialog between the participants. Rodden et al. [204] emphasized that the use of videos allowed them to explore the complexity and invisible nature of a not yet existing infrastructure by visualizing its broad socio-technical nature and core concepts. This visualization, in turn, supported the users to articulate their concerns with a focus on the lack of trust towards commercial entities in the future infrastructure.

Karras et al. [140] proposed an approach to generate videos, which demonstrate interaction sequences on hand-drawn and digitally created mockups, as additional support for textual scenarios. These videos are produced as a by-product of digital prototyping by capturing and replaying interaction events of responsive controls without any implementation (see Figure 3.1f). They found that such videos allow a slightly faster understanding of textual scenarios by developers compared to static mockups.

Darby et al. [64] reported on an ongoing case study where they applied design fiction using videos to gather feedback on visionary scenarios of a system for supporting consultations in dementia care (see Figure 3.1g). Besides some early insights on the future system, they identified important issues regarding the design fiction process itself. In particular, the stimulation of creative solutions by the stakeholders and the traceability between stakeholders' solutions and their implementation in the video are crucial issues.

Schneider et al. [217] investigated the use of videos in combination with text to support the elicitation of feedback. Requirements engineers produced videos showing an envisioned ordering and delivery process from a first-person and third-person perspective (see Figure 3.1h). These videos were presented to stakeholders to gather feedback on the refinement of the vision. Schneider et al. [217] found that the use of videos and text resulted in more feedback than the mere use of individual media. Regarding the first- and third-person perspectives, they found no significant preference for either of the two perspectives.

Busch et al. [45] compared the use of animated and real videos representing the same vision of a system to elicit feedback from stakeholders (see Figure 3.1i). Their results did not show any difference between the two types of videos regarding the amount of feedback. Thus, Busch et al. [45] concluded that animated videos offer a viable alternative to real videos for communicating a vision.

Xu et al. [258] proposed the evolutionary scenario-based design which uses vision videos of unimplemented parts of a system for requirements elicitation and system demonstration purposes throughout the project lifecycle. These videos were produced by members of the development team using virtual world technology (see Figure 3.1j). Xu et al. [258] report five short lessons learned about how to produce videos using virtual reality. These lessons suggest the use of a storyboard to tell a story-driven video, the involvement of developers and customers to achieve a better understanding, and the full use of text or audio to express ideas. However, they stated explicitly that detailed guidance on the design and evaluation of videos of visionary scenarios remains future work. Xu et al. [259] extended their approach of the evolutionary scenario-based design to represent the mental models of users. They described how they have employed videos to illustrate as-is, visionary, and demonstration scenarios for elicitation and validation (see Figure 3.1k). They provide five short lessons learned, similar to their previous ones [258], to produce videos of demonstration scenarios.

Fricker et al. [86] proposed the use of video recording to document the discussions between stakeholders and representatives of the development team about a future system in requirements workshops (see Figure 3.1l). According to the approach, an additional film crew produces the video that serves team members who are often only involved in the development but not in the workshops, such as developers, as more comprehensive documentation than mere textual minutes. In a first evaluation, Fricker et al. [86] found that developers appreciated such a video despite some weaknesses since the video allowed a better understanding of the stakeholders' needs. Based on the positive and negative feedback from their subjects, they derived recommendations for the production and use of videos of workshops in practice.

The presented examples illustrate how different vision videos of various approaches can be. While some vision videos show real-world scenes, others present animations of computer-generated content. There are also clear differences in the representation of persons, systems, and interactions. As a consequence, vision videos of the individual approaches seem to have their specific characteristics. However, only three out of these twelve approaches provided some guidance on how to produce videos with the required characteristics so that the videos are suitable for their respective approach. Besides the twelve previously presented approaches with concrete examples of vision videos, I found 18 further approaches that also deal with the use of vision videos in requirements engineering but do not include examples of vision videos.

In appendix A, Table A.1 and Table A.2 summarize all 30 approaches related to the application of vision videos in requirements engineering regarding supported activities, focused parts of a vision, video content, target audience, target video producer, and given guidance on video production and use. All approaches used vision videos mainly to support the requirements engineering activities: elicitation, validation, and documentation. The videos illustrated (1) problems, that need to be solved, (2) proposed solutions for a given problem, or (3) both problem and solution. Videos of problems mainly presented environmental contexts and observations of users' work practice. Videos of proposed solutions showed scenarios of the future system, prototypes, and software project visions. In the case of approaches presenting a problem and solution, the produced videos could contain all previously mentioned contents and presentations of implemented parts of the future systems as well as recorded meetings. The target audience consisted of stakeholders and members of the development team, i.e., decision-makers, users, managers, customers, domain experts, requirements engineers, developers, and designers. The target video producers were mainly members of the development team, i.e., requirements engineers or arbitrary team members. Two approaches [198, 215] focused on the use of videos created by users, and six approaches [34, 38, 39, 60, 86, 167] introduced the role of a video producer that was fulfilled by either a member of the development team or an external video professional. Only eight out of 30 approaches [34, 86, 118, 164, 204, 216, 258, 259] provided a few brief tips, hints, recommendations, or lessons learned for the production and use of videos for the respective approach. However, this guidance remains too abstract for a reader to understand how the specific videos need to be produced to be of sufficient quality.

Despite all these approaches to the application of vision videos in requirements engineering and their benefits shown, videos are not an established documentation option for communication in requirements engineering [136]. This thesis addresses this topic by examining why videos are neglected and developing a candidate solution to integrate videos into requirements engineering practices and techniques that support requirements communication for shared understanding.

4

A Survey on Videos as a Documentation Option in Requirements Engineering

Although the idea of using videos as a communication mechanism in requirements engineering is more than 35 years old [136], videos are still not an established documentation option for communication [124, 129, 139, 143, 209]. According to the scientific approach presented in section 1.3, I examine the state of practice and science (see Figure 1.1, ③) to answer Research Question 1.1 by conducting an explanatory survey with an online questionnaire. A survey is a suitable research method for collecting information to describe, compare, and explain knowledge, attitudes, and behavior [78]. This survey gathers software professionals' attitudes towards videos as a documentation option as well as the production and use of videos in requirements engineering. The survey results enable to identify and describe the reasons why software professionals neglect videos as a communication mechanism. These reasons provide explanations for potential issues that impede the production and use of videos in requirements engineering. Based on the obtained insights, I develop the concepts of a candidate solution for integrating videos into requirements engineering practices to support effective requirements communication for shared understanding.

Related Publication. *The survey is based on "Karras, O.: Software Professionals' Attitudes towards Video as a Medium in Requirements Engineering. International Conference on Product-Focused Software Process Improvement, Springer, 2018" [124].*

4.1 Survey Objective

The research goal underlying the survey is formulated by applying the goal definition template [18] to ensure that the research context and objective are well-defined.

31

Research Goal 4.1

Analyze videos as a documentation option in requirements engineering

for the purpose of identifying the reasons why videos are neglected as a communication mechanism

with respect to the attitude towards videos as well as the production and use

from the point of view of software professionals

in the context of an international survey conducted in academia and industry.

The following two research questions emerge from Research Goal 4.1.

Research Question 4.1

What is the attitude of software professionals towards videos as a documentation option in requirements engineering?

Research Question 4.1 considers the attitude of software professionals towards videos to investigate whether software professionals neglect videos as a documentation option due to a fundamental rejection. Such a rejection would be reflected in a negative attitude including the mention of weaknesses and threats of videos. In the case of no fundamental rejection, there should be a neutral or positive attitude including the mention of strengths and opportunities.

Research Question 4.2

How do software professionals produce and use videos as a documentation option in requirements engineering?

Research Question 4.2 deals with the production and use of videos by software professionals in requirements engineering. This investigation examines how intensively software professionals apply videos for which purposes. If software professionals do not produce and use videos, the obstacles that prevented them from applying videos are examined.

I developed a goal tree (see Figure 4.1) to express the Research Goal 4.1 in measurable terms [174]. The derived sub-goals are more concrete and thus facilitate the design of the survey and its questions. In addition to the attitude of software professionals towards videos, the particular strengths, weaknesses, opportunities, and threats of videos perceived by software professionals are of essential interest (see left part of Figure 4.1). The production and use of videos are described by the number of videos applied, their intended purposes as well as the frequent flaws that occurred during the application. In the case of no application of videos, the obstacles that prevent the production and use are gathered (see right part of Figure 4.1).

Besides the research goal and questions, it is important to specify the target population as part of the survey objective [203]. The target population of this survey includes software professionals from academia and industry. Videos and, in particular, vision videos are often applied in the research and development stage to communicate ideas and visions to the public to gather feedback and investigate the interest of future users [246]. Both groups have relevant

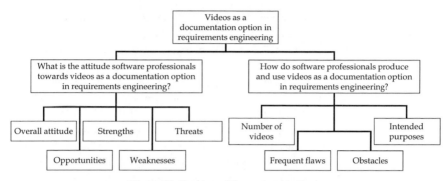

Figure 4.1: Goal tree of the survey objectives

attitudes towards videos as a documentation option in requirements engineering. While practitioners report an industrial project-oriented point of view, researchers can state a scientific project-oriented one. Since 2017, research and innovation projects supported by the European Union through Horizon 2020 and previous framework programs produced and used videos to show the future impact of their work on the life of Europe's citizens and the society as a whole[8].

Remark. *The YouTube channel "EU Science and Innovation" provides a playlist[9] of all so far published videos of research and innovation projects funded by the European Union. This playlist contains 376 videos illustrating the impact of different projects.*

4.2   Survey Design

I developed the survey design by following the process for conducting a questionnaire survey by Robson and McCartan [203], whose individual steps I explain in detail below.

4.2.1   Development of the Survey Instrument

The development of the survey instrument includes the creation of the questionnaire as well as its pre-test and refinement. However, before creating the questionnaire, the type and administration of the survey must be determined since these factors influence the questions that can be addressed [147]. This survey is cross-sectional since the subjects have been asked for information only at one fixed point in time. Furthermore, it is self-administered by using a self-hosted LimeSurvey[10] to have full control over the entire survey and all collected data.

---

[8]www.ec.europa.eu/research/investeuresearch/index.cfm
[9]www.youtube.com/playlist?list=PLvpwIjZTs-LjHDvRTqlyjfLeflXDak5er, accessed 02.10.2020
[10]www.limesurvey.org

A first draft of the questionnaire was iteratively developed in consideration of the guidelines for survey data collection by Robson and McCartan [203, p. 244 ff.]. Based on the goal tree (see Figure 4.1), the single questions were designed by following the recommendations of Kitchenham and Pfleeger [147]. I developed open-ended questions on the strengths, weaknesses, opportunities, threats, frequent flaws, and obstacles to capture the respondents' ideas and experiences in their own words. For the overall attitude, the number of videos, and the intended purposes, I used closed questions. The overall attitude was assessed based on a 3-point scale (positive, neutral, negative). For the number of videos, I used a numerical response that ranges from zero to infinity. The intended purposes are based on the findings of Hanjalic et al. [101] who identified five high-level intended purposes for videos (see Definition 4.1). I decided to use these defined high-level intended purposes of videos since they have been widely applied by other researchers to classify videos [152, 153, 201]. The questionnaire only considers the first four purposes since they are perceived very similarly by producers and viewers, and all of them can be fulfilled without a video by using other documentation options. The fifth purpose is a default category covering all cases that can only be fulfilled by a video. Thus, this purpose is too general to provide concrete insights.

Definition 4.1 (*Intended purposes of videos; according to Hanjalic et al. [101, p. 1243]*)

The five high-level intended purposes of videos are:

(1) **Information**: *Convey or obtain knowledge and information (declarative knowledge).*

(2) **Experience learning**: *Convey or obtain skills or something practically by experience (procedural knowledge).*

(3) **Experience exposure**: *Convey or obtain particular experiences. The video serves as a replacement of an actual person, place, entity, or event.*

(4) **Affect**: *Convey or obtain a mood or affective state. The video serves for relaxation or entertainment purposes.*

(5) **Object**: *Convey or obtain content in form of a video to serve a particular purpose in a real-life situation.*

Each question was first reviewed using the checklist of Leßmann [156]. Subsequently, there were five rounds of pre-tests. In each pre-test, a software professional from the target population completed the survey and we discussed how the questionnaire could have been improved. The final questionnaire and the question order are included in appendix B.1 and B.2.

4.2.2 Data Collection

For the sampling of the target population, two non-probabilistic sampling methods were combined: *snowball sampling* and *convenience sampling* [147].

For snowball sampling, I directly contacted 25 persons from my network who belong to the target population. These 25 persons were asked to participate in the survey and to distribute the survey in their network to people who also belong to the target population. I also applied convenience sampling by using several communication channels to advertise the survey to obtain responses from those persons who are available and willing to take part. Thus, the survey was accessible to everyone. For this reason, I included filtering questions to ensure that potential respondents belong to the target population of software professionals from academia or industry and have the experience and knowledge to answer the questions. Due to these filtering questions (cf. appendix B) , not all questions were answered by each respondent. As a consequence, the sample size per question may vary which is why the sample size for each sample statistic is reported below separately [147].

The survey was conducted in the second half of 2017, starting on August 7th and closing on December 12th. The survey invitation was disseminated via various online communities such as LinkedIn[11], ResearchGate[12], and Twitter[13] as well as a mailing list of a German professionals group on requirements engineering. I also personally advertised the survey at the 25th *IEEE International Requirements Engineering Conference*. A response rate cannot be reported since the total size of the sample approached is unknown due to the communication channels used.

4.2.3 Data Analysis

During the design of the questionnaire, I decided to leave the control of all the data entered to the respondents to increase their trust in the research process. When the questionnaire was aborted, all entered data was deleted. As a consequence, there could only be complete entries.

The analysis of the data set combines descriptive and inferential statistics. All responses were first analyzed by using descriptive statistics, including frequency, mean, minimum and maximum value, to describe and summarize the sample. The questionnaire contained several open-ended questions with free-text answers. These responses were analyzed via manual coding [211] to convert the individual answers into countable categories. An answer could belong to more than one category. Manual coding is a qualitative data analysis method consisting of two consecutive coding cycles each of which can be repeated iteratively. While the first coding cycle includes the initial coding of the data, the second cycle focuses on classifying, synthesizing, abstracting, and conceptualizing categories from the coded data.

Figure 4.2 shows the manual coding process with two examples of coded free-text answers. In the first coding cycle, I applied *in vivo* coding which assigns a word or phrase found in a response as a code to the respective data (see Figure 4.2, bold highlighting). The use of *in vivo* cod-

---

[11]www.linkedin.com
[12]www.researchgate.net
[13]www.twitter.com

ing allows adhering closely to the respondents' actual language. According to Saldaña [211], this method is a good starting point for manual coding since it provides the essential basis for the second coding cycle. In the second coding cycle, I applied *pattern* coding. This method groups the coded data into a smaller number of themes to develop categories (see Figure 4.2, italic highlighting). I iterated three times through each cycle which took a total of three weeks. The detailed results of the manual coding are in appendix B.3.

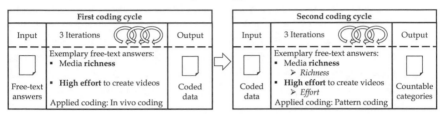

Figure 4.2: Manuel coding process

In addition to the descriptive statistics, I used inferential statistics to draw conclusions about the target population by analyzing the sample. I examined the frequency distribution of the answers given by academia and industry. Pearson's χ^2 goodness-of-fit test [65] with a significance level of $\alpha = .05$ was used to examine whether there is a difference between the observed frequency distribution of the given answers and the expected frequency distribution. I expected an equal frequency distribution of the answers, i.e., a ratio of 1 : 1, since I assumed that software professionals from academia and industry give similar answers meaning that the answers do not depend on the perspective. In the case of this frequency distribution, both groups can be treated as one which, in turn, allows drawing more general conclusions. Otherwise, one of the two groups would have given a specific answer more frequently indicating a higher relevance of this answer for the corresponding group.

Remark. *The entire data set is published in "Karras, O.: Survey Data Set Part 1 – Attitudes Towards Videos as a Documentation Option for Communication in Requirements Engineering. Zenodo, Version: 1.1, 2018" [125] and "Karras, O.: Survey Data Set Part 2 – Attitudes Towards Videos as a Documentation Option for Communication in Requirements Engineering. Zenodo, Version: 1.0, 2020" [127].*

4.3 Sample

In total, 64 out of 106 respondents completed the survey within an average of 19 minutes. Figure 4.3 summarizes the demographics of the sample. Of the 64 respondents, 34 were from industry and 30 were from academia. Eight practitioners stated their business role as a *requirements engineer*, seven as a *project manager*, five as a *developer*, two as a *software architect*, and 12 as other business roles only mentioned once. The researchers mainly stated two research areas: 16 times *requirements engineering* and ten times *software engineering*. Four researchers named other research areas in computer science but these have been mentioned only once. On average, the practitioners had 9.2 years of experience and the researchers 7.4 years. The respondents worked in 11 different countries: 40 in Germany, 16 in other European countries, six in North America, and two in Asia including the Middle East.

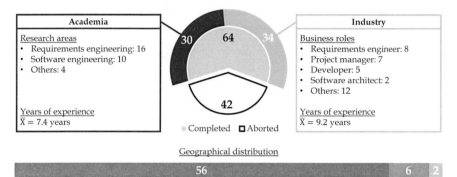

Figure 4.3: Demographics of the sample (Sample size: $N = 64$)

4.4 Results: Descriptive Statistics

4.4.1 Attitude Towards Videos

All 64 respondents reported their attitude towards video as a documentation option in requirements engineering. Of the 64 respondents, 38 had a positive, 25 a neutral, and one a negative attitude. While 59 respondents stated that videos have the potential to improve requirements engineering, 34 respondents mentioned threats of videos for requirements engineering (see Table 4.1). All 64 respondents mentioned at least one strength and one weakness of videos.

Table 4.1: Videos as a documentation option: Attitude, potential, and threats (Sample size: $N = 64$)

Groups	Attitude towards videos			Potential for RE?		Threats for RE?	
	Positive	Neutral	Negative	Yes	No	Yes	No
Academia	21	9	0	28	2	17	13
Industry	17	16	1	31	3	17	17
In total	38	25	1	59	5	34	30

In the following, I report on the identified strengths, weaknesses, opportunities, and threats of videos perceived by the respondents. Figure 4.4 shows the coding frequencies (CF) of the manual coding per identified strength (see Figure 4.4a), weakness (see Figure 4.4b), opportunity (see Figure 4.4c), and threat (see Figure 4.4d) divided into academia and industry. The detailed results of manual coding are in appendix B.3, Figure B.2 – Figure B.5.

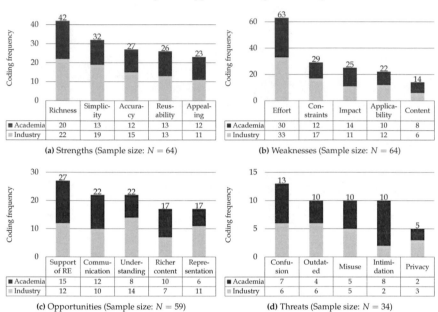

(a) Strengths (Sample size: $N = 64$)

	Richness	Simplicity	Accuracy	Reusability	Appealing
■ Academia	20	13	12	13	12
▨ Industry	22	19	15	13	11

(b) Weaknesses (Sample size: $N = 64$)

	Effort	Constraints	Impact	Applicability	Content
■ Academia	30	12	14	10	8
▨ Industry	33	17	11	12	6

(c) Opportunities (Sample size: $N = 59$)

	Support of RE	Communication	Understanding	Richer content	Representation
■ Academia	15	12	8	10	6
▨ Industry	12	10	14	7	11

(d) Threats (Sample size: $N = 34$)

	Confusion	Outdated	Misuse	Intimidation	Privacy
■ Academia	7	4	5	8	2
▨ Industry	6	6	5	2	3

Figure 4.4: Coding frequencies of the strengths, weaknesses, opportunities, and threats of videos

Strengths. Videos are most appreciated for their *richness* (CF = 42) of detailed and comprehensive information such as gestures, facial expressions, decisions, requirements, and rationals. Anyone can easily use and understand this information due to the *simplicity* (CF = 32) of videos. The respondents emphasized the *accuracy* (CF = 27) of videos since videos capture exact statements and visualize concrete examples, problems, and solutions. Videos have increased *reusability* (CF = 26) for subsequent analyses and sharing due to their long-term accessibility and persistence. The respondents stated that videos are an *appealing* (CF = 23) medium since their visualizations are less ambiguous and more tangible than textual representations.

Weaknesses. The most mentioned weakness of videos is the high *effort* (CF = 63) in terms of costs and time for planning, producing, and watching a video. There are several technical *constraints* (CF = 29) of videos such as file format, file size, or necessary equipment which impede the application of videos. Videos may have a negative *impact* (CF = 25) on people with different effects, e.g., too high expectations, intimidation, or low acceptance. In particular, the respondents stated that people who are recorded on a video tend to change their behavior since they are afraid of making mistakes or saying something wrong. Furthermore, the respondents expected that people who watch a video tend to be less attentive due to inactivity. The *applicability* (CF = 22) of videos is a general problem. In addition to legal and privacy issues, videos also do not seem to be suitable for every kind of content and context. The *content* (CF = 14) of videos is a further weakness. Videos should contain the right amount of relevant and detailed information. However, videos often contain too much irrelevant and abstract information which makes it difficult for the target audience to understand the videos.

Opportunities. The most mentioned opportunity of videos is the *support of requirements engineering* (CF = 27) in terms of improving activities, i.a., elicitation, interpretation, validation, and documentation, and techniques, i.a., interview, workshop, focus group, and observation. Especially, the techniques may benefit from videos since more information, results, and rationales can be captured and accessed. According to the respondents, videos may facilitate *communication* (CF = 22) and *understanding* (CF = 22) of processes, problem domains, interdependencies, project visions, or contexts among stakeholders and a development team. Videos may also provide *richer content* (CF = 17) than textual descriptions due to their richness, i.e., their detailed content with comprehensive information. The respondents also emphasized that videos may allow an improved *representation* (CF = 17) of workflows, interactions, environments, and scenarios due to a better description by visualization.

Threats. The most mentioned threat of videos is their *confusion* (CF = 13) since they contain a lot of unstructured data. Therefore, it is difficult to identify the right, important, and meaningful information in addition to the less relevant content. The management of videos is cumbersome since frequent changes are difficult to handle and can easily lead to *outdated* (CF = 10) information. The *misuse* (CF = 10) of videos is a further threat since they should not be used as the single documentation option to convey information. Videos may cause *intimidation* (CF = 10) of people. In particular, the respondents stated that the use of videos may lead to changed behavior and untrue statements by people who feel uncomfortable or do not want to appear in a video. Some respondents also mentioned *privacy* (CF = 5) concerns regarding the misuse of recorded information or the violation of privacy.

Finding 4.1

> *The majority of the respondents has a positive attitude towards videos and highlighted the potential of videos to improve requirements engineering. Nevertheless, more than half of the respondents mentioned threats from applying videos in requirements engineering.*
>
> *Although the respondents mentioned in detail the strengths and opportunities of videos for requirements engineering, they also identified several weaknesses and threats that impede the application of videos. In particular, the respondents indicated that videos may support requirements engineering by facilitating the communication and understanding between all parties involved due to their richness, simplicity, and accuracy. However, the effort and technical constraints are potential issues for the application of videos. Furthermore, the inappropriate use of videos as well as their extensive information content poses potential threats for requirements engineering, especially as videos may intimidate people and their contents may be easily outdated.*

4.4.2 Production of Videos

Thirty out of the 64 respondents have produced at least one video in a requirements engineering context. On average, the respondents produced 3.4 videos.

Intended Purposes of Produced Videos. Out of the 30 respondents, 23 produced videos to convey declarative knowledge (*information*) and 17 to convey procedural knowledge (*experience learning*). Thirteen respondents produced videos to convey a particular experience replacing a person, place, entity, or event by the corresponding video (*experience exposure*). Only 2 respondents produced a video to change the mood or affective state of their target audience (*affect*). Table 4.2 summarizes these findings grouped by academia and industry.

Table 4.2: Intended purposes of produced videos (Sample size: $N = 30$). Remark: The intended purposes of produced videos were gathered using a multiple-choice question since the respondents may have produced more than one video for more than one purpose.

Groups	Intended purposes of videos			
	Information	Experience learning	Experience exposure	Affect
Academia	11	5	4	1
Industry	12	12	9	1
In total	23	17	13	2

Frequent Flaws. Sixteen out of the 30 respondents who produced at least one video reported frequent flaws which they experienced in the video production. Figure 4.5 presents the coding frequencies (CF) of the manual coding per identified frequent flaw. The detailed results in terms of codes and the derived categories are in appendix B.3, Figure B.6.

In total, the respondents reported seven frequent flaws from their experience. The most frequent flaw of produced videos concerns the *content* (CF = 7) of a video. The respondents were faced with the problem that their videos were often too complex due to too much information. Furthermore, they encountered problems concerning the *image quality* (CF = 5) and *sound quality* (CF = 5) of their videos such as blurred images and poor sound. The *plot* (CF = 5) of the produced videos is another frequent flaw since the videos often had a poorly structured presentation of the content. The respondents also presupposed *prior knowledge* (CF = 4) by their target audience which the viewers lacked. Thus, they omitted tacit and contextual knowledge that was necessary to understand the videos. Some respondents reported an insufficient *preparation* (CF = 4) of their video production which caused technical problems and impeded the whole process. In some cases, the respondents indicated that the *video length* (CF = 3) was too long resulting in a loss of attention for their target audience.

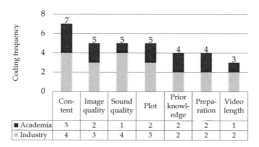

Figure 4.5: Coding frequencies of the frequent flaws of produced videos (Sample size: $N = 16$)

Obstacles. Thirty-four out of the 64 respondents have never produced a video in a requirements engineering context. These respondents were asked about the obstacles that prevented them from producing videos. Figure 4.6 shows the coding frequencies (CF) per identified obstacle. The detailed results of manual coding are in appendix B.3, Figure B.7.

The most mentioned obstacle to video production is a high *effort* (CF = 14) in terms of costs and time. Especially, the respondents stated that video production is time-consuming since they are inexperienced and thus have a *lack of knowledge* (CF = 9) about how to produce a video. Furthermore, the respondents have *no equipment* (CF = 8) such as cameras and video editing software to produce a video. Another important obstacle to the production of videos is the *low added value* (CF = 8) expected by the respondents. They explained that videos did not provide enough benefits compared to the effort required to produce them. Besides the low added value, the respondents also expected the *antipathy of others* (CF = 4) who might reject video production due to a missing understanding of its advantages. In some cases, the respondents indicated *limited applicability* (CF = 4) of video production since they lacked a suitable context in which they could have produced a video.

41

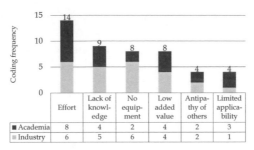

Figure 4.6: Coding frequencies of the obstacles to the production of videos (Sample size: $N = 34$)

Finding 4.2

> *The respondents mainly produced videos to convey declarative and procedural knowledge. They seldom created a video to change the affective state of their target audience. The produced videos often contained too much poorly structured information and had quality issues concerning the image and sound. Despite the abundance of information, the videos presupposed prior knowledge which the target audience did not have. These flaws can be attributed to the inadequate preparation of video production.*
>
> *The respondents cited as the main obstacle to video production the alleged high effort. This effort is likely to be perceived high due to the other two frequently mentioned obstacles: a lack of knowledge about how to produce a video and missing equipment. As a consequence of the alleged effort, the potential benefits and added value of videos seemed to be too low.*

4.4.3 Use of Videos

Thirty out of the 64 respondents have used at least one video in a requirements engineering context. On average, the respondents used 5.4 videos.

Intended Purposes of Used Videos. Out of the 30 respondents, 24 used videos to convey declarative knowledge (*information*) and 23 to convey procedural knowledge (*experience learning*). Twelve respondents also used videos to convey a particular experience with the video replacing a person, place, entity, or event (*experience exposure*). Only four respondents used a video to change the mood or affective state of their target audience (*affect*) (see Table 4.3).

Frequent Flaws. Twenty-one of the 30 respondents who used at least one video reported frequent flaws. Figure 4.7 shows the coding frequencies (CF) of the manual coding per identified frequent flaw. In appendix B.3, Figure B.8 presents the results of the manual coding.

The most frequent flaw of a used video concerns the *representation* (CF = 9) of its contents. According to the respondents, used videos often insufficiently visualized the content and thus

Table 4.3: Intended purposes of used videos (Sample size: $N = 30$). Remark: The intended purposes of used videos were gathered using a multiple-choice question since the respondents may have used more than one video for more than one purpose.

Groups	Intended purposes of videos			
	Information	Experience learning	Experience exposure	Affect
Academia	10	9	4	1
Industry	14	14	8	3
In total	24	23	12	4

lacked clarity. The *sound quality* (CF = 8) is a further problem of used videos since they frequently had a poor auditory quality of their sound. Furthermore, the *content* (CF = 7) of videos often consisted of too much irrelevant information. Thus, the videos were not focusing on the essence. As a consequence, the *video length* (CF = 7) was problematic since the duration of the videos were often too long. In addition to the poor sound quality, the *image quality* (CF = 6) of the used videos was often insufficient due to light problems, inadequate perspectives, or blurred images. In some cases, the videos used had a negative *impact* (CF = 5) on the target audience since they bored the viewers and thus lost their interest.

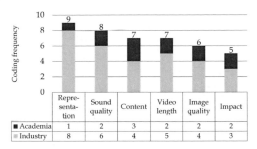

Figure 4.7: Coding frequencies of the frequent flaws of used videos (Sample size: $N = 21$)

Obstacles. Thirty-four of the 64 respondents never used a video in a requirements engineering context. These 34 respondents reported about the obstacles that prevented them from using videos. In Figure 4.8, I present the coding frequencies (CF) per identified obstacle. The detailed results of the manual coding are presented in appendix B.3, Figure B.9.

The most mentioned obstacle for using videos is that there were *no videos* (CF = 13) that could have been used. According to the respondents, no one had made videos available to them in their companies. The respondents also did not consider videos as necessary since they expected a *low added value* (CF = 11) from videos compared to other documentation options. The low added value might be accompanied by the further obstacle of *limited applicability*

43

(CF = 9). Several respondents stated that they lacked the opportunity to use videos in their context. Another obstacle to the use of videos is the *effort* (CF = 4) of watching a video. Some respondents mentioned that the viewing and processing of videos require too much time.

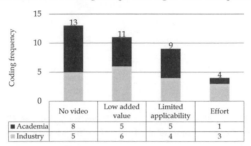

Figure 4.8: Coding frequencies of the obstacles to the use of videos (Sample size: $N = 34$)

Finding 4.3

The respondents mainly used videos to convey declarative and procedural knowledge. They seldom used a video to change the affective state of their target audience. The videos used often did not adequately visualize their contents and had quality issues in terms of image and sound. Furthermore, the videos frequently contained too much irrelevant information resulting in a too long video duration which, in turn, bored the target audience.

According to the respondents, the main obstacle to the use of videos is the lack of videos that could be used. Besides the missing opportunities to use videos in their context, several respondents expected the added value of videos to be too low. The value of videos seemed even lower due to the effort in terms of time for watching and processing a video.

4.5 Results: Inferential Statistics

I examine the frequency distribution of the answers given by the respondents from academia and industry to analyze whether the two groups gave similar answers or not. In the case of an equal frequency distribution of the given answers, i.e., a ratio of 1 : 1, the answers do not depend on the perspective. In this case, the two groups of the sample can be treated as one group which allows drawing more general conclusions about the target population. In particular, I test the following null and alternative hypothesis:

H_0: The observed ratio of the frequencies per answer given by the respondents from academia and industry equals the ratio of 1 : 1 in the sample.

H_1: The observed ratio of the frequencies per answer given by the respondents from academia and industry equals another ratio than 1 : 1 in the sample.

44

4.5.1 Test and Assumptions

The null hypothesis is tested by using Pearson's χ^2 goodness-of-fit test [186]. This test determines whether an observed frequency distribution differs from an expected frequency distribution. Two assumptions need to be fulfilled to perform Pearson's χ^2 goodness-of-fit test:

(1) The investigated variable is categorical, i.e., nominal or ordinal scaled.
In this case, the investigated variable is nominally scaled since a respondent can belong to one of the two categories: *academia* or *industry*.

(2) The expected frequency of each category needs to be at least one. For a maximum of 20% of all categories, the expected frequency may be less than five to ensure that the test statistic follows approximately a χ^2 distribution.
Regarding the expected equal frequency distribution, i.e., a ratio of 1 : 1, the second assumption requires that the expected frequency of the two categories *academia* and *industry* is at least five and thus the total observed frequency per answer is at least ten. Otherwise, more than 20% of all categories would have an expected frequency of less than five.

4.5.2 Statistical Results

The Pearson's χ^2 goodness-of-fit test was applied to each answer by the respondents with a significance level of $\alpha = .05$ if the two assumptions were fulfilled. In total, I performed 33 Pearson's χ^2 goodness-of-fit tests which cause the problem of multiple testing. This problem increases the probability of erroneously obtaining statistically significant results. Therefore, the *Bonferroni-Holm* correction method [107] was used to counteract this problem by adjusting each calculated p-value in consideration of the number of performed tests. The *Bonferroni-Holm* correction method was used since this method considers the type 1 and type 2 errors [65].

Table 4.4, Table 4.5, and Table 4.6 report the details of each test grouped by the attitude towards videos, the production of videos, and the use of videos. Each table shows the observed and expected ratio of the frequencies per answer given by the respondents from academia and industry, the total observed frequency per answer, the calculated χ^2-value as well as the calculated and adjusted p-value. The results of all tests carried out ($p_a > .05$) indicate that the observed ratio of the frequencies per answer given by the respondents from *academia* and *industry* is not statistically different from the expected ratio of 1 : 1. The null hypothesis H_0 cannot be rejected. Therefore, I can assume an equal frequency distribution of the answers given by the respondents from academia and industry. This distribution implies that the two groups gave similar answers which means that the surveyed software professionals from academia and industry can be treated as one group of software professionals. As a consequence, the findings of previous sections can be generalized across both groups of target population which in turn allows drawing more general conclusions.

Finding 4.4

> *According to the results, the answers given by the respondents from academia and industry do not depend on the perspective. Therefore, the two groups can be treated as one group which means that the findings can be generalized across both groups. Thus, more general conclusions about the target population of software professionals can be drawn.*

4.6 Threats to Validity

In the following, I report the threats to construct, external, internal, and conclusion validity that accompany with this kind of study [257].

Construct Validity. All data were collected by using a single online questionnaire which causes a mono-method bias. The data only enables limited explanations of the results since the respondents' rationales and thoughts remain unknown behind their answers. Nevertheless, an explanatory survey is one of the most suitable research methods for collecting information to describe, compare, and explain knowledge, attitudes, and behavior to obtain a broader overview of the state of practice and science [78]. The findings might also be subjectively affected since I performed the whole study on my own. This potential researcher bias has particular implications for the coding and analysis on which the results are based. This threat to validity is mitigated by using *in vivo* coding to adhere closely to the respondents' actual language found in the qualitative data. Furthermore, the questionnaire and all collected and analyzed data are published online (cf. Karras [125, 127]) to increase the transparency of the findings.

External Validity. According to the respondents' answers, all of them were software professionals from either academia or industry. Thus, they are representatives of the target population. However, the survey was open to anyone to achieve a heterogeneity of responses. The questionnaire included filter questions (cf. appendix B) to ensure that the respondents belong to the target population and have the experience and knowledge to provide relevant answers to the questions (cf. section 4.2.2). Nevertheless, I cannot foreclose that the respondents made false statements. There were no monetary rewards or gifts since these incentives usually do not increase the response rate and motivation of the respondents [147]. Therefore, there was no incentive to participate in the survey without giving honest answers. The survey is also completely replicable since the entire questionnaire is accessible online (cf. Karras [125, 127]).

Internal Validity. Maturation and mortality are two of the important threats to validity for a survey. The time taken to complete the questionnaire is crucial. In the case of too many questions, respondents may be affected negatively and abort. Thus, the development of the survey instrument is important for internal validity. I mitigated these threats to validity by carefully designing the questionnaire in consideration of the research questions and goal to ensure good

Table 4.4: Results of Pearson's χ^2 goodness-of-fit tests: Attitude towards videos

Answer	Observed ratio (Academia : Industry)	Expected ratio	Total frequency	χ^2	Calculated p	Adjusted p_a
Attitude towards video						
Positive	21 : 17	19 : 19	38	0.42	.52	1.0
Neutral	09 : 16	12.5 : 12.5	25	1.96	.16	1.0
Negative	violates of the second assumption of a total frequency of at least ten.					
Potential for requirements engineering						
Yes	28 : 31	29.5 : 29.5	59	0.15	.70	1.0
No	violates of the second assumption of a total frequency of at least ten.					
Threats for requirements engineering						
Yes	17 : 17	17 : 17	34	0.00	1.0	1.0
No	13 : 17	15 : 15	30	0.53	.47	1.0
Strengths						
Richness	20 : 22	21 : 21	42	0.10	.76	1.0
Simplicity	13 : 19	16 : 16	32	1.13	.29	1.0
Accuracy	12 : 15	13.5 : 13.5	27	0.33	.56	1.0
Reusability	13 : 13	13 : 13	26	0.00	1.0	1.0
Appealing	12 : 11	11.5 : 11.5	23	0.04	.84	1.0
Weaknesses						
Effort	30 : 33	31.5 : 31.5	63	0.14	.71	1.0
Constraints	12 : 17	14.5 : 14.5	29	0.86	.35	1.0
Impact	14 : 11	12.5 : 12.5	25	0.36	.55	1.0
Applicability	10 : 12	11 : 11	22	0.18	.67	1.0
Content	08 : 06	07 : 07	14	0.18	.67	1.0
Opportunities						
Support of RE	15 : 12	13.5 : 13.5	27	0.33	.56	1.0
Communication	12 : 10	11 : 11	22	0.18	.67	1.0
Understanding	08 : 14	11 : 11	22	1.63	.20	1.0
Richer content	10 : 07	8.5 : 8.5	17	0.53	.47	1.0
Representation	06 : 11	8.5 : 8.5	17	1.47	.23	1.0
Threats						
Confusion	07 : 06	6.5 : 6.5	13	0.08	.78	1.0
Outdated	04 : 06	05 : 05	10	0.40	.53	1.0
Misuse	05 : 05	05 : 05	10	0.00	1.0	1.0
Intimidation	08 : 02	05 : 05	10	3.60	.06	1.0
Privacy	violates of the second assumption of a total frequency of at least ten.					

Table 4.5: Results of Pearson's χ^2 goodness-of-fit tests: Production of videos

Answer	Observed ratio	Expected ratio	Total frequency	χ^2	Calculated p	Adjusted p_a
	(Academia : Industry)					
Intended purposes of produced videos						
Information	11 : 12	11.5 : 11.5	23	0.04	.83	1.0
Exp. learning	05 : 12	8.5 : 8.5	17	2.88	.09	1.0
Exp. exposure	04 : 09	6.5 : 6.5	13	1.92	.17	1.0
Affect	violates of the second assumption of a total frequency of at least ten.					
Frequent flaws of produced videos						
All answers violate the second assumption of a total frequency of at least ten.						
Obstacles to the production of videos						
Effort	08 : 06	7 : 7	14	0.29	.59	1.0
The other answers violate the second assumption of a total frequency of at least ten.						

Table 4.6: Results of Pearson's χ^2 goodness-of-fit tests: Use of videos

Answer	Observed ratio	Expected ratio	Total frequency	χ^2	Calculated p	Adjusted p_a
	(Academia : Industry)					
Intended purposes of used videos						
Information	10 : 14	12 : 12	24	0.67	.41	1.0
Exp. learning	09 : 14	11.5 : 11.5	23	1.09	.30	1.0
Exp. exposure	04 : 08	6 : 6	12	1.33	.25	1.0
Affect	violates of the second assumption of a total frequency of at least ten.					
Frequent flaws of used videos						
All answers violate the second assumption of a total frequency of at least ten.						
Obstacles to the use of videos						
No video	08 : 05	6.5 : 6.5	13	0.69	.41	1.0
Low added value	05 : 06	5.5 : 5.5	11	0.09	.76	1.0
Limited applicability	violates of the second assumption of a total frequency of at least ten.					
Effort	violates of the second assumption of a total frequency of at least ten.					

instrumentation (see section 4.2.1). The questions and answers were carefully designed to ensure good wording to mitigate ambiguity and complexity. I have used the professional software LimeSurvey[14] to provide a standardized questionnaire format that includes an explanation of the purpose of the study, the indication of the responsible person, and the estimated duration

---

[14]www.limesurvey.org

of the survey. A further threat to internal validity is the sampling in terms of selection, sample size, and response rate. The respondents were volunteers who are generally more motivated to participate which may have affected the results. For the sample size, all subgroups of the target population must be approximately the same size. This could be ensured since 30 software professionals from *academia* and 34 form *industry* completed the questionnaire. The response rate cannot be reported due to the selected convenience sampling and the anonymous answering of the questionnaire. Therefore, I do not know how many people have been approached and thus cannot determine the proportion of those who were approached and participated in the survey. This may have compromised the validity of the survey.

Conclusion Validity. The validity of any scientific evaluation highly depends on the reliability of measures. Good instrumentation is crucial for the results of a survey. I followed guidelines for carrying out a survey and conducted five rounds of pre-tests to ensure good instrumentation. In total, I spent four weeks on the entire design of the questionnaire. Although the heterogeneity of the respondents in terms of knowledge and background might have affected the findings, I deliberately chose this heterogeneity to increase external validity. According to the results of the inferential statistics, an equal frequency distribution of the answers given by the respondents from academia and industry can be assumed. These results imply that the two groups can be treated as one group. Therefore, I am confident that the respondents' variations in terms of knowledge and background have little influence on the conclusion validity.

4.7 Discussion

The findings of the survey provide important insights into the state of practice and science regarding the attitude of software professionals towards videos as well as their video production and use. These insights substantiate that the application of videos as a documentation option in requirements engineering especially requires support in the production of videos to facilitate requirements communication for shared understanding.

First, *the respondents from academia and industry gave similar answers regarding videos as a documentation option in requirements engineering* (cf. Finding 4.4). This finding implies that the two groups can be treated as one group. Thus, the subsequent statements can be generalized across both groups of the target population.

Attitude. *Software professionals have a positive attitude towards videos as a documentation option in requirements engineering* (cf. Finding 4.1). Fifty-nine out of 64 software professionals emphasized the potential of videos to improve requirements engineering by supporting multiple activities and techniques through richer content as well as a better representation than textual and pictorial descriptions. The identified strengths (*richness, simplicity, accuracy, reusability,* and *appealing*ness) underline the benefits of videos as a powerful, simple, and appealing documentation option. Especially, the top three opportunities (*support of RE*, improved *communication*, and improved *understanding*) emphasize the suitability of videos as a communication mechanism in requirements engineering. However, the surveyed software professionals stated several weaknesses and threats that impede the application of videos in requirements engineering. In particular, the high effort to plan, produce, view, and process videos was the most frequently identified issue overall. In addition to this primary weakness, further mentioned weaknesses and threats of videos were, i.a., technical *constraints*, negative *impact*, *misuse*, and extensive information *content*. All of them indicate a lack of knowledge of software professionals about how to produce and use good videos that are suitable for effective requirements communication. These insights lead to the following answer to the Research Question 4.1:

Answer to Research Question 4.1

The attitude of software professionals towards videos as a documentation option in requirements engineering is positive. They do not fundamentally reject videos as a communication mechanism. Several strengths and opportunities underline the benefits of videos as a communication mechanism. However, the stated weaknesses and threats of videos impede their application in requirements engineering.

Production. *Software professionals already produce videos in requirements engineering but, in particular, a lack of knowledge about video production is the main obstacle to the application and often leads to frequent flaws in the videos produced* (cf. Finding 4.2). Almost half of the 64 software professionals produced at least one video in requirements engineering. These videos mainly conveyed *declarative* as well as *procedural knowledge* and rarely had the intent to influence the *affective state* of the target audience. Therefore, software professionals rarely seem to consider the emotional impact of videos, e.g., to convince stakeholders. Furthermore, the videos produced often had a poor *plot*, too much *content*, and obvious flaws in the *image* and *sound quality*. These flaws can be attributed to inadequate preparation which results from insufficient knowledge of the video production process by software professionals. Although some surveyed software professionals already produced videos, more than half of them never produced one. The main obstacles to the production are an alleged high *effort*, a *lack of knowledge*, and missing *equipment*. These obstacles lead again to the same insight: A lack of knowledge about the process and equipment required for video production is the key reason why software professionals neglect videos as a communication mechanism in requirements engineering, even though they are aware of the strengths and opportunities of videos for effective requirements communication.

Use. *Software professionals already use videos in requirements engineering but, in particular, there is a lack of videos that could be used at all, and in case of existing videos, these videos have frequent flaws concerning the quality of their content and representation* (cf. Finding 4.3). Almost half of the surveyed software professionals used at least one video in requirements engineering. As in the production, videos are mainly used to convey *declarative* as well as *procedural knowledge* and rarely to influence the *affective state* of the target audience. Thus, videos are seldom used as a means for emotional impact. The videos used often had quality issues concerning their *content*, *image*, *sound*, and *duration*. These flaws coincide with the frequently mentioned flaws of produced videos. Despite the existing use of videos, more than half of the software professionals stated several obstacles that prevent them from using videos. Especially, a *lack of videos* that could be used and a *low added value* are crucial concerns of software professionals. The lack of videos implies that the surveyed software professionals do not understand the production of videos as part of their work since they assume to receive the videos from someone else. However, video production is only a further supporting technique that they could apply, such as workshops, scenarios, or audio and video recording [208]. Furthermore, the software professionals mainly justify the expected low added value of videos with the argument of high production effort.

Based on the results on the production and use of videos by software professionals, I can summarize the findings as the following answer to the Research Question 4.2:

Answer to Research Question 4.2

> *Software professionals produce and use videos as a documentation option in requirements engineering to convey declarative and procedural knowledge. The conscious application of videos to emotionally influence the target audience is a rather subordinate topic. However, these produced and used videos often have flaws concerning the quality of their contents and representations. In many cases, there is a lack of videos that could be used at all. This lack of videos can be attributed to a high production effort perceived by software professionals. Besides, some software professionals do not understand video production as part of their work, even though it is just another supporting technique, such as video recording. The only difference between recording and production is that a video is used not just to capture, but essentially to illustrate information.*

4.8 Conclusion

Videos are not fundamentally rejected by software professionals. Instead, software professionals have a positive attitude towards videos and know about their strengths and opportunities for effective requirements communication and thus shared understanding.

Nevertheless, videos are a communication mechanism with a neglected potential. In particular, the main weakness and most frequently mentioned obstacle for producing videos is a high effort. This obstacle results in a lack of videos that can be used at all which, in turn, mainly impairs the use of videos. The findings of the survey support the insight that software professionals lack knowledge about how to produce and use good videos for visual communication. This insight coincides with the conclusion and assumptions of different researchers [48, 136, 185]. According to Owens and Millerson, "*what was considered a professional quality camera* 10 *years ago has been dwarfed by the quality of small, low-cost high-definition pocket-sized cameras available today.* [...] *So now, no one can blame the lack of quality on his or her camera gear because almost anyone can afford the equipment. For all the cool technological advancements, keep in mind that the important thing is to know how to visually communicate*" [185, p. 80]. Carter and Karatsolis [48] also emphasized that using videos properly as a documentation option for communication in requirements engineering could provide significant benefits.

However, many existing approaches only focused on the use of videos in requirements engineering but omitted the details about how to produce good videos that are suitable for their respective purpose (cf. section 3.2). So far, little research encountered the challenge of enabling software professionals with the necessary knowledge and skills to produce good videos for visual communication. This emphasizes the need for research that focuses on the production of videos to establish them as an effective communication mechanism in requirements engineering. This thesis addresses the challenge of supporting software professionals to produce and use videos on their own at moderate costs and with sufficient quality. I assume the necessity to focus on simplicity regarding the used process, technology, knowledge, and skills due to the alleged high production effort. This should enable software professionals to more easily apply videos in requirements engineering. Based on the insights obtained, the following chapter 5 introduces a candidate solution (see section 1.3, Figure 1.1, ④) consisting of two concepts for integrating videos as a communications mechanism in requirements engineering practices. These two concepts (cf. chapter 6 and chapter 7) serve to mitigate the perceived high production effort and to bridge the knowledge and skill gap of software professionals to produce and use good videos as a documentation option in requirements engineering to support for effective requirements communication for shared understanding.

5

A Candidate Solution to Integrate Videos into Requirements Engineering Practices

The insights of the survey in chapter 4 substantiate three main issues that impede the production and use of videos as a communication mechanism in requirements engineering.

Issue (1): Software professionals associate the production and use of videos as a communication mechanism in requirements engineering with a high effort.

Issue (2): Software professionals lack knowledge and skills to produce and use good videos for visual communication.

Issue (3): Software professionals either lack videos that could be used at all or they produce and use videos that are likely to have frequent flaws and thus insufficient quality.

These three issues are related to each other in the overall context of the cognitive planning and execution activities within the video production and use process. The fundamental human information processing model of Reason [199], the so-called *human errors model*, explains the relationships. These relationships must be understood to develop concepts for a candidate solution (see Figure 1.1, ④) that aims to meet the underlying Research Goal 1.1 of this thesis.

5.1 A Candidate Solution Based on the Human Errors Model

When humans are faced with a situation that requires them to solve a problem or task, e.g., producing a vision video, they always perform the two cognitive activities of planning and execution [199]. Both activities are sources of cognitive failures which Reason [199, 200] calls *human errors*. First, a human error (see Definition 5.1) can be skill-based, rule-based, or knowledge-based, i.e., in the case of insufficient or missing knowledge and skills, a human is likely to fail in solving a problem or task. The lack of knowledge and skills of software professionals on how to produce and use good videos (**Issue (2)**) can be a cause of human errors. Humans are afraid of making mistakes, which affects their behavior. There are two strategies how humans handle this fear of human errors [10]. Either humans avoid situations that cause this fear to protect themselves from making mistakes, or they invest enormous effort to ensure that they have not made mistakes, which is not guaranteed despite the effort. The *avoidance strategy* corresponds to **Issue (3)** since software professionals do not understand video production as part of their work, resulting in a lack of videos. The *effort strategy* corresponds to **Issue (1)** and **Issue (3)**, resulting in a high effort for producing and using videos that are still likely to have insufficient quality. For this reason, a candidate solution must address the lack of knowledge and skills of software professionals as well as guide and support software professionals in the production and use of videos during their normal work so that all three issues are considered.

Definition 5.1 (*Human error; based on Reason [199]*)

> *A human error is a cognitive failure resulting from a human's decision (planning) or action (execution) in a situation where the human has to solve a problem or task.*

The human errors model provides two approaches (*person approach* and *system approach*) that explain how human errors are caused and how they can be managed to reduce the risk of their occurrence [200]. Both approaches have different but important practical implications for coping with the risk of human errors [200].

Table 5.1 summarizes the differences between both approaches which are briefly explained below. The person approach assumes that unsafe decisions and actions of humans can cause human errors due to inattention, forgetfulness, poor motivation, carelessness, negligence, recklessness, and thoughtlessness [200]. In contrast, the system approach has the premise that humans are fallible and errors occur even in the best organizations. Therefore, the system approach assumes that human errors do not originate in human nature but in potential error traps

Table 5.1: Differences between the person approach and system approach; based on Reason [200, p. 768]

Human errors	Person approach	System approach
Causes	Unsafe decisions and actions of humans due to inattention, forgetfulness, poor motivation, carelessness, negligence, recklessness, and thoughtlessness	Potential error traps in organizational processes due to complex, complicated, and long-winded tasks with unnatural sequences of process steps
Countermeasures	Reduce variability in human behavior by: • Creating awareness • Providing a guideline	Provide effective practices by: • Developing new practices • Revising existing practices

in organizational processes. The two approaches provide different countermeasures on how to manage and prevent the risk of human errors due to their different causes. While the person approach is intended to reduce variability in human behavior, i.e., by creating awareness or providing a guideline, the system approach focuses on changing the conditions under which humans work, i.e., by developing new practices or revising existing ones.

Both approaches must be considered to address all three issues identified. While the person approach helps to provide the necessary knowledge and skills to produce and use videos with sufficient quality, the system approach helps to support software professionals in the production and use of videos during their normal work. For this reason, this thesis proposes a candidate solution that consists of two concepts called *video as a by-product* (**Concept 1**) and *awareness and guidance* (**Concept 2**). While **Concept 1** is based on the system approach, **Concept 2** is based on the person approach. Figure 5.1 summarizes the previously elaborated relationships of the issues found, based on the human errors model by Reason [199,200]. Furthermore, Figure 5.1 also shows the two concepts of the candidate solution related to the respective issues addressed. The objective and an overview of each concept are explained in the following sections.

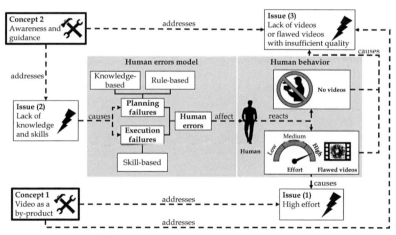

Figure 5.1: Relationships between the issues found and the concepts of the candidate solution

5.2 Concept 1: Video as a By-Product

This concept is based on the system approach and thus counteracts potential error traps in organizational processes by providing effective practices for producing and using videos as a documentation option for effective requirements communication. However, any new practice would increase the effort perceived by the parties involved since they would be unfamiliar with the new practice. Instead of developing new practices for applying videos in requirements engineering, the concept *video as a by-product* supports the selection and revision of requirements engineering practices by integrating the production and use of videos into corresponding techniques. A practice is only an abstract task that should lead to a qualitative improvement of the requirements engineering process (cf. Definition 2.3). Therefore, it is necessary to consider the corresponding techniques of a practice since these techniques are concrete methods that can directly be applied to implement a practice (cf. Definition 2.4). The research goal underlying this concept can be summarized as follows:

Research Goal 5.1

> **Analyze** the *rationale as a by-product* approach of Schneider *[213]*
>
> **for the purpose of** developing an approach to provide effective practices by revising requirements engineering practices
>
> **with respect to** reducing the effort for producing and using videos at moderate costs and with sufficient quality in the corresponding techniques
>
> **from the point of view of** this researcher
>
> **in the context of** requirements engineers who coordinate and communicate the stakeholders' needs between stakeholders and a development team to proactively develop and negotiate shared understanding by aligning their mental models of a future system.

A suitable starting point for Research Goal 5.1 is the *rationale as a by-product* approach of Schneider [213]. This approach has its origin in capturing rationale as a by-product of arbitrary practices within software projects. Several researchers have already adopted this approach to other aspects such as experience and knowledge [14], information flows [236], design decisions [44], contexts [71], and feedback [214]. The idea of the rationale as a by-product approach is to support the selection and revision of practices to integrate the capture of the rationale during the practice at different levels by being as little intrusive as possible to the experts and bearers of the rationale. As a consequence, experts and bearers of the rationale have the impression that the rationale emerges as a by-product of the normal work [213].

This thesis adopts the rationale as a by-product approach [213] by focusing on *video as a by-product*. The proposed approach supports the selection and revision of requirements engineering practices by integrating the production and use of videos at moderate costs and with sufficient quality into corresponding techniques. As a consequence, the parties involved in such a revised practice and corresponding technique have the impression that the video emerges as a by-product of the normal work. In this way, the concept *video as a by-product* addresses the alleged high effort (**Issue (1)**) and the lack of videos (**Issue (3)**) by keeping the effort low and increasing the number of videos produced.

The following section 5.3 presents the objective and an overview of the concept *awareness and guidance*. This concept addresses the lack of knowledge and skills of software professionals to produce and use good videos for visual communication (**Issue (2)**).

5.3 Concept 2: Awareness and Guidance

This concept is based on the person approach and thus counteracts unsafe decisions and actions of humans by reducing variability in their behavior when they produce and use videos as a documentation option for effective requirements communication. According to Reason [200], there are two options for addressing variability in human behavior: Creating awareness (Option (a)) and providing a guideline (Option (b)). The concept *awareness and guidance* supports both options since decisions and actions result from two different activities according to the human errors model [200]. While unsafe decisions are made in planning activities, actions result from execution activities (cf. Definition 5.1). Each activity can be more easily addressed by one of the two options. In particular, making safe decisions in video production and use requires an awareness of what constitutes a good video (Option (a)) [139]. In contrast, safe actions in video production and use can be ensured with a guideline (Option (b)) that specifies how actions should be performed to achieve a particular result. Both options are necessary to reduce the variability in human behavior and thus the risk of human errors when producing and using videos in requirements engineering practices. Below, I summarize the research goal underlying this concept:

Research Goal 5.2

> **Analyze** generic video production guidelines
> **for the purpose of** developing an approach to reduce the risk of human errors when software professionals produce and use videos in requirements engineering practices
> **with respect to** creating awareness regarding video quality and providing a condensed guideline to produce and use videos at moderate costs and with sufficient quality
> **from the point of view of** this researcher
> **in the context of** requirements engineers who coordinate and communicate the stakeholders' needs between stakeholders and a development team to proactively develop and negotiate shared understanding by aligning their mental models of a future system.

As introduced in section 2.3.2, the concept of video quality is rather ill-defined due to numerous factors. Although there are no universal rules for the production and use of high-quality videos, the discipline of video production provides a variety of guiding recommendations [185]. These generic video production guidelines have been discovered through years of experience and thus represent best practices on how to produce a good video with specific characteristics [136, 185]. An analysis of generic video production guidelines is a suitable starting point for Research Goal 5.2. As stated by Karras and Schneider [136], an analysis of the existing know-how of the discipline video production can help to learn what constitutes a good video and how to achieve these characteristics in requirements engineering practices.

On the one hand, the analysis of generic video production guidelines allows identifying individual quality characteristics of videos. Based on these characteristics, a quality model for videos can be developed that provides a clearer definition of the hitherto ill-defined concept of video quality. Such a quality model for videos enables to create awareness regarding video quality (Option (a)) since software professionals can use the quality model to identify relevant video characteristics for their respective project context. These video characteristics can be further used to establish requirements, satisfaction criteria, and measures for a particular video. Thus, software professionals obtain a basis for their planning activities that supports them in estimating and deciding on the consequent effort and activities required during the video production and use by using the defined characteristics as a checklist for the comprehensive treatment of video quality.

On the other hand, the analysis of generic video production guidelines allows operationalizing the quality model for videos by revealing how individual quality characteristics can be achieved. The analysis provides a comprehensive set of recommendations on how to produce and use a good video with specific characteristics. This set of recommendations allows providing a condensed guideline for video production and use (Option (b)) that is grounded and reflected on a valid body of knowledge. Software professionals can use this guideline to control their execution activities and thus their actions by achieving the fundamental knowledge and skills to produce and use videos at moderate costs and with sufficient quality.

This thesis presents the analysis of generic video production guidelines and its two results. In the context of producing and using videos in requirements engineering practices, I propose a quality model for videos to create awareness regarding the video quality among software professionals (Option (a)) as well as a condensed guideline for video production and use by software professionals (Option (b)). In this way, the concept *awareness and guidance* addresses the flawed videos with insufficient quality (**Issue (3)**) and the lack of knowledge and skills of software professionals (**Issue (2)**) by creating awareness of what constitutes the quality of a video and providing the fundamental knowledge and skills to produce and use videos at moderate costs and with sufficient quality.

In the following, I elaborate the details of the individual concepts of the candidate solution and their validations in academia (see Figure 1.1, ⑤). While chapter 6 presents the concept *video as a by-product*, chapter 7 presents the concept *awareness and guidance*.

6

Revising Requirements Engineering Practices to Apply Videos as a By-Product

According to the Research Goal 5.1, this chapter presents the concept *video as a by-product* of the candidate solution. This concept supports the selection and revision of requirements engineering practices by integrating the production and use of videos into corresponding techniques. The concept focuses on keeping the alleged effort for producing and using videos low and increasing the number of produced videos. Thus, the concept addresses the two issues *high effort* (**Issue (1)**) and *lack of videos* (**Issue (3)**) (see chapter 5).

Related Publications. *The concept 'video as a by-product' and its instantiation in two requirements engineering practices are based on "Karras, O. et al.: Video as a By-Product of Digital Prototyping: Capturing the Dynamic Aspect of Interaction. 2017 IEEE 25th International Requirements Engineering Conference Workshops (REW), IEEE, 2017" [140] and "Karras, O. et al.: Supporting Requirements Elicitation by Tool-Supported Video Analysis. 2016 IEEE 24th International Requirements Engineering Conference (RE), IEEE, 2016" [130].*

6.1 Developing the Video as a By-Product Approach

A suitable starting point for the development of this concept is the *rationale as a by-product* approach by Schneider [213] (cf. section 5.2). This approach supports the selection and revision of arbitrary practices within software projects to capture the rationale of decisions with reduced effort. Schneider [213] successfully applied his approach to two different practices, and several researchers [14, 44, 71, 214, 236] have already adopted Schneider's approach to other aspects, i.a., information flows and contexts. I followed their line of thought by adopting the *rationale as a by-product* approach to produce and use videos as a by-product in requirements engineering practices. In this way, I want to support requirements communication for shared understanding. Below, I briefly summarize the objective, structure, and application of the *rationale as a by-product* approach to facilitate the understanding of my concept *video as a by-product*.

6.1.1 Starting Point: The Rationale as a By-Product Approach

The rationale of decisions is an asset in software engineering since a development team needs to know why a decision was made, e.g., why one specific design or solution was preferred to another. However, the systematic creation and capturing of rationale is a complex task in software engineering that requires effort, time, and resources to build and maintain the corresponding documentation. Therefore, the *rationale paradox* is a frequently observable inevitability: When most rationale is created, the chances of capturing the rationale are lowest [213]. Schneider [213] proposed the *rationale as a by-product* approach to addresses this inherent tension between creating and capturing rationale to externalize this important information.

Objective. The underlying objective of the *rationale as a by-product* approach is to shift the effort away from (1) the time of carrying out a practice and (2) the parties involved in this practice. Thus, the parties involved have the impression that *"the rationale is really 'captured as a by-product of doing normal work'"* [213, p. 95]. Schneider [213] achieves this reduction of effort by using substantial preparation and tailored software tools to capture the rationale at different levels on the side while working on practices as usual. The trick is to select and revise the right practice by developing a tool-supported solution [213].

Structure. Schneider [213] developed his approach in analogy to agile methods in software engineering [19, 54] to propose a light-weight approach that supports the selection and revision of a practice according to the objective described above. In particular, the *rationale as a by-product* approach is defined by two goals and seven principles [213]. The two goals represent the values that Schneider [213] is striving for with his approach. This way of structuring an approach is inspired by the widely known method *extreme programming* by Beck [19]. According to Beck [19], this structure results from the relationship between values, principles, and practices. Values are abstract, large-scale, and universal criteria used by everyone to judge, decide, and justify their actions in a practice. Consequently, values set the direction for a person's actions and thus shape the practice by giving it a purpose. While values are expressed at a high level of abstraction, practices are concrete, clear, and objective. A practice is, therefore, the proof of values since a practice entails accountability for values. However, *"values and practices are an ocean apart"* [19, p. 14] from each other. This gap is bridged by principles that concretize values by providing recommendations to guide a person's actions in a practice. These principles allow to better understand what a practice is intended to accomplish. As a consequence, a defined set of principles forms a domain-specific guideline that supports the selection and revision of a practice that is consistent with the associated values. The application of a practice that implements the defined principles ensures to achieve the corresponding values.

Application. The strength of the *rationale as a by-product* approach lies in its structure [213]. The higher level of abstraction of the values and their concretization through principles allow the application of the approach in a wide variety of different situations and activities in software engineering [213]. In particular, the approach helps to select a rewarding practice for capturing rationale and to revise this practice by developing an individual software tool to support the practice. Although such a software tool requires substantial preparation of the practice, its support reduces the effort during the actual practice so that the rationale seems to be captured as a by-product. The concrete instantiation of the approach requires to implement the principles in a particular practice through their operationalization in a corresponding technique. However, the implementation of the principles can be done in several ways depending on the selected practice [213]. Consequently, the actual outcome of the approach in terms of the revised practice and the resulting software tool cannot be described more precisely.

Schneider [213] defined his values and principles with a clear reference to the capture of rationale. Therefore, the *rationale as a by-product* approach cannot be applied directly to revise requirements engineering practices to produce and use videos as a by-product. However, this approach provides a sound basis as an orientation to develop the *video as a by-product* approach.

6.1.2 The Video as a By-Product Approach

Below, I present the *video as a by-product* approach inspired by the *rationale as a by-product* approach [213]. The underlying objective of the *video as a by-product* approach is to keep the effort for producing and using a video low (1) at the time of carrying out a practice and (2) for the parties involved by using substantial preparation and tailored software tools.

The *video as a by-product* approach is defined by four values and nine principles which are based on the insights that I gained through the analysis of the *rationale as a by-product* approach [213]. I have refined these values and principles by using my experience and knowledge from applying the *video as a by-product* approach to two different requirements engineering practices [130, 140]. In Table 6.1, I present the values that are explained in the following.

Integration. According to the objective, the effort for producing and using a video needs to be kept low at the time of carrying out a practice. For this purpose, the production and use of a video need to be integrated into the actual practice and the corresponding technique. In this way, the parties involved in this practice perceive the production and use of a video as part of their work and not as additional actions which are only inserted in favor of applying a video.

Table 6.1: Values of the video as a by-product approach

Values
V1 **Integration**: The production and use of a video are part of a practice that belongs to an activity within the software development process.
V2 **Involvement**: The production and use of a video concern only the parties who are already involved in a practice, and are as little intrusive as possible to those involved.
V3 **Simplicity**: The production and use of a video must be easy for the parties involved regarding the process and technology used as well as the knowledge and skills required.
V4 **Supplementation**: The video is only supplementary material in addition to the actual results of a practice.

Involvement. The involvement of persons in a practice is a crucial concern. Any additional action in a practice lowers the chance that the parties involved accept the practice [213]. Therefore, the effort for producing and using a video needs to be kept low for the parties involved. The literature mentions two options for handling the video production and use in requirements engineering: Either these actions are delegated to video professionals or software professionals perform these actions themselves [136]. Both options have their advantages and disadvantages. However, Karras and Schneider [136] concluded that it is easier to counteract the disadvantages associated with the production and use of a video by software professionals themselves. For this purpose, video production and use must be as little intrusive as possible to those involved.

Simplicity. According to the results of the survey (cf. section 4.4.1), the most mentioned weakness of videos as a communication mechanism in requirements engineering is the alleged high effort for their production and use. For this reason, I assume the necessity to focus on simplicity regarding the processes and technologies used as well as the knowledge and skills required. In this way, the parties involved in a practice can produce and use a video more easily which in turn lowers the threshold for applying videos in requirements engineering.

Supplementation. A video shall only be supplementary material in addition to the actual results of a practice. According to the survey results (cf. section 4.4.1, section 4.4.2, and section 4.4.3), the applicability of videos to any context and content is questionable, and videos may be rejected by the parties involved. The consideration of videos as supplementary material is advisable since the occurrence of such cases is not predictable. If no video can be produced and used, the original practice must still be applicable as a fallback option, even spontaneously.

Based on these values, I defined nine principles that provide recommendations to guide a person's actions in a practice that shall achieve the corresponding values. In particular, a practice implementing these nine principles is intended to accomplish the production and use of a video as a by-product. Thus, this defined set of principles forms a domain-specific guideline that supports the selection and revision of requirements engineering practices that are consistent with the associated values. In Table 6.2, I present a comprehensive list of the nine principles. Each principle is subsequently explained in detail.

Table 6.2: Principles of the video as a by-product approach

Principles
P1 **Focus**: Focus on one particular practice in which you want to produce and use a video.
P2 **Concurrency**: Produce and use a video during that particular practice.
P3 **Parties involved**: Involve only the parties who are already involved in the particular practice to produce and use a video.
P4 **Relief**: Relieve the parties involved as much as possible of the burden of producing and using a video.
P5 **Separation**: Separate the two actions production and use of a video from each other during the particular practice.
P6 **Technology**: Use a mobile device (notebook, tablet, or smartphone) to produce and use a video as well as to capture practice-specific information.
P7 **Combination**: Combine the video with practice-specific information and results so that the parties involved can process and understand all collected materials together.
P8 **Fallback option**: Ensure that in addition to the video, the actual results of the particular practice are always created.
P9 **Further use**: Allow the further use of the video beyond the particular practice, but do not insist.

Focus. The first principle relates to the values *integration* and *supplementation*. The *video as a by-product* approach supports the selection and revision of requirements engineering practices by integrating the production and use of a video into corresponding techniques. This integration requires a defined context and content. First, a defined context facilitates the revision of a practice due to a focused scope and perspective. Second, a defined content supports the decision of how a video can be applied as supplementary material that enhances the results of the practice selected. Therefore, it is important to focus on only one particular practice at a time.

Concurrency. The second principle relates to the values *integration, simplicity*, and *supplementation*. The production and use of a video must be integrated as a part of the particular practice and must not be an independent task. At best, the actions are so well integrated into the particular practice that they can easily be carried out on the side by those involved so that the video emerges as supplementary material in addition to the actual results of the practice.

Parties Involved. The third principle relates to the values *involvement* and *simplicity*. The costs and effort for a particular practice can be kept low if only the parties already involved are considered for the production and use of a video. Any additional person increases the costs and effort due to a further indirection in communication and coordination. Instead of involving additional persons, this principle recommends considering only those who are already involved in a practice. The production and use of a video must be as little intrusive as possible to those involved so that as few parties involved as possible are burdened by the additional actions.

Relief. The fourth principle relates to the values *involvement* and *simplicity*. Any additional action in a practice lowers the chance that the parties involved accept this practice. Therefore, the way of involving the parties involved in the production and use of a video must be well thought out. In general, the persons who are the sources of information for the actual results of the particular practice shall not be unnecessarily burdened. Their motivation to carry out these actions is low since they do not benefit from sharing and documenting their knowledge. Instead, the effort shall mainly be shifted to a person who benefits most from applying a video in the particular practice. This person is more motivated due to the personal added value and thus best suited to carry out the production and use of a video.

Separation. The fifth principle relates to the values *integration* and *simplicity*. The production and use of a video are complex actions with which especially software professionals are not necessarily familiar. For this reason, both actions shall be separated from each other in the particular practice. Thus, the parties involved only have to deal with one of the two actions at a time which in turn lowers their burden by simplifying the practice.

Technology. The sixth principle relates to *integration* and *simplicity*. The use of a mobile device is necessary to produce and use a video. The integration of a mobile device in the particular practice can be simplified by using the knowledge about the practice in advance for planning the revision. On the one hand, the mobile device must be integrated in the practice to efficiently support the production and use of a video. On the hand, it is important to decide how to apply a video as supplementary material in addition to the actual results of the practice.

Combination. The seventh principle relates to the values *integration* and *supplementation*. A video shall be combined with practice-specific information and results to be truly integrated into the practice. This combination is advisable since any information that belongs together and is divided into two or more artifacts must be processed together by its recipients to be well understood [134, 135, 239]. Successive processing of the individual artifacts only enables the understanding of the single materials but not necessarily of their interrelationships. Therefore, the combination of the video with practice-specific information and results is essential for their common understanding by the parties involved.

Fallback Option. The eighth principle relates to the values *integration* and *supplementation*. The applicability of a video in a practice is sometimes uncertain. Although the practice is revised to produce and use a video as a by-product, a video may not be applied either due to the context or due to, even spontaneous, rejection by the parties involved. Especially in the case of spontaneous rejection, the original practice must still be applicable as a fallback option.

Further Use. The ninth principle relates to the values *integration, simplicity,* and *supplementation*. Although the objective is to keep the effort for producing and using a video low, the additional actions always require extra work. Due to this effort, the video should be able to be used beyond the particular practice to achieve as much benefit as possible. However, this further use should not be insisted on since otherwise the development process may depend on the existence of the video. If no video can be produced, the further development process is delayed.

Table 6.3 summarizes the individual relationships between the four values and nine principles of the *video as a by-product* approach for an overview.

Table 6.3: Relationships between the values and principles of the video as a by-product approach

Principles	Values			
	Integration	Involvement	Simplicity	Supplementation
Focus	✓			✓
Concurrency	✓		✓	✓
Parties involved		✓	✓	
Relief		✓	✓	
Separation	✓		✓	
Technology	✓		✓	
Combination	✓			✓
Fallback option	✓			✓
Further use	✓		✓	✓

Like the *rationale as a by-product* approach, the application of the *video as a by-product* approach requires its concrete instantiation by implementing the principles in a particular practice through their operationalization in a corresponding technique. In the following section 6.2, I outline my procedure for selecting two different requirements engineering practices and corresponding techniques in which I applied the *video as a by-product* approach.

6.2 Selecting Practices for Revision to Apply Videos as a By-Product

The definition of *video as a by-product* approach allows its application in a wide variety of different situations and activities in software engineering. For this reason, the instantiation of the *video as a by-product* approach requires a defined context to limit the number of practices and corresponding techniques for selection. According to Research Goal 1.1, the context of this thesis deals with the coordination and communication of stakeholders' needs by requirements engineers between stakeholders and a development team to proactively develop and negotiate shared understanding by aligning their mental models of a future system. This context can be defined more precisely by clarifying the affected requirements engineering activities.

This thesis applies vision videos, as one specific kind of video, as a documentation option to support requirements communication for shared understanding. Vision videos are intended to share an integrated view of a future system and its use among all parties involved for two intended purposes: (1) for documenting the integrated view to align the actions and views of the parties involved; and (2) for eliciting and validating the integrated view with the parties involved regarding new or diverging aspects [137, 139]. Thus, vision videos are applied in the requirements engineering activities elicitation, validation, and documentation. The related work on the use of vision videos in requirements engineering (cf. section 3.2) substantiates that vision videos are essentially used in these activities. The respondents of the survey also emphasized the opportunity of videos to support these three activities (cf. section 4.4.1).

Although these activities include a variety of practices, several researchers [66, 84, 248, 251] coincided that *prototyping* and *facilitated meetings*, such as workshops, are common and well-known practices of these activities. I decided to apply the *video as a by-product* approach to these two practices due to the following three reasons. First, both practices are well-known for enabling, building, and assessing shared understanding among stakeholders and a development team [92, 248]. While prototyping supports shared understanding by experiencing how the future system will look and work, facilitated meetings focus on achieving shared understanding by discussing an artifact or topic, such as a vision. Second, both practices are known to enable the application of videos [96, 208], but the effort for producing and using a video in these practices is high [84,130,143,171,230]. The *video as a by-product* approach addresses exactly this high effort by using substantial preparation and tailored software tools to keep the effort as low as possible (cf. section 6.1.2). According to Gulliksen and Lantz [96] as well as Carter and Karatsolis [48], such software tools and methods are needed to integrate videos in activities and practices. Third, both practices are established in the industry. In the last 15 years, various researchers [84,206,248,264] have repeatedly shown that these two practices are widespread and frequently used in the industry. For these three reasons, the practice *prototyping* and *facilitated meetings* are promising for the application of the *videos as a by-product* approach.

In addition to the practices, corresponding techniques must be selected to operationalize the principles. Fricker et al. [84] found that the techniques *scenarios* and *workshops* significantly correlate with successful requirements engineering in industry projects. Each technique is a corresponding technique of one of the two practices selected. On the one hand, *prototyping* is a highly valued practice to elicit, analyze, and understand *scenarios* about how users want to interact with a future system in typical situations [92, 206]. On the other hand, *workshops* are one specific kind of *facilitated meetings* [92,195]. I decided to select these two techniques due to their significant relationships to requirements engineering success in the industry.

In the following sections, I present the application of the *video as a by-product* approach to *prototyping of scenarios* and *facilitated workshops* with the instantiation and validation in academia.

6.3 Revising Prototyping to Apply Videos as a By-Product

Stakeholders and development teams value prototyping of scenarios since they gain a better shared understanding of the future system and its use [169]. A scenario (see Definition 6.1) is an established technique for refining an abstract vision by providing a concrete example that is easier to understand by all parties involved [92, 195, 208]. The most common documentation option of scenarios in practice are textual descriptions [6, 53, 84]. As explained in section 2.2.2, *"it is far from certain that this* [textual documentation option] *is optimal in all cases"* [6, p. 467]. For this reason, I apply the *video as a by-product* approach to prototyping of scenarios to obtain vision videos as supplementary material. These videos are suitable for illustrating interaction processes between a user and a future system and thus can supplement the textual descriptions of scenarios to support requirements communication for shared understanding [88, 132, 234].

Definition 6.1 (*Scenario; based on Alexander and Maiden [6, p. 510], Carroll [47]*)

> *A scenario is a description of an individual, concrete, linear, and deterministic interaction process between a user and a system to achieve a particular goal of the user.*

In the following, I present the developed concepts that implement the principles of the *video as a by-product* approach to instantiate the approach in scenario prototyping.

6.3.1 Implementing Videos as a By-Product of Prototyping

According to the related work (see section 3.2), several approaches [32, 34, 61, 192, 235, 258] have already combined scenarios and videos to support requirements communication for shared understanding. However, the major problem of these approaches is the high effort for producing and modifying videos [140]. These approaches handle the production and use of videos as individual actions in addition to the usual actions of the respective practice. In contrast to these approaches, my underlying idea for implementing the principles of the *video as a by-product* approach is to represent the dynamic aspect of interaction in digital prototyping of scenarios in a way that can easily be created, modified, and is always repeatedly playable without the necessity of having a video. Thus, the prototyping of scenarios does not depend on the existence of videos but integrates the opportunity to automatically produce and use them.

In particular, I represent interactions as sequences of events generated by responsive controls in hand-drawn and digitally created mockups. Based on the combination of event sequences and mockups, vision videos can be produced automatically as a by-product by playing and recording the event sequences on the mockups. Changes and alternative scenarios are unproblematic since videos can be produced automatically from modified event sequences and mockups. In this way, vision videos can be produced and used at low effort.

67

6.3.1.1 Concepts for Producing and Using Videos as a By-Product of Prototyping

Based on the idea explained above, the implementation of the principles of the *video as a by-product* approach resulted in three concepts. First, I present all three concepts in detail before I reveal how these concepts relate to the principles (see Table 6.2) to achieve the corresponding values (see Table 6.1) in section 6.3.1.2.

Concept 1 – Support of Arbitrarily Created Mockups. Prototyping of scenarios can be done by using hand-drawn and digitally created mockups with different levels of detail and visual refinement [235]. Therefore, it is necessary to support any kind of mockup. I realize the support of arbitrarily created mockups by digitizing them, if necessary, and adding responsive controls with a user interface builder, such as the Gluon Scene Builder[15]. These responsive controls provide the benefit that they always generate their events, i.a., mouse, keyboard, and touch events, even without any implementation. Besides, the responsive controls can be styled individually by using cascading style sheets[16]. Figure 6.1 shows the same mockup of a graphical user interface for a login screen at three different levels of detail and visual refinement. In all three cases, the mockup contains the same three responsive controls ((1) text field, (2) password field, and (3) button). However, each mockup uses another cascading style sheet. While Figure 6.1a shows the hand-drawn mockup with transparently styled responsive controls, Figure 6.1b and Figure 6.1c show the digitally created mockup with wireframe- respectively custom-styled responsive controls.

(a) Hand-drawn mockup of a graphical user interface for a login screen with transparently styled responsive controls

(b) Digitally created mockup of a graphical user interface for a login screen with wireframe- styled responsive controls

(c) Digitally created mockup of a graphical user interface for a login screen with custom-styled responsive controls

Figure 6.1: Exemplary levels of detail and visual refinement of a mockup for a login screen. Remark: All three mockups contain the same three responsive controls: (1) a text field for an email address, (2) a password field for a password, and (3) a button to sign in.

---

[15]https://gluonhq.com/products/scene-builder/
[16]https://www.w3.org/Style/CSS/Overview.en.html

Concept 2 – Evolutionary Specification of Scenarios. In a prototyping session, a requirements engineer either elicits scenarios of how a user wants to interact with a future system or validates specified scenarios by presenting them to a user to obtain feedback for modification [235]. Both purposes require that scenarios can be specified and modified fast and easily to evolve during their specification. I realize the evolutionary specification of scenarios by capturing practice-specific information to produce and use vision videos. For one scenario, this specific information includes the order of the mockups and the interactions represented as sequences of events generated by responsive controls. Figure 6.2 shows the structure and relationships between the information captured. The order of the mockups defines the *scenario sequence*. Each mockup has its own *event sequence* which contains the events belonging to the respective mockup in their execution order. A scenario sequence can be modified by adding, rearranging, and deleting mockups. While added mockups require their associated event sequences to be specified, rearranged mockups retain their previously specified event sequences. The event sequences can be modified for each mockup individually. This management of the events facilitates changes of interactions since not the entire scenario sequence is affected by changes but only the respective mockup. There are two options to modify an event sequence: Either (1) deleting the existing event sequence and capturing a new event sequence; or (2) capturing new individual events and arranging them in the order of the existing events.

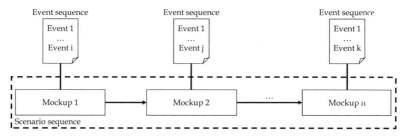

Figure 6.2: Structure of a scenario sequence and its individual event sequences. Remark: $i, j, k, n \in \mathbb{N}$.

Concept 3 – Independence from Videos. The time of the parties involved in a practice is always valuable. For this reason, no time should be wasted waiting for a video to be produced in order to be used. I realize the independence from videos by using the captured scenario sequence and its associated event sequences. Based on this information, the procedure of a scenario and its interactions can be visualized at any time without a video. A specified scenario can be visualized by displaying one mockup after the other according to the *scenario sequence*. The interactions are visualized by executing the events, which are computer-generated, according to the *event sequence* on the responsive controls of the corresponding mockup. Each responsive control can always be identified in each mockup due to a unique identification number.

Therefore, the execution and visualization of the events do not depend on the absolute position of the responsive controls. Thus, the responsive controls can be resized and rearranged (cf. Figure 6.1) and still allow the execution and visualization of the events. Although independence from videos is necessary during a prototyping session, the production of a video is an important feature to use the results of such a session independently from a software tool that implements these concepts. A scenario and its interactions can be exported as a vision video by executing and visualizing the scenario and event sequences as explained above and recording this visualization using screencasting. In this way, a video is only an exportable documentation option of the practice. As a part of his bachelor thesis, Hausmann [104] extended this concept by adding audio comments to a produced video. For each mockup in a scenario sequence, an audio comment can be recorded which is maximum as long as the duration of the interactions. This duration can be calculated in advance since each event has a defined but adjustable duration for playback. The audio comments are added to the video during the export.

The key features of the three concepts for implementing the *video as a by-product* approach are:

C1: Support of arbitrarily created mockups

- Mockups can be hand-drawn and digitally created
- Support of different levels of detail
- Support of visual refinement

C2: Evolutionary specification of scenarios

- Fast and easy definition and modification of a scenario
- Manage the scenario sequence by adding, rearranging, and deleting mockups
- Manage the event sequence for each mockup individually

C3: Independence from Videos

- Playback interactions at any time without a video
- A video is only an exportable documentation option
- An audio comment can be recorded for each mockup in a scenario sequence

I developed these concepts taking into account the principles of the *video as a by-product* approach. The relationships between the concepts and principles are explained below to show how the principles have been implemented in the revised practice.

6.3.1.2 Relationships between the Developed Concepts and Principles

The subsequent explanation refers to the overall implementation of the principles (see Table 6.2) in the revised practice highlighting the individual concepts and principles addressed. Table 6.4 presents a detailed overview of the relationships between each developed concept and principle of the *video as a by-product* approach.

Table 6.4: Relationships between the developed concepts for videos as a by-product of scenario proto-typing and the principles of the video as a by-product approach

Principles	Concepts		
	C1: Support of arbitrarily created mockups	C2: Evolutionary specifi- cation of scenarios	C3: Independence from videos
P1: Focus	✓	✓	
P2: Concurrency			✓
P3: Parties involved	✓	✓	✓
P4: Relief		✓	✓
P5: Separation		✓	✓
P6: Technology	✓	✓	✓
P7: Combination	✓	✓	✓
P8: Fallback option	✓		
P9: Further use			✓

First of all, the *video as a by-product* approach is applied to digital prototyping of scenarios (C1 and C2) which are one particular practice and corresponding technique (P1). Although the visualization of a scenario and its interactions is independent of the existence of a video (C3), a vision video can be exported at all times during a prototyping session (P2). No additional person is required to conduct such a prototyping session (P3) due to the selected way of specifying, visualizing, and exporting a scenario (C1, C2, and C3). Nevertheless, the parties involved are relieved from the burden of producing and using a video (P4) since the visualization is independent of the existence of a video (C2) and the export of a video can be done at any time (C3). These two concepts (C2 and C3) also separate the production and use of a vision video as a by-product of digital prototyping of scenarios to simplify the revised practice for the parties involved (P5). The application of digital prototyping by using responsive controls on mockups (C1, C2, and C3) implies the use of a mobile device such as a notebook or tablet (P6) to capture and play the interaction events in order to produce a vision video. The combination of mockups, interaction events, and audio comments (C1, C2, and C3) in a video allows the parties involved to process and understand all collected materials together (P7). However, the actual results of a prototyping session can always be achieved even without using a mobile device and producing a video since hand-drawn and printed, digitally created mockups (C1) can be used as a fallback option (P8). A produced video is only an exportable documentation option to make the collected materials and practice-specific information accessible independently from a software tool that implements the developed concepts (C3). Thus, the further use of produced vision videos beyond the revised practice is enabled but not insisted on (P9).

All nine principles were considered in the development of the three concepts to achieve the four defined values of the *video as a by-product* approach. Based on these three concepts, a tailored software tool, the so-called *Mockup Recorder*, has been developed that facilitates the production and use of vision videos as a by-product of scenario prototyping to support requirements communication for shared understanding. In the following, I present the details of the prototypical implementation of the three concepts in the *Mockup Recorder*.

6.3.2 The Tailored Software Tool: Mockup Recorder

The *Mockup Recorder* has been developed by Glauer [90] as a part of his bachelor thesis. The *Mockup Recorder* imports mockups either as FXML source files or as PNG / JPEG files that are automatically embedded in FXML source files. FXML is a markup language for defining graphical user interfaces of JavaFX applications [49]. The FXML format is necessary for adding the responsive controls to hand-drawn and digitally created mockups to generate the interaction events to be captured. Figure 6.3 shows the graphical user interface of the *Mockup Recorder* with its three main components: (1) *mockup chooser*, (2) *scenario timeline*, and (3) *mockup preview*.

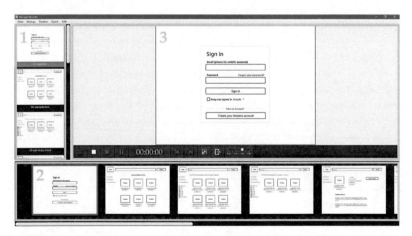

Figure 6.3: Mockup Recorder: (1) mockup chooser for selecting mockups, (2) scenario timeline for planning a scenario, and (3) mockup preview for capturing and playing interaction events

The *mockup chooser* (see Figure 6.3, 1) is a list of preview images of all mockups which have been imported to a project in the *Mockup Recorder*. This list provides an overview of all available mockups of one project. Each mockup in this list can be displayed in its original size in the *mockup preview* (Figure 6.3, 3) by double-clicking on the preview image of a mockup. The mockups can be edited with the Gluon Scene Builder[17] by right-clicking on its preview image and selecting the menu item "Edit" from the opened context menu. The mockups can be placed in the scenario timeline (see Figure 6.3, 2) using drag and drop. The *scenario timeline* (see Figure 6.3, 2) is a list of all mockups contained in a scenario. Based on the metaphor of a "filmstrip", each mockup in the *scenario timeline* represents a "keyframe" of a vision video. The order of these mockups defines the *scenario sequence* which can be edited by deleting or dragging and dropping a "key frame" in the "filmstrip". For capturing and playback interaction events, a mockup of the *scenario timeline* must be displayed in the *mockup preview* by left-clicking on the corresponding "key frame". The *mockup preview* (Figure 6.3, 3) consists of two components. Besides a view for displaying a mockup, the *mockup preview* has a toolbar for capturing and playing interaction events on the displayed mockup. The *Mockup Recorder* supports mouse, keyboard, and touch events. The export function is the key feature of the *Mockup Recorder* and is therefore presented separately. The toolbar of the *mockup preview* provides the export function for the scenario specified in the *scenario timeline*. The scenario and its interactions are exported by displaying one mockup after the other in the *mockup preview* and executing the interaction events generated by the computer. This visualization is recorded using screencasting to produce a vision video. In addition to the video, the *Mockup Recorder* exports each mockup in the scenario as a PNG file, e.g., to include these images in the corresponding specification.

Remark. *All details of the Mockup Recorder can be found in "Glauer, L.: Specification of GUI Interactions as Videos. Leibniz Universität Hannover, Bachelor thesis, 2017" [90].*

Besides the prototypical implementation, it is important to understand how the *Mockup Recorder* is applied. For this purpose, I explain its two main use cases below.

6.3.3 Use Cases of Mockup Recorder

In general, the *Mockup Recorder* is used for digital prototyping of scenarios using mockups to specify and document the dynamic aspect of interaction as videos. These videos are produced and used as a by-product in this practice and its corresponding technique to support requirements communication for shared understanding. However, prototyping can be used either to elicit scenarios with a user or to validate specified scenarios by a user. Based on these two purposes, I describe both use cases of the *Mockup Recorder* for each situation.

Use Case 1 – Elicitation of Scenarios. A requirements engineer uses the *Mockup Recorder* together with a user of the future system in close collaboration during a prototyping session. They create mockups which are used in the *Mockup Recorder* to specify interaction processes between the user and the system, i.e., scenarios. Each specified scenario can be exported both as a vision video as well as an image set of the mockups used in the scenario.

---

[17]https://gluonhq.com/products/scene-builder/

In a prototyping session, the requirements engineer elicits required functionalities and associated controls for the user interface regarding the interaction processes between the user and the system based on the user's goals. The requirements engineer and user use the identified functionalities and associated controls to jointly create mockups of the graphical user interface for the future system. These mockups can be created either with any editor and even hand-drawn, as long as PNG / JPEG files of the created mockups can be provided for import into the *Mockup Recorder*, or directly as FXML source files using the Gluon Scene Builder[18]. In the case of imported images, the automatically created FXML source files need to be refined by adding the required responsive controls. This step is not necessary if the mockups are directly created and imported as FXML source files (cf. section 6.3.2). After the mockups are created and imported, the requirements engineer and the user specify scenarios. A scenario is specified by arranging the required mockups from the *mockup chooser* (see Figure 6.3, 1) in the *scenario timeline* (see Figure 6.3, 2). Once the scenario sequence is specified, the requirements engineer and the user can specify the interactions for each mockup. For this purpose, the requirements engineer starts the capturing function in the toolbar of the *mockup preview* (see Figure 6.3, 3) and either the requirements engineer or even the user interacts with the mockup displayed in the *mockup preview* according to his idea of the interaction process. When the event sequence of the mockup is specified, the parties involved select the next mockup in the *scenario timeline* and repeat the process. Once the event sequences of all mockups in the *scenario timeline* are specified, the requirements engineer and user can review the entire scenario and its interactions by playing them in the *Mockup Recorder*. If they are satisfied with their result, the specified scenario can be exported as a vision video and an image set. This entire process for specifying a scenario can be repeated as often as required until all scenarios are specified.

Use Case 2 – Validation of Scenarios. The validation of scenarios can be done either in a meeting with the users or independently of a meeting by the users. In both cases, the exported vision videos of specified scenarios are viewed by the users for validation. The users give feedback either by confirming the scenarios or providing improvement suggestions for modifying the scenarios according to their needs. Based on the suggestions, the requirements engineer revises the scenarios and repeats the process until all scenarios are confirmed.

In both cases, the requirements engineer first uses the *Mockup Recorder* to specify each scenario for validation as described above (cf. **Use Case 1 – Elicitation of Scenarios.**). These scenarios are based on previously elicited information such as goals, use cases, and requirements. Once the scenarios are specified and exported as vision videos, the requirements engineer either presents the videos to the users in a meeting or distributes the videos among the users, e.g., by email. A meeting is not necessary since every user can play the videos and give feedback. Based on this feedback, the requirements engineer can revise the scenarios if necessary. How-

---

[18]https://gluonhq.com/products/scene-builder/

ever, in the case of a meeting, the requirements engineer can directly use the *Mockup Recorder* to revise the scenarios in close collaboration with the users. At the end of both cases, all specified scenarios are validated by the users and documented as vision videos for further use, e.g., as supplementary material in addition to a written specification for the development team.

After the introduction of the first instantiation of the *video as a by-product* approach with its prototypical implementation and use cases, it is necessary to validate the benefit of videos as a by-product of scenario prototyping.

6.4 Validating the Benefit of Videos as a By-Product of Prototyping

Although the approach enables the production and use of vision videos as a by-product of scenario prototyping, the benefit of these videos is unknown. According to the scientific approach presented in section 1.3 (see Figure 1.1, ⑤), I conducted a controlled experiment in academia to initially evaluate the support of these videos for requirements communication for shared understanding. This step is crucial to ensure that the concept *video as a by-product* is valid and sound to contribute to the fundamental relevance of the candidate solution before the candidate solution is applied in an industrial context. Therefore, the experiment is necessary to lay the foundation for the technology transfer from academia to industry.

6.4.1 Experimental Objective

According to the defined value *supplementation* of the *video as a by-product* approach, videos shall only be considered as supplementary material in addition to the actual results of a practice. This value coincides with the line of thought of different researchers [2, 5, 48] who concluded that written documentation needs to be supplemented by other media to turn it into an effective means of communication (cf. section 2.2.2). Therefore, the produced vision videos are only additional support for understanding the textual descriptions of scenarios similar to image sets of mockups used in a prototyping session of scenarios [140]. Based on this context, the research goal underlying the controlled experiment can be summarized as follows:

Research Goal 6.1

> **Analyze** vision videos produced as a by-product of scenario prototyping
> **for the purpose of** supplementing textual descriptions of scenarios
> **with respect to** understanding scenarios
> **from the point of view of** students who have the role of a developer
> **in the context of** a controlled off-line setting of a fictitious project in academia.

The produced vision videos capture the dynamic aspect of interactions between a user and a future system. This dynamic interaction is lost if only image sets of static mockups are used as supplementary material for textual descriptions of scenarios [140]. Both media, vision videos and image sets of static mockups, are only supplementary material for textual descriptions of scenarios. Therefore, the question rises how the use of vision videos as supplementary material differs from the use of image sets of static mockups regarding the understanding of scenarios. In particular, I ask the following research question:

Research Question 6.1

How does the use of a vision video as supplementary material for a textual description of a scenario affect the understanding of the scenario compared to the use of an image set of static mockups?

6.4.2 Experimental Design

The experimental design is developed by following the recommendations and process for experimentation in software engineering by Wohlin et al. [257]. Below, I present the important details of the resulting experimental design.

6.4.2.1 Hypotheses

In consideration of Research Goal 6.1 and Research Question 6.1, I examine the influence of the two different supplementary materials (a video and an image set of static mockups) for a textual description of a scenario on the subjects' understanding of the scenario. In particular, I test the following null and alternative hypothesis:

H_0: There is no difference between the use of a vision video and an image set of static mockups as supplementary material for a textual description of a scenario regarding the subjects' understanding of the scenario.

H_1: There is a difference between the use of a vision video and an image set of static mockups as supplementary material for a textual description of a scenario regarding the subjects' understanding of the scenario.

6.4.2.2 Independent and Dependent Variables

Based on the hypotheses, the independent variable of this experiment is the supplementary material with two levels: *vision video* and *image set of static mockups*. The dependent variable under investigation is the subjects' understanding of the scenario. However, the understanding of any material by a human is a theoretical construct that cannot be measured directly [17]. Thus, the subjects' understanding of the scenario is a latent variable which needs to be operationalized by indicators, so-called manifest variables. The operationalization ensures that the experiment delivers comparable results when repeated (cf. Bartholomew et al. [17, p.175 ff]).

I used three manifest variables as indicators for the subjects' understanding of the scenario: *familiarization time*, *extraction time*, and the number of *correct answers*. Table 6.5 presents an overview of the variables with their meaning.

Table 6.5: Overview of the independent and dependent variables

	Variables	Meaning
Independent	Supplementary material	The supplementary material has two levels: Vision video and image set of static mockups.
Dependent	Familiarization time	The time a subject needs to become familiar with the textual description of the scenario and supplementary material.
	Extraction time	The time a subject needs to extract information from the textual description of the scenario and supplementary material to answer questions.
	Number of correct answers	The number of questions that a subject has answered correctly.

6.4.2.3 Material

The textual description and the supplementary materials (vision video and image set of static mockups) are based on a scenario that deals with the purchase of a product by a customer in a webshop. I decided to use the same scenario for all subjects in the experiment to ensure the comparability of the results. However, I must remark that this decision restricts the validity of the results. Below, I describe the three materials used.

The textual description consists of 19 steps that describe in detail the interaction process between a user and a webshop to purchase a product (cf. appendix C.1). If a step initiates an event sequence on a particular mockup (cf. Figure 6.2), there is a reference from this step to the respective mockup of the image set. I used the *Mockup Recorder* to produce the vision video. This vision video has a total duration of 64 seconds and shows the described interaction process on ten different mockups. The vision video is published online [128]. The image set of the static mockups consists of the ten different mockups that were used in the *Mockup Recorder* to specify the interaction process. The ten mockups can be found in appendix C.2.

6.4.2.4 Subject Selection

This experiment serves the first validation of the instantiation of the *video as a by-product* approach in prototyping of scenarios in academia. Although experiments with students are often associated with a lack of realism [227], I consciously decided to select students as subjects for this experiment due to the following three reasons. First, students are often used as subjects for validation in academia since *"they are more accessible and easier to organize* [than professionals from the industry]" [227, p. 4]. Second, students form a more homogeneous group than professionals from the industry since they have comparable knowledge, experience, and skills. Despite reduced external validity, a more homogeneous group increases the conclusion validity since the risk of variation due to subjects' heterogeneity is mitigated. Third, there are only minor differences between students, which are close to their graduation, and software professionals concerning their ability to perform small but non-trivial assessment tasks [109].

The selection of subjects was carried out using convenience sampling. Potential subjects were personally invited to participate in the experiment on various occasions. All contacted subjects were undergraduate and graduate students of computer science, computer engineering, or business informatics. The only limitation in the selection of subjects was that a subject had to have at least one year of experience as a developer to be representative of a developer from the industry. The selected subjects participated in the experiment voluntarily. There was no financial reward and thus little incentive to participate without being self-motivated.

6.4.2.5 Experimental Procedure

The experiment has a between-subjects design with two groups (G_{Video} and $G_{Image\ set}$) due to the use of only one scenario for better comparability of the results. Therefore, each subject belonged to only one group. Each group received either only the vision video (G_{Video}) or only the image set of the ten static mockups ($G_{Image\ set}$) as supplementary material in addition to the textual description of the scenario. The subjects were randomly assigned to one of the two groups, whereby only the even distribution of undergraduate and graduate students between the two groups was ensured. The experimental procedure for one session with a subject was composed of three steps: *introduction, familiarization,* and *extraction*.

Before running the experiment, each subject got an *introduction* to the experimental procedure with its two tasks of familiarizing oneself with the provided materials (*familiarization*) and extracting information from the materials to answer questions (*extraction*). Afterward, the subject read and signed the consent form for participation (see appendix C.3)

For the experiment, each subject was put in the situation of being a developer who has to understand a scenario of how a customer wants to purchase a product in a webshop to implement the corresponding software. The scenario was provided as a textual description supplemented by either the vision video or the image set of ten static mockups. The two tasks *familiarization* and *extraction* have been carried out one after the other to measure the *familiarization time* and the *extraction time* separately. For the first task, the *familiarization time* was measured from the beginning of the task until the subject explicitly stated to be familiar with the scenario.

For the second task, the *extraction time* was measured from the beginning of the task until the subject answered all ten questions of the questionnaire (see appendix C.3). These questions focused on detailed aspects of the scenario such as particular presented information, e.g., delivery options, and specific steps of the interaction process, e.g., the order of entering customer data. The subjects were permitted to use all provided materials for answering the questions since the experiment focused on how they work with the materials and not how much they memorize. Each session with one subject lasted no longer than 30 minutes. The experiment was carried out with 16 subjects as described above within one week in February 2017 [90].

6.4.2.6 Data Analysis Methods

The data analysis combines descriptive and inferential statistics. All collected data (see appendix C.4) have a ratio scale. Thus, the data can be analyzed either with the parametric *t*-test for two independent means [237] or the non-parametric independent 2-group *Mann Whitney U* test [168] due to the experimental design. Both tests can be used to determine whether statistically significant differences between the two groups (G_{Video} and $G_{Image\ set}$) can be observed under the given experimental conditions. The choice of the test depends on whether the data of the respective dependent variable is normally distributed or not. Data is normally distributed if the normality of the residuals is met which can be tested with the *Shapiro-Wilk* test [225]. In the case of a normal distribution, the *t*-test is used, and otherwise, the *Mann Whitney U* test, both with a significance level of $\alpha = .05$.

6.4.3 Sample

In total, 16 subjects participated in the experiment, 14 of whom were undergraduate and two were graduate students. All subjects have a computer science background and had at least one year of experience as a developer at the time of the experiment. The subjects were between the 2nd and 5th academic year with an average academic year of 2.88, indicating that the subjects were close to their graduation. Therefore, I expected the subjects to be suitable as representatives of developers from the industry.

6.4.4 Results

Figure 6.4 shows the boxplots of collected data of the three dependent variables for both groups. Figure 6.4a illustrates that all subjects of the group G_{Video} familiarized themselves faster with the scenario than half of the subjects of the group $G_{Image\ set}$. Besides one outlier in the group G_{Video}, both boxplots of Figure 6.4b and Figure 6.4c are very similar indicating that the data of each of the two dependent variables (*extraction time* and *number of correct answers*) are similarly distributed for both groups.

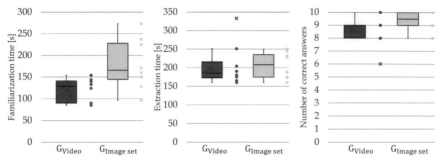

(a) Boxplots of the familiarization time of the two groups

(b) Boxplots of the extraction time of the two groups

(c) Boxplots of the number of correct answers of the two groups

Figure 6.4: Boxplots of the analyzed data. Remark: The ●-symbol visualizes the collected data points. The ×-symbol marks outliers in the data that are more than 1.5 times the interquartile range above or below the upper respectively lower quartile. The exact values of the collected data points and boxplots can be found in appendix C.4, Table C.1 and Table C.2.

With regard to the hypotheses (see section 6.4.2.1), the data analysis procedure was applied to all three dependent variables (*familiarization time*, *extraction time*, and *number of correct answers*). For this reason, I performed a total of three statistical tests to analyze the collected data for differences between the two groups, independent of the result of the respective *Shapiro-Wilk* test for normal distribution. These three statistical tests cause the problem of multiple testing which increases the probability of erroneously obtaining statistically significant results. Therefore, the *Bonferroni-Holm* correction method [65, 107] was used to counteract this problem by adjusting each calculated *p*-value in consideration of the number of performed tests.

Table 6.6 reports the details of each *Shapiro-Wilk* test, the respective *t*-test or *Mann Whitney U* test, and the adjusted *p*-value. The results of all three statistical tests carried out ($p_a > .05$) indicate that the subjects' understanding of a scenario is not statistically different between the two groups (G_{Video} and $G_{Image\ set}$). Thus, the null hypothesis H_0 cannot be rejected. Therefore, I assume that there is no difference between the use of a vision video and an image set of static mockups as supplementary material for the textual description of a scenario regarding the subjects' understanding of the scenario. This finding implies that a vision video is as good as an image set of static mockups to supplement a textual description of a scenario since both materials support an equally good understanding of the scenario by the subjects.

Finding 6.1

According to the results of the statistical analysis, there is no difference between the use of a vision video and an image set of static mockups as supplementary material for a textual description of a scenario regarding the subjects' understanding of the scenario. Therefore, both media seem to support an equally good understanding of a scenario by the subjects.

Table 6.6: Results of the statistical analysis

Dependent variable	Shapiro-Wilk		t-test		Mann Whitney U		Adjusted
	W	p	$t(7)$	p	U	p	p_a
Familiarization time	0.90	.08	-2.57	.02	-	-	.06
Extraction time	0.86	.02	-	-	31	.96	.96
Correct answers	0.82	.01	-	-	17	.11	.22

6.4.5 Threats to Validity

In the following, I report the threats to construct, external, internal, and conclusion validity that accompany with this kind of study [257].

Construct Validity. There is a mono-operation bias due to the use of only one scenario that deals with the purchase of a product by a customer in a webshop. As a consequence, the experiment does not convey a comprehensive representation of the complexity in practice. Nevertheless, the selected scenario represents a challenging situation in the real world. The dependent variables were only measured with objective measures, which represents a mono-method bias. This threat to validity only allows a restricted explanation of the findings. However, I decided to focus only on objective measures since they are easier to reproduce and thus more reliable than subjective measures. The second task of extracting information from the provided materials to answer questions caused an interaction of testing and treatment. The answering of questions implies measuring the number of correct answers. Humans are afraid of being evaluated. Therefore, the subjects may have been more careful to avoid incorrect answers which in turn may have affected the *process time* since the subjects might have taken more time to answer the questions than necessary. This effect should cancel out in the experiment since this threat to validity applies to both groups.

External Validity. I expect the subjects to be suitable as representatives of developers from the industry since they were on average close to their graduation and had at least one year of experience as a developer. However, the laboratory environment endangers external validity since this controlled off-line setting only represents a fictitious situation that is different from the real world. The selected scenario of the purchase of a product in a webshop had no pragmatic value for the subjects since none of them had a genuine working task with the provided materials. The webshop scenario is also a scenario that probably all subjects have already experienced by themselves. This prior knowledge of the subjects could have affected their answers to the questions. This threat to validity was counteracted by changing the steps in the interaction process and the presented data in the mockups compared to known webshops such as Amazon[19].

---

[19]http://www.amazon.de

Internal Validity. The selected between-subjects design with two groups (G_{Video} and $G_{Image\ set}$) caused interactions with selection since different groups have different behaviors. I consciously decided to use this experimental design to use the same textual scenario for both groups. Thus, I counteracted possible learning effects and achieved better comparability. In contrast, a within-subjects design, where each subject would have used both supplementary materials, would have required two different but comparable complex scenarios to avoid learning effects. However, it is difficult to ensure that two different scenarios have similar complexity for all subjects. Therefore, I expected the between-subjects design to be the better choice. The distribution of the sessions with the subjects over one week is a further threat to validity. The respective day-time could have affected the subjects and their motivation to contribute to the experiment. For this reason, the sessions were only held at regular times of day between 8 and 17 o'clock.

Conclusion Validity. The use of objective measures increases the reliability of the experimental results since these measures are easier to reproduce and more reliable than subjective measures. However, the numbers of correct answers were determined by using a questionnaire. A poor question wording could have affected the subjects' understanding of the questions. In the case of ambiguity, I allowed the subjects to ask questions at any time. All subjects had a comparable computer science background and at least one year of experience as a developer. Thus, the subjects formed a homogeneous group that counteracts the threat of erroneous conclusions. A more homogeneous group mitigates the risk that variation due to the subjects' heterogeneity is larger than due to the investigated supplementary materials for the textual scenario.

6.4.6 Discussion

The experiment provides important insights into the use of vision videos as supplementary material for written documentation. These insights substantiate that a vision video offers the same benefits as an image set of static mockups regarding the understanding of a textual description of a scenario. Thus, a vision video is a suitable medium to supplement written documentation.

A vision video, produced as a by-product of scenario prototyping, is as good as an image set of static mockups as supplementary material for a textual description of a scenario. The statistical analysis of all three dependent variables showed no difference between the use of a vision video and an image set of static mockups as supplementary material for understanding of a scenario. Both media are equally well suited for familiarizing oneself with a scenario, extracting information, and answering questions about details of the content and interactions process of a scenario. The subjects' understanding of a textual description of a scenario with the support of a video is as good as with the support of an image set of static mockups (see Finding 6.1).

However, I must emphasize that video is known to be the richer and more effective documentation option for communication (see Figure 2.2). For this reason, vision videos should be preferred over image sets of static mockups. These videos support an equally good understanding as image sets but are better suited to support requirements communication for *shared understanding* due to their richness and effectiveness for communication.

The instantiation of the *video as a by-product* approach in prototyping of scenarios (see section 6.3) enables the production of corresponding vision videos at low effort. This kind of video captures the dynamic aspect of interactions between a user and a future system. Once this information is specified, the produced vision videos contain important and consistent information that is valid and traceable by being related to stakeholders' needs. Therefore, these vision videos are a stable reference with *good enough specification quality* (see Definition 2.8). In contrast to a bare interactive prototype, the videos offer a clear benefit due to the strictly defined interaction processes. In this way, scenarios can be played repeatedly without any deviation from their original sequence and no user is required to perform the interactions with the prototype. In addition, videos can be easily shared and used by everyone since the vision videos can be played independently from the software tool *Mockup Recorder*.

Despite these benefits, the finding and insights of the experiment should not be overgeneralized due to the laboratory environment and threats to validity. This experiment is a first validation in academia which contributes to the fundamental relevance of the candidate solution by showing the validity and soundness of the concept *video as a by-product* and its instantiation in prototyping of scenarios. This validation is a necessary step to justify the validation of the candidate solution in the industry. As an answer to the Research Question 6.1, I can summarize:

Answer to Research Question 6.1

> *The use of a vision video as supplementary material for a textual description of a scenario does not differ from the use of an image set of static mockups regarding the understanding of the scenario. Both supplementary materials support an equally good understanding of a scenario. Therefore, vision videos produced as a by-product of scenario prototyping offer the same benefits as image sets of static mockups but are better suited to support requirements communication for shared understanding.*

6.4.7 Conclusion

This controlled experiment shows that a vision video produced as a by-product of scenario prototyping is a suitable medium to supplement the written documentation of a scenario. The statistical analysis of three different indicators for the understanding of a scenario exhibits no differences between the use of a vision video and an image set of static mockups as supplementary material for a textual description of a scenario. Thus, this kind of video is a promising supplementary material to turn written documentation into an effective means for communication. In contrast to image sets of static mockups, the produced vision videos better support requirements communication due to their higher richness and effectiveness for communication. Therefore, these vision videos contribute to *shared understanding* among all parties involved, offer a *good enough specification quality* and thus help to achieve a *clear scope*. As a consequence, these videos can help to establish the vision of the system in the relevant system context, which is the overall goal of the requirements engineering process (see Figure 2.3).

6.5   Revising Workshops to Apply Videos as a By-Product

As I explained in section 6.2, I have selected two practices and corresponding techniques for the application of the *video as a by-product* approach. Besides *prototyping of scenarios*, I also applied the *video as a by-product* approach to *facilitated workshops*. The following sections present this second application of the approach with its instantiation and validation in academia.

Facilitated workshops (see Definition 6.2) are an established technique in requirements engineering to engage stakeholders in joint decision-making on artifacts, e.g., the system vision, to foster requirements communication for shared understanding [86,92]. However, only a small group of selected stakeholders and members of the development team are involved in these workshops [86]. All other stakeholders and team members, who are not involved in the workshop, cannot benefit from the direct communication and the in-depth understanding during the workshop [86]. These non-involved persons have to rely on the documented workshop results which are summarized by a scribe in textual minutes. The creation and use of textual minutes are problematic since it is based on self-written notes [130]. Gall et al. pointed out: *"The notes are seldom complete and accurate as the scribe cannot take down everything or may omit or misinterpret important statements of a stakeholder"* [88, p. 3]. Different researchers [86, 88, 119] addressed this problem by using video recording as an additional action in a workshop to document the entire meeting. The produced videos were used as additional artifact to elaborate and supplement the textual minutes since they provide the documented information nearly as rich and trustworthy as the actual participation in the workshop [86]. For this reason, these videos are well-suited to support requirements communication for shared understanding.

However, these videos are long, unstructured, and disconnected from the scribes' notes and textual minutes which is why the motivation for using the videos is low [86,130]. Fricker et al. [86] concluded the necessity to complement the video with other artifacts of a workshop, e.g., the scribes' notes, to increase the acceptance of the videos. Based on this conclusion, I extended the approach of Fricker et al. [86] by applying the *video as a by-product* approach to facilitated workshops. In this way, the effort for producing and using videos is lowered and the video is better integrated into this requirements engineering practice. The produced video is a vision video (cf. Definition 2.11) since it documents the vision or parts of it in the form of discussions among the workshop participants about the future system (cf. section 6.2).

Definition 6.2 (*Facilitated workshop; based on Gottesdiener [94], Rupp et al. [208]*)

> *A facilitated workshop is a structured meeting of some selected stakeholders and members of the development team to develop and elaborate particular results, i.a., goals, scenarios, storyboards, use cases, and prototypes, in close collaboration.*
>
> *A facilitated workshop is moderated by a neutral moderator who guides the participants through the workshop based on a fixed agenda and clear rules to support the participants in their joint decision-making.*
>
> *A scribe supports the moderator by taking notes to capture all decisions and results during the workshop. Based on these notes, the scribe creates the textual minutes of the workshop.*

In the following, I present the developed concepts that implement the principles of the *video as a by-product* approach for its instantiation in facilitated workshops.

6.5.1 Implementing Videos as a By-Product of Workshops

Based on the approach of Fricker et al. [86], my underlying idea for implementing the principles of the *video as a by-product* approach is to combine the scribe's notes and the textual minutes with the video. In this way, a structuring of the artifacts can be achieved which allows an easy and fast access to the relevant information of all artifacts. In particular, I combine the scribe's work of taking notes and writing the textual minutes with the actions of producing and using a video. During a workshop, the scribe starts the video recording and directly connects his notes and textual minutes with the video by using annotations and timestamps. After a workshop, the scribe analyzes the annotated video to elaborate his notes and the textual minutes. In this way, the produced video is closely connected with the notes and textual minutes which keeps the effort for producing and using the video low.

6.5.1.1 Concepts for Producing and Using Videos as a By-Product of Workshops

Based on the idea explained above, the implementation of the principles of the *video as a by-product* approach resulted in four concepts. First, I present all four concepts in detail before I reveal how these concepts relate to the principles (see Table 6.2) to achieve the corresponding values (see Table 6.1) in section 6.5.1.2.

Concept 1 – Workflow Integration. A scribe has two tasks: Taking notes during a workshop and writing the textual minutes after a workshop [94]. Video recording and analysis must be integrated into the workflow of a scribe without restricting any former tasks [98]. This integration increases the chance that a scribe accepts the revised practice. I realize this integration by developing one tailored graphical user interface for each of the two main tasks of a scribe. The two developed views, so-called *Recorder* and *Analyzer*, consider the specific circumstances during a workshop and afterward in the follow-up analysis. The *Recorder* view assists a scribe in taking notes, recording, and annotating a video to connect the created artifacts during a workshop. The *Analyzer* view assists a scribe in elaborating the notes, writing the textual minutes, and viewing the annotated video to analyze the created artifacts after a workshop. Each view offers only the features that a scribe needs in the respective situation to focus his attention on the task at hand. In section 6.5.2, I present both views (see Figure 6.6 and Figure 6.7) in detail.

Concept 2 – Overview of the Structure. Facilitated workshops can last up to several hours. Thus, a resulting video has a long duration and contains a large amount of information. According to the survey results (cf. section 4.4), this large amount of information is the most mentioned threat of videos for requirements engineering since it is a typical source of frequent flaws in the production and use of a video. The respondents emphasized that a video often contains a lot of irrelevant information besides the few relevant parts. These few relevant parts are difficult to find since a video lacks a clear visible structure [130]. Therefore, there is a need to create an overview of the structure of a video regarding its relevant parts. I realize this overview of the structure by using annotations (see Definition 6.3), a timeline, and timestamps to highlight, visualize, and connect the relevant parts of a video with the notes. An annotation always belongs to one specific timestamp in the video to highlight this part as relevant. This annotation can contain arbitrary information such as a comment, an explanation, and a note to enrich the respective part of a video. Figure 6.5 shows an exemplary extract of a timeline of an analyzed video of a workshop. The annotations are represented as points in the timeline arranged by timestamps and grouped by type. The information of an annotation is displayed by another component of the graphical user interface (cf. section 6.5.2). This visual overview of the structure of a video facilitates the navigation of a scribe in a video to elaborate the notes and write the textual minutes of the workshop. As a part of his dissertation, Kiesling [143] extended this concept by additionally connecting the textual minutes with the annotations and the video based on timestamps. In this way, all created artifacts are interconnected with each other so that a scribe can navigate from each artifact to another one.

Definition 6.3 (*Annotation; according to Karras [123, p. 41]*)

An annotation is a marker that can contain a comment, note, explanation, and other arbitrary information to highlight and enrich a relevant part of a video.

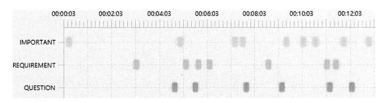

Figure 6.5: Exemplary extract from a timeline of an analyzed video of a workshop

Concept 3 – Customizable Annotation System. A facilitated workshop does not have a standard procedure since it is only a framework for individual processes, plans, and techniques [94]. Therefore, each workshop is unique. For this reason, there is a wide range of possible information, results, and thus contents for annotations in a corresponding video. Therefore, there is a need for a customizable annotation system that applies to the wide variety of different workshop situations to capture the required data suitably [98, 102]. I realize this customizable annotation system by using settings to freely define annotations with individual attributes and shortcuts for their creation. These settings allow a scribe to customize the annotations and their use according to his individual needs. As a result of the defined settings, a scribe can create annotations, possibly with predefined contents, by using shortcuts. Thus, a scribe can fast and easily create annotations on the side while taking notes since he only needs the keyboard. In this way, I consider the individuality of facilitated workshops as well as the working behavior of a scribe to ensure the applicability of the revised practice to the wide variety of different workshop situations.

Concept 4 – Export of the Created Artifacts. The results of a facilitated workshop are summarized and documented in the textual minutes by a scribe. This documentation is especially important for all those who cannot participate in the workshop. Different researchers [86, 88, 119] recorded workshops on video to use the video as additional artifact to elaborate and supplement the textual minutes of a workshop. However, these researchers did not connect the textual minutes and the video. Thus, the artifacts, that are complementary and should therefore be processed together, are separated which impedes the understanding of their interrelationships by the recipients [134, 239]. I realize the combination of the individual artifacts, e.g., textual minutes, annotations, notes, and video, by using the structures created on the basis of timestamps (cf. **Concept 2 – Overview of the Structure.**) to automatically export the comprehensive textual minutes. These individual connections allow to supplement the textual minutes with information from the different artifacts, for example by including annotations with their individual attributes and snapshots from the video. In addition to the comprehensive textual minutes, the individual export of the single artifacts created is also necessary to support their further use independently of a tailored software that implements the presented concepts.

The key features of the four concepts for implementing the *video as a by-product* approach are:

C1: Workflow integration

- A tailored graphical user interface for each task of a scribe (*Recorder* and *Analyzer*)
- The *Recorder* view assists a scribe in taking notes, recording a video, and annotating a video to connect the created artifacts during a workshop
- The *Analyzer* view assists a scribe in elaborating notes, writing the textual minutes, and viewing an annotated video to analyze the created artifacts after a workshop

C2: Overview of the structure

- Annotations highlight the relevant parts of a video
- The timeline offers an visual overview of an annotated video
- Timestamps connect a video, annotations, notes, and the textual minutes
- Annotations, timeline, and timestamps facilitate the navigation of a scribe in a video to elaborate the notes and write the textual minutes of a workshop

C3: Customizable annotation system

- Settings to customize annotations and their use according to a scribe's needs
- Arbitrary annotations with individual attributes can be freely defined
- Arbitrary shortcuts for creating annotations, possibly with predefined content, can be freely defined

C4: Export of the created artifacts

- Export of the comprehensive textual minutes supplemented with information from the annotations, notes, and video
- Individual export of the created artifacts, such as lists of annotations with all their information, notes, as well as video snapshots and clips

I developed these concepts taking into account the principles of the *video as a by-product* approach. The relationships between the concepts and principles are explained below to show how the principles have been implemented in the revised practice.

6.5.1.2 Relationships between the Developed Concepts and Principles

Based on the overall implementation of the principles (see Table 6.2), I explain the relationships between the developed concepts and principles of the *video as a by-product* approach. Table 6.7 shows the relationships between each concept and principle in detail.

The *video as a by-product* approach is applied to facilitated workshops (C1, C2, and C3) which is one particular practice and corresponding technique (P1). The production and use of a video are integrated into the entire process of a facilitated workshop (C1 and C3) which consists of the three phases planning, conduct, and follow-up analysis (P2). In the planning phase, a scribe can predefine annotations that he uses during the conduct of a workshop and afterward in the follow-up analysis. No additional person is required in the practice (P3) due to the integration of video production and use in a scribe's workflow (C1). Thus, the other parties involved (moderator and participants of a workshop) are relieved from the burden of producing and using a video (P4) since only the scribe, who benefits most from the resulting video in this practice, is burdened with its production and use (C1). This workflow integration (C1) considers the separation of the production and the use of a video to focus the scribe's attention on the task at hand (P5). The underlying idea of combining a scribe's notes and the

Table 6.7: Relationships between the concepts for videos as a by-product of facilitated workshops and the principles of the video as a by-product approach

Principles	Concepts			
	C1: Workflow integration	C2: Overview of the structure	C3: Customizable annotation system	C4: Export of the created artifacts
P1: Focus	✓	✓	✓	
P2: Concurrency	✓		✓	
P3: Parties involved	✓			
P4: Relief	✓			
P5: Separation	✓			
P6: Technology	✓	✓	✓	✓
P7: Combination	✓	✓	✓	✓
P8: Fallback option	✓			✓
P9: Further use	✓			✓

textual minutes with a video (P7) is reflected in all four concepts (C1, C2, C3, and C4). All four concepts (C1, C2, C3, and C4) require the use of a mobile device such as a notebook (P6) to take notes, write the textual minutes, record and view a video, and to connect all these artifacts. However, I must emphasize that the workflow integration (C1) as well as the export (C4) only provide the opportunity to produce and use a video but do not require its existence. Thus, the original practice with its actual results, i.a., notes and the textual minutes, is still applicable as a fallback option (P8). In this way, the concepts (C1 and C4) allow the further use of a video beyond the particular practice but do not insist on (P9).

According to these explanations, I considered all nine principles in the development of the four concepts to achieve the four defined values of the *video as a by-product* approach. Based on these four concepts, I developed a tailored software tool, the so-called *Requirements Video Analyzer* (*ReqVidA*), that facilitates the production and use of videos as a by-product of facilitated workshops to support requirements communication for shared understanding. In the following, I present the details of the prototypical implementation of the four concepts in *ReqVidA*.

6.5.2   The Tailored Software Tool: ReqVidA

I developed *ReqVidA* as a part of my master thesis [123]. *ReqVidA* provides the two tailored graphical user interfaces *Recorder* and *Analyzer* (cf. **Concept 1 – Workflow Integration.**). Both views allow a scribe to create annotations, take notes, and write the textual minutes. Furthermore, a scribe can export all these artifacts at any time during or after a workshop. However, both views have their specific features. Below, I present each view with its features in detail.

6.5.2.1 Recorder

Figure 6.6 shows the graphical user interface of the *Recorder*. In the *Recorder*, a scribe can record one or more videos of a workshop. During the workshop, the scribe always sees a real-time display of the video image to monitor the recording, e.g., to ensure that all participants of the workshop are captured by the video camera (see Figure 6.6, 1). The *Recorder* supports the use of webcams and digital camcorders. A camcorder has to be connected with the mobile device, e.g., a notebook or Microsoft Surface, via a so-called "capture device" to transfer the video and audio data. In the case of multiple connected video and audio devices, the *Recorder* offers the opportunity to select the specific devices. This selection option is important to consider internal webcams of notebooks, front and back cameras of tablets, and the use of external microphones. Each created annotation with all its attributes is presented in an individual tab in the detail view (see Figure 6.6, 2). Although custom annotations can have arbitrary attributes, all annotations have a common set of attributes: a unique identification number, a name, a reference to the corresponding video, a timestamp in the video, a type, and a comment. The identification number, reference, and timestamp are automatically created by the software. All other attributes are optional and therefore do not need to be filled in at the time an annotation is created. Thus, the workflow of a scribe is not interrupted due to missing inputs. Besides the detail view of annotations, the *Recorder* provides a list of all created annotations sorted by their timestamps in the corresponding video (see Figure 6.6, 3). This list offers a simple overview

Figure 6.6: ReqVidA – Recorder: (1) video recorder with real-time video display, (2) detail view of annotations, (3) list of created annotations, and (4) editor for notes and the textual minutes

of all annotations created so that a scribe can fast and easily access a specific annotation when needed. The *Recorder* also has an internal text editor to take notes and write the textual minutes (see Figure 6.6, 4). This editor helps to focus the scribe's attention only on *ReqVidA* since no additional software is necessary for a scribe to perform his task.

6.5.2.2 Analyzer

Figure 6.7 shows the graphical user interface of the *Analyzer*. The *Analyzer* enables the analysis of a video by providing an integrated video player (see Figure 6.7, 1). Besides the basic functionalities, this video player has a snapshot function to extract images from the video to supplement the textual minutes. As explained above, the *Analyzer* and the *Recorder* allow a scribe to create annotations, take notes, and write the textual minutes. Therefore, the *Analyzer* also has the detail view of annotations (Figure 6.7, 2), the sorted list of created annotations (Figure 6.7, 3), and the internal text editor (Figure 6.7, 4). These three components provide the same functionalities in both views. In addition, the *Analyzer* has an interactive timeline that offers a visual overview of the annotations to facilitate a scribe's navigation in the video (see Figure 6.7, 5). Based on three interaction options, i.e., single-clicking, double-clicking, as well as drag and drop, a scribe can interact with all points in the timeline which represent the created annotations. A scribe can open a specific annotation in the detail view by single-clicking on the corresponding point. He can use double-clicking to open the annotation in the detail

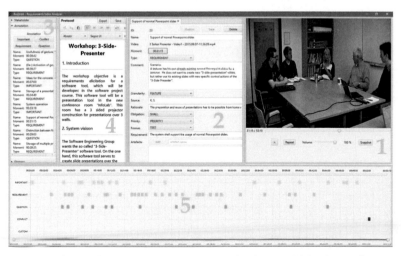

Figure 6.7: ReqVidA – Analyzer: (1) video player with snapshot function, (2) detail view of annotations, (3) list of annotations, (4) editor for notes and the textual minutes, and (5) interactive timeline

view and navigate directly to the corresponding part in the video. Last but not least, he can adjust the timestamp of the annotation by using drag and drop on the respective point. A special feature of the *Analyzer* is its flexibility in the analysis of any video, even if the video was not recorded with the *Recorder*. This flexibility and the customizable annotation system allow the applicability of *ReqVidA* in a variety of other scenarios beyond its original purposes.

Remark. *All details of ReqVidA can be found in "Karras, O.: Tool-Supported Analysis of Requirements Workshop Videos. Leibniz Universität Hannover, Master thesis, 2015" [123] and "Kiesling, S. et al.: ReqVidA – Requirements Video Analyzer. Softwaretechnik-Trends 36 (2015), No. 3" [144].*

Besides the prototypical implementation, it is important to understand how *ReqVidA* is applied. For this purpose, I explain its use case below.

6.5.3 Use Case of ReqVidA

ReqVidA serves the documentation of facilitated workshops as videos which are used as additional artifacts to elaborate and supplement the textual minutes. These videos are produced and used as a by-product in this practice and its corresponding technique. Figure 6.8 shows a FLOW diagram [236] of the typical use case of *ReqVidA* to support requirements communication for shared understanding between stakeholders and a development team. During a facilitated workshop, a scribe uses *ReqVidA* to record the meeting on video which he connects with his notes and textual minutes. Based on these artifacts, the scribe uses *ReqVidA* to elaborate and supplement the textual minutes in the follow-up analysis.

In a facilitated workshop, the moderator guides the participants through the workshop based on a fixed agenda and his experience to support the participating stakeholders in their joint decision-making. The scribe uses the *Recorder* of *ReqVidA* to record the entire workshop with its dynamic discussions and interactions of the workshop participants on video. During the recording, the scribe connects the video with his notes and draft version of the textual minutes by using annotations. Besides other documents that are created in the workshop, e.g., storyboards and prototypes, the scribe obtains one or more annotated videos, the draft version of the textual minutes, and his notes as a result of using *ReqVidA*.

After the workshop, the scribe performs a follow-up analysis to create the final textual minutes based on all workshop results. For this purpose, the scribe uses his knowledge and insights gained in the workshop and the *Analyzer* of *ReqVidA*. The scribe analyzes the annotated video(s) to elaborate the comprehensive textual minutes that is supplemented with information from the annotations, notes, and video(s). As a result of the analysis, the scribe obtains the comprehensive textual minutes and the video(s) with elaborated annotations. However, the scribe has also the opportunity to export further results such as lists of annotations with all

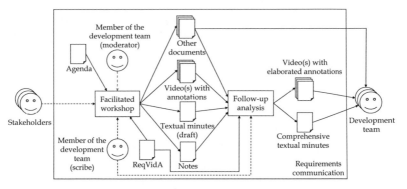

Figure 6.8: Information flow diagram of the use case of ReqVidA

their information, notes, and video snapshots. The comprehensive textual minutes, the video(s) with elaborated annotations, and the other documents resulted from the workshop are made available to the entire development team, especially to those who could not participate in the workshop. In this way, the development team can compensate for the lack of presence of all team members in the workshop and still gain an in-depth understanding of the stakeholders' needs to implement a solution that is accepted by the stakeholders, or in other words, achieve effective requirements communication for shared understanding (cf. Definition 2.5).

6.6 Validating the Benefit of Videos as a By-Product of Workshops

After the introduction of the second instantiation of the *video as a by-product* approach with its prototypical implementation and use case, it is necessary to evaluate the benefit of videos as a by-product of facilitated workshops. For this purpose, I conducted a controlled experiment in academia (cf. section 1.3 and Figure 1.1, ⑤) to examine the support of these videos for requirements communication for shared understanding. This step is part of the initial validation of the concept *video as a by-product* to increase its validity and soundness. The experiment contributes to the fundamental relevance of the candidate solution which must be ensured for its transfer from academia to industry.

6.6.1 Experimental Objective

The basic idea for producing and using videos as a by-product of facilitated workshops is to document the discussions among the workshop participants about the future system. These videos provide richer and more trustworthy information for a scribe to elaborate and supplement the textual minutes than using only textual notes. Therefore, the production and use of these videos serve to improve the quality of the textual minutes. However, the production and use of videos require a high effort which is the most mentioned weakness of videos according to the results of the survey in section 4.4.1. Especially, the ratio between the required effort and the potential benefits of applying videos is one of the identified obstacles preventing software professionals from using videos (cf. section 4.4.3). Based on this context, the underlying research goal of the controlled experiment can be summarized as follows:

Research Goal 6.2

> *Analyze* videos produced as a by-product of facilitated workshops
> *for the purpose of* elaborating and supplementing textual minutes
> *with respect to* the effort for writing the textual minutes and its quality
> *from the point of view of* software professionals and students who have the role of a scribe
> *in the context of* a controlled off-line setting of a fictitious project in academia.

I applied the *Goal Question Metric Paradigm* (GQM) [18, 244] to prepare the development of the experimental design. GQM is a method to identify one or more metrics for the operationalization of a specified goal by asking one or more questions. This method facilitates the identification, selection, and interpretation of metrics since the collected data is associated with the question(s), that characterize the goal, to provide quantitative answers [244, 257]. Based on the Research Goal 6.2, I ask the following research question:

Research Question 6.2

> *How does the use of a video as an additional artifact for elaborating and supplementing the textual minutes affect the effort of writing the textual minutes and its quality compared to the mere use of textual notes?*

Remark. *All detailed results of the applied GQM method can be found in "Karras, O.: Tool-Supported Analysis of Requirements Workshop Videos. Leibniz Universität Hannover, Master thesis, 2015" [123].*

6.6.2 Experimental Design

I develop the experimental design by following the recommendations and process for experimentation on software engineering by Wohlin et al. [257].

6.6.2.1 Hypotheses

According to Research Goal 6.2 and Research Question 6.2, I examine the differences between the use of videos (*ReqVidA*) compared to the mere use of textual notes (text editor) on the subjects' effort of writing the textual minutes and its quality. In particular, I investigate whether the use of *ReqVidA* differs from the use of a text editor regarding the effort and quality. Thus, I test the following two null and alternative hypotheses:

$H1_0$: There is no difference between the use of a video as an additional artifact (*ReqVidA*) for elaborating and supplementing the textual minutes and the mere use textual notes (text editor) regarding the subjects' effort of writing the textual minutes.

$H2_0$: There is no difference between the use of a video as an additional artifact (*ReqVidA*) for elaborating and supplementing the textual minutes and the mere use textual notes (text editor) regarding the quality of the textual minutes.

$H1_1$: There is a difference between the use of a video as an additional artifact (*ReqVidA*) for elaborating and supplementing the textual minutes and the mere use textual notes (text editor) regarding the subjects' effort of writing the textual minutes.

$H2_1$: There is a difference between the use of a video as an additional artifact (*ReqVidA*) for elaborating and supplementing the textual minutes and the mere use textual notes (text editor) regarding the quality of the textual minutes.

6.6.2.2 Independent and Dependent Variables

Based on the hypotheses, the independent variable of this experiment is the used technique for writing the textual minutes with two levels: *ReqVidA* and *text editor*. The dependent variables under investigation are the subjects' effort of writing the textual minutes and the quality of the textual minutes. As a result of the applied GQM method, I identified and selected one metric for each of the two dependent variables. The effort of writing the textual minutes is measured as the time a subject needs to write the textual minutes (*writing time*). The quality of the textual minutes is measured as the ratio between fulfilled and checked quality characteristics (*quality ratio*). Table 6.8 presents an overview of the variables with their meaning.

Table 6.8: Overview of the independent and dependent variables

Variables		Meaning
Independent	Used technique	The used software tool has two levels: *ReqVidA* and text editor.
Dependent	Writing time	The time a subject needs to write the textual minutes.
	Quality ratio	The ratio between the fulfilled and checked quality characteristics applied to the textual minutes.

6.6.2.3 Material

Instead of a real workshop, I used a ten-minute video clip from a one-hour video of a real workshop. I used this video clip due to the following three reasons. First, it was not possible to organize a workshop with all subjects as scribes at the same time. The subjects' presence would have affected the procedure and participants of the workshop. Second, it was also not feasible to conduct the same workshop for each subject individually since the workshop would never have been the same which endangered the comparability of the experimental results. Third, the analysis of a one-hour video takes up to three times as much effort [105]. This effort had to be limited to increase the chance that subjects would be willing to participate in the experiment. Despite these reasons, I must remark that this decision restricts the validity of the results.

In the video clip, the participants discuss their visions and requirements for a future software system. These requirements are important contents of the workshop which must be included in the textual minutes. In agreement with the workshop participants, I verified that the video clip contains eleven requirements that should be included in the textual minutes. This video clip does not allow the subjects to write the complete textual minutes. Therefore, I used these requirements as representative for the textual minutes. The quality of the textual minutes is represented by the average quality of the elicited and elaborated requirements whose quality can be assessed by using established quality characteristics for requirements [123, 130].

Remark. *Based on different publications [113, 208, 251], I created a list of quality characteristics for requirements. From this list, I selected six quality characteristics (traceability, priority, legal obligation, rationale, granularity, and atomic) whose fulfillment can be objectively assessed. All details on the quality characteristics and the selection process can be found in "Karras, O.: Tool-Supported Analysis of Requirements Workshop Videos. Leibniz Universität Hannover, Master thesis, 2015" [123].*

6.6.2.4 Subject Selection

The target population of this experiment includes members of a development team in industry who can take on the role of a scribe in a facilitated workshop. These subjects should have basic knowledge about requirements and their quality characteristics and, at best, have already taken the role of a scribe in a workshop.

I combined the two non-probabilistic sampling methods *snowball sampling* and *convenience sampling* to address potential subjects from the target population [147]. For snowball sampling, I directly contacted 15 software professionals from my network who belong to the target population. These 15 persons were asked to participate in the experiment and to distribute the invitation to participate in the experiment to people who also belong to the target population. However, software professionals are difficult to access and organize for experiments in academia [227]. Therefore, I also used convenience sampling to personally invite students to participate in the experiment on various occasions at the university. All contacted students were undergraduate and graduate students of computer science and were close to their graduation. These students are most similar to software professionals from industry regarding the required basic knowledge. All subjects participated voluntarily in the experiment. There was no financial reward and thus little incentive to participate without being self-motivated.

6.6.2.5 Experimental Procedure

The experiment has a between-subjects design with two groups ($G_{ReqVidA}$ and $G_{Text\ editor}$) due to the use of the same ten-minute video clip for better comparability of the experimental results. Therefore, each subject belonged to only one group of the two groups. Each group used either only *ReqVidA* ($G_{ReqVidA}$) or only a text editor ($G_{Text\ editor}$) to write the textual minutes. The subjects were randomly assigned to one of the two groups, whereby only the even distribution of undergraduate and graduate students as well as software professionals was ensured. The experimental procedure for one session with a subject was composed of three steps: *introduction*, *workshop session*, and *follow-up analysis*.

Before running the experiment, each subject got an *introduction* to the experimental procedure and the recorded workshop with its topic and content. Afterward, the subject read and signed the consent form for participation (see appendix D.1 and D.2).

For the experiment, each subject was put in the situation of being a scribe who has to write the textual minutes of a workshop. In particular, the subject had two tasks. First, the subject used the assigned technique to take notes regarding requirements for the future system stated by the participants during the *workshop session*. The workshop session was simulated by showing the subject the full ten-minute video clip once. Second, the subject used the assigned technique to elicit and elaborate high-quality requirements for the final textual minutes in the *follow-up analysis*. While the group $G_{ReqVidA}$ used *ReqVidA* with all its features and thus had the video clip of the workshop in addition to their created textual notes, the group $G_{Text\ editor}$ had only their created textual notes. After each task, I conducted a semi-structured interview with the subject by using a developed questionnaire (see appendix D.1 and D.2). While the questionnaire served to collect specific information, the method of questioning as a semi-structured interview encouraged the subjects to reveal their thoughts and suggestions.

The *writing time* was only measured from the beginning of the second task until the subject explicitly stated that he had finished the elicitation and elaboration of high-quality requirements. I excluded the time for the first task since it was the same for all subjects. The quality of the textual minutes was measured as the average quality of the elicited and elaborated requirements. After the session with a subject, I checked the fulfillment of the selected quality characteristics (cf. **Remark.**, p. 96) for each requirement to calculate the average *quality ratio*. Each session with one subject lasted no longer than 60 minutes. The experiment was carried out with twelve subjects as described above within two weeks in September 2015.

6.6.2.6 Data Analysis Methods

The data analysis combines descriptive and inferential statistics. All collected data (see appendix D.3) have a ratio scale. Therefore, the data can be analyzed either with the parametric *t*-test for two independent means [237] or the non-parametric independent 2-group *Mann Whitney U* test [168] due to the experimental design. These tests determine whether statistically significant differences between the two groups ($G_{ReqVidA}$ and $G_{Text\ editor}$) can be observed under the given experimental conditions. The choice of the test depends on whether the data of the respective dependent variable is normally distributed or not. The *Shapiro-Wilk* test [225] allows determining whether data is normally distributed. In the case of a normal distribution, the *t*-test is used, and otherwise, the *Mann Whitney U* test, both with a significance level of $\alpha = .05$.

6.6.3 Sample

In total, twelve subjects participated in the experiment: two undergraduate students, six graduate students, and four software professionals. All subjects have a computer science background and ten of them were already involved in at least one workshop. Five of these ten subjects had experience as a scribe. All involved students were close to their graduation. Therefore, I expected the subjects to be suitable representatives of the target population.

6.6.4 Results

According to the data analysis (cf. section 6.6.2.6), I checked whether the collected data is normally distributed by using the *Shapiro-Wilk* test. Depending on the respective result, I performed the corresponding statistical test whose results are summarized in Table 6.9.

In total, I performed three statistical tests to analyze the collected data for differences between the two groups. These three statistical tests cause the problem of multiple testing which increases the probability of erroneously obtaining statistically significant results. Therefore, the *Bonferroni-Holm* correction method [107] was used to counteract this problem by adjusting each calculated *p*-value in consideration of the number of performed tests. The *Bonferroni-Holm* correction method was used since this method considers the type 1 and type 2 errors [65].

Writing Time. The *Shapiro-Wilk* test ($W = 0.90, p = .15$) indicated that the *writing time* is normally distributed. The performed *t*-test showed that the *writing time* to elicit and elaborate high-quality requirements was significantly longer for group $G_{ReqVidA}$ ($M = 1270.5, SD = 397.28$) than for group $G_{Text\ editor}$ ($M = 460.2, SD = 193.66$), $t(5) = -4.49, p_a = .003$. The null hypothesis $H1_0$ can be rejected. The use of a video as an additional artifact (*ReqVidA*) for elaborating and supplementing the textual minutes requires more time than the mere use of textual notes (text editor). Figure 6.9a shows the boxplots of the writing time which illustrates that all subjects of the group $G_{ReqVidA}$ required more time to elicit and elaborate requirements than all subjects of the group $G_{Text\ editor}$. The comparison of the average writing times shows that the group $G_{ReqVidA}$ required almost three times longer than the group $G_{Text\ editor}$.

Finding 6.2

According to the results of the statistical analysis, there is a significant difference between the use of ReqVidA and a text editor for eliciting and elaborating high-quality requirements regarding the subjects' effort of writing the textual minutes. The use of ReqVidA requires on average almost three times more time than the use of a text editor.

Table 6.9: Results of the statistical analysis

Dependent variable	Shapiro-Wilk		t-test		Mann Whitney U		Adjusted
	W	p	$t(5)$	p	U	p	p_a
Writing time	0.90	.15	-4.49	.001	-	-	.003
Quality ratio	0.81	.01	-	-	0	.005	.01
Standardized quality ratio	0.93	.42	2.30	.04	-	-	.04

Quality Ratio. The *Shapiro-Wilk* test ($W = 0.81, p = .01$) showed that the average *quality ratio* is not normally distributed. The corresponding *Mann Whitney U* test yielded that the average *quality ratio* of the elicited and elaborated requirements was significantly higher for the group $G_{ReqVidA}$ ($Mdn = 95.8$) than for the group $G_{Text\ editor}$ ($Mdn = 16.7$), $U = 0, p_a = .01$. The null hypothesis $H2_0$ can be rejected. The use of a video as an additional artifact (*ReqVidA*) for elaborating and supplementing the textual minutes leads to qualitatively better requirements than the mere use of textual notes (text editor). Figure 6.9b illustrates that all subjects of the group $G_{ReqVidA}$ elicited and elaborated qualitatively better requirements than all subjects of the group $G_{Text\ editor}$. On average, the quality ratio of the requirements of the group $G_{ReqVidA}$ is more than five times higher than the quality ratio of the requirements of the group $G_{Text\ editor}$.

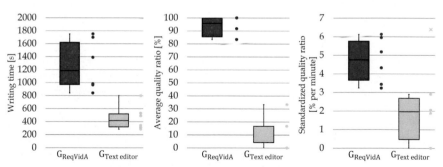

(a) Boxplots of the writing time of the two groups

(b) Boxplots of the average quality ratio of the two groups

(c) Boxplots of the standardized quality ratio of the two groups

Figure 6.9: Boxplots of the analyzed data. Remark: The •-symbol visualizes the collected data points. The ×-symbol marks outliers in the data that are more than 1.5 times the interquartile range above or below the upper respectively lower quartile. The exact values of the collected data points and boxplots can be found in appendix D.3, Table D.1 and Table D.2.

The average quality ratio of the group $G_{ReqVidA}$ might only be higher than the average quality ratio of the group $G_{Text\ editor}$ due to the increased writing time. Therefore, I standardized the average quality ratio regarding the writing time and performed its statistical analysis.

Standardized Quality Ratio. According to the *Shapiro-Wilk* test ($W = 0.93, p = .42$), the *standardized quality ratio* is normally distributed. The performed t-test showed that the *standardized quality ratio* was significantly higher for the group $G_{ReqVidA}$ ($M = 4.7, SD = 1.13$) than for the group $G_{Text\ editor}$ ($M = 2.2, SD = 2.15$), $t(5) = 2.30, p_a = .04$. Thus, the average quality ratio of the group $G_{ReqVidA}$ is higher than the average quality ratio of the group $G_{Text\ editor}$ for the same time range. Figure 6.9c presents the corresponding boxplots of the standardized quality ratio for each group. Besides one subject of the group $G_{Text\ editor}$, which is an outlier, all other subjects of this group achieved a lower standardized quality ratio than all subjects of the group $G_{ReqVidA}$. On average, the group $G_{ReqVidA}$ achieved a more than two times higher standardized quality ratio than the group $G_{Text\ editor}$.

Finding 6.3

> *According to the results of the statistical analysis, there is a significant difference between the use of ReqVidA and a text editor for eliciting and elaborating high-quality requirements regarding the quality. On average, the use of ReqVidA leads to a more than five times higher quality ratio and a more than two times higher standardized quality ratio of the elicited and elaborated requirements than the use of a text editor.*

6.6.5 Threats to Validity

Below, I report the threats to construct, external, internal, and conclusion validity [257].

Construct Validity. Instead of a real workshop, I only used a ten-minute video clip from a one-hour video of a real workshop. This use of only one short video clip causes a mono-operation bias since it does not convey the complexity in practice. However, I have to emphasize that the video clip showed a part of a real workshop. The dependent variables were only measured by using objective measures. The mere use of objective measures represents a mono-method bias. Nevertheless, I consciously decided to use objective measures since these measures are easier to reproduce and more reliable than subjective measures. The given tasks of taking notes of stated requirements as well as eliciting and elaborating requirements based on these notes caused an interaction of testing and treatment. The subjects might have been aware that the requirements and their quality have been under investigation due to the given tasks. This might have affected their behavior. However, I assume that the interaction of testing and treatment is a minor threat to validity since some subjects elicited and elaborated requirements with very low quality despite the given tasks.

External Validity. I expected the subjects to be suitable representatives of the target population since most of them had workshop experience and five of them have already been a scribe in a workshop. However, the controlled off-line setting endangers the external validity since the subjects were put in a fictitious situation. Although the video clip shows a part of a real workshop, it is still only a video. Furthermore, the situation had no pragmatic value for the subjects since none of them had a genuine working task. This lack of pragmatic value might have also affected the quality of the elicited and elaborated requirements since there was no real need for them. Besides the simplified textual minutes in the form of requirements, I also had to simplify the process of a workshop and its follow-up analysis. Instead of some hours or even a working day, the subjects had only a five-minute interruption between both tasks. Thus, their time to forget information was much shorter than in reality. However, both simplifications were necessary to reduce the effort of the subjects and not to waste their valuable time.

Internal Validity. The use of *ReqVidA* compared to the use of a text editor caused interactions with selection regarding the instrumentation. For three of the six assessed quality characteristics of requirements, *ReqVidA* supports its user with default values. One could argue that these default values caused higher requirements quality. I investigated this assumption in my master thesis [123] as well as in the corresponding publication [130]. I showed that even if the quality characteristics that are affected by default values are excluded in the analysis the subjects of the group $G_{ReqVidA}$ still achieved a significantly higher quality ratio and standardized quality ratio than the subjects of the group $G_{Text\ editor}$. I decided to include all quality characteristics in the analysis since exactly this support was part of the investigation. A further threat to internal validity is the assignment of the subjects to the two groups. Although the order of the subjects was completely random, I balanced the two groups to ensure that both groups have the same number of subjects who were undergraduate students, graduate students, and software professionals. I did this balancing to have more homogeneous groups for comparison.

Conclusion Validity. The validity of an experiment highly depends on the reliability of the measures. I used objective measures to increase the reliability of the experimental results. In contrast to subjective measures, objective measures are easier to reproduce and thus more reliable. The selected and assessed quality characteristics are objective measures since their fulfillment can be judged based on the presence and absence of specific information in the elicited and elaborated requirements [123]. A further threat to conclusion validity is the reliability of treatment implementation. While *ReqVidA* supported the subjects by providing specific attributes for annotations of requirements with some default values, the subjects who used the text editor had only their knowledge and skills to elicit and elaborate requirements. One could argue that an additional list of quality characteristics for requirements might have helped the subjects of the group $G_{Text\ editor}$ to elicit and elaborate qualitatively better requirements. However, this additional support by *ReqVidA*, as opposed to the text editor, was part of the investigation. Thus, providing such a list of quality characteristics would have distorted the experimental results. All subjects of the experiment (undergraduate students, graduate students, and software professionals) together formed a heterogeneous group. This heterogeneity increases the risk that the variation due to the subjects' differences is larger than due to the investigated treatment. I mitigated this threat to validity by evenly distributing the undergraduate students, graduate students, and software professionals among the two groups $G_{ReqVidA}$ and $G_{Text\ editor}$.

6.6.6 Discussion

The experiment provides important insights into the use of videos for elaborating and supplementing textual minutes of workshops. In contrast to the mere use of textual notes, a scribe needs more time to elicit and elaborate requirements for the textual minutes if he uses a video as an additional artifact. However, the average quality of these requirements is significantly higher when a video is additionally used instead of only textual notes. Thus, a video produced as a by-product is a suitable medium to elaborate and supplement the textual minutes.

The combination of a video, produced as a by-product of a facilitates workshop, and textual notes enables the elicitation and elaboration of qualitatively better requirements than the mere use of textual notes. The basic idea of using videos as additional artifacts is to relieve the scribe during a workshop and to better support him in the follow-up analysis. A scribe is relieved from the pressure of having to comprehensively record all stated information during a workshop since the video recording captures all verbal and non-verbal information in its actual context. Thus, a scribe can later reconsider the notes regarding their accuracy and completeness in their concrete context. In contrast to previous approaches [86, 88, 119], the instantiation of the *video as a by-product* approach, i.e., *ReqVidA*, facilitates the access, structure, and navigation between a video, the notes, and the textual minutes by using annotations and timestamps.

The statistical analysis showed two important findings. First, the use of a video in addition to textual notes needs more time to write parts of the textual minutes than the mere use of textual notes (see Finding 6.2). However, this finding is not surprising since any additional tasks and artifacts increase the effort. The important insight of this higher effort is reflected in the way the subjects worked with the additional video. While the subjects of the group $G_{Text\ editor}$ only elaborated their notes to requirements by formulating them to sentences, the subjects of the group $G_{ReqVidA}$ viewed several parts of the video clip multiple times to revise their notes and elaborate their requirements. Thus, the subjects who used *ReqVidA* processed all artifacts together which is the necessary and aspired way of working. In this way, these subjects were able to obtain a more comprehensive understanding of the interrelationships between the artifacts and the contained information which enabled them to elicit and elaborate qualitatively better requirements. This higher quality of the requirements is the second important finding (see Finding 6.3). The statistical analysis showed that the average quality ratio and the standardized average quality ratio of the requirements are significantly higher if using *ReqVidA* than using a text editor. The subjects of the group $G_{ReqVidA}$ used the opportunity to reconsider their notes in the corresponding workshop context due to the video. Thus, they revised their notes and requirements by supplementing them with further information from the video which their notes lacked. The subjects of the group $G_{Text\ editor}$ did not have this opportunity which is reflected in the significantly lower quality of their requirements.

Despite the higher effort, the higher average quality ratio and the implementation of the intended way of interrelating the video, the notes, and the textual minutes substantiate the validity and soundness of the instantiation of the *video as a by-product* approach in facilitated workshops. Once recorded, the videos of facilitated workshops contain important and consistent information that is valid and traceable by being related to stakeholders' needs. Therefore, these videos, the notes, and the textual minutes, which are all closely connected, are a stable reference with *good enough specification quality* (cf. Definition 2.8) for the further development process to support requirements communication for *shared understanding*.

This experiment contributes to the fundamental relevance of the candidate solution by showing the validity and soundness of the concept *video as a by-product* and its second instantiation in facilitated workshops. As an answer to the Research Question 6.2, I can summarize:

Answer to Research Question 6.2

The use of a video as an additional artifact for elaborating and supplementing the textual minutes increases the effort of writing the textual minutes but also its quality compared to the mere use of textual notes. The increased effort results from the implementation of the aspired way of working with the video and the notes by interrelating them to better understand their relationships and contained information. This better understanding, in turn, leads to the qualitatively better textual minutes since it contains more comprehensive information. Therefore, videos produced as a by-product of facilitated workshops offer in combination with textual notes and the textual minutes a suited documentation option to support requirements communication for shared understanding.

6.6.7 Conclusion

According to the results, a video produced as a by-product of facilitated workshops is a suitable medium to elaborate and supplement the textual minutes. Despite a higher effort of writing the textual minutes, the use of a video is beneficial for facilitated workshops and their follow-up analysis. On the one hand, the higher effort results from in-depth processing of the interrelated artifacts to understand them and their information. On the other hand, this better understanding helps a scribe to reconsider the artifacts regarding their accuracy and completeness and to revise them accordingly. The revised artifacts have a higher quality which better supports the further development process. The obtained insights point to the conclusion that these videos in combination with the notes and textual minutes offer a *good enough specification quality* of explicit documentation suited for communication. Therefore, these interrelated artifacts support requirements communication for *shared understanding* and thus help to achieve a *clear scope*. In this way, the three most important requirements engineering objectives are addressed which helps to achieve the overall goal of the requirements engineering process, i.e., establishing the vision of the system in the relevant system context (cf. Figure 2.3).

6.7 Summary of the Chapter

This chapter presents the concept *video as a by-product* of the candidate solution for revising requirements engineering practices to apply videos as a by-product. Based on Schneider's *rationale as a by-product* approach [213], I introduced the *video as a by-product* approach with its four values (see Table 6.1) and nine principles (see Table 6.2). I applied the *video as a by-product* approach to two different requirements engineering practices and corresponding techniques: (1) prototyping of scenarios and (2) facilitated workshops. Each instantiation of the *video as a by-product* approach was validated in academia to ensure the validity and soundness of this concept, which thus contributes to the fundamental relevance of the candidate solution.

Regarding Research Goal 5.1, I can summarize that I developed an approach to provide effective practices by revising requirements engineering practices to produce and use videos at moderate costs and with sufficient quality in corresponding techniques. The findings and insights of the controlled experiments show that videos produced as a by-product are a suitable medium to supplement written documentation. In contrast to merely written documentation, these videos better support requirements communication for shared understanding due to their communication richness and effectiveness. Overall, I am confident that the concept *video as a by-product* is valid and sound. However, the candidate solution consists of two concepts. The following chapter first presents the second concept *awareness and guidance* and its validation in academia before the entire candidate solution is validated in industry (see chapter 8).

7

Awareness and Guidance to Apply Videos in Requirements Engineering Practices

According to Research Goal 5.2, this chapter presents the concept *awareness and guidance* of the candidate solution. This concept serves to create awareness of video quality and to provide guidance in the production and use of videos. In this way, the concept supports software professionals to produce and use good videos in requirements engineering practices by addressing the two issues *lack of knowledge and skills* (**Issue (2)**) and *flawed videos with insufficient quality* (**Issue (3)**) (see chapter 5) deduced from the insights of the survey (see chapter 4).

Related Publications. *The concept 'awareness and guidance' is based on "Karras, O. and Schneider, K.: Software Professionals are Not Directors: What Constitutes a Good Video? 2018 1st International Workshop on Learning from other Disciplines for Requirements Engineering (D4RE), IEEE, 2018" [136], "Karras, O. et al.: Representing Software Project Vision by Means of Video: A Quality Model for Vision Videos. Journal of Systems and Software 162 (2020)" [139], and "Karras, O. and Schneider, K.: An Interdisciplinary Guideline for the Production of Videos and Vision Videos by Software Professionals, Technical Report – Version: 1.0, Software Engineering Group, Leibniz Universität Hannover, 2020" [137].*

7.1 The Need for Awareness and Guidance

According to the related work (see section 3.2), several approaches apply videos in requirements engineering. Although these approaches use videos, the required video production is often considered as a secondary task [136]. At first, this neglect of video production does not seem to be a problem since viewers of a video are mainly interested in what a video shows and tells. Therefore, it is unlikely that the viewers are concerned about how the video production was done unless they get bored or the technology becomes obtrusive and distracting [185]. Every video producer needs to be aware of the video quality to avoid any defects in a video [139]. Thus, the video producer can focus the viewers' attention on the conveyed content so that viewers can fulfill the goals of their individual underlying information needs [139]. However, software professionals are not directors and thus lack the knowledge and skills (**Issue (2)**) to produce and use good videos on their own. As a consequence, videos produced by software professionals are frequently flawed and thus have insufficient quality (**Issue (3)**).

While some researchers [32, 258] clearly state to give no guidance for producing videos, other researchers [61,262] only focus on the use of videos but omit the details on how to produce videos that are suitable for their respective purpose [136].

For example, the approach of Creighton [61], so-called video-based requirements engineering, provides a comprehensive process for producing and using videos in requirements engineering. Figure 7.1 shows this process in a simplified manner, which I specified for the application of vision videos. Creighton [61] solves the issue of video production by introducing the role *video producer* which "*is in charge of shooting video clips*" [61, p. 80]. Although Creighton [61] explains that this role can be fulfilled by a member of the development team, he suggests hiring a specialized film agency to outsource video production to video professionals due to their knowledge, skills, and equipment. This role is introduced to shift the effort of producing videos away from the requirements engineer. However, this shift complicates the process since outsourcing is expensive and requires additional in-depth communication between the requirements engineer and the video professional [136]. This additional indirection in the communication can cause further misunderstandings, besides the potential misunderstandings between the stakeholder and the requirements engineer. The entire process can be facilitated if the *requirements engineer* can produce and use videos on his own. Thus, the activity "Produce vision video" can be moved to the lane of the role *requirements engineer* and the role *video producer* is not necessary anymore (see Figure 7.1).

So far, little research encountered the challenge to encourage and enable software professionals to produce and use good videos on their own [136]. Software professionals could enrich their communication and thus requirements engineering abilities if they knew what constitutes a good video and how to achieve it [136,139]. For this purpose, I developed the concept *awareness and guidance*. On the one hand, the concept provides a quality model for videos to create awareness of which individual quality characteristics constitute the overall quality of a video. On the other hand, the concept provides a guideline to operationalize the quality model for videos by revealing how individual quality characteristics can be achieved in the video production and use process (cf. section 5.3).

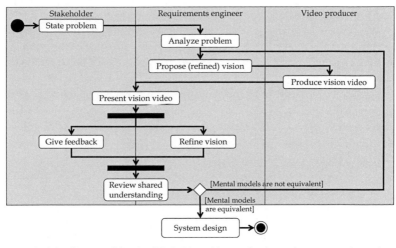

Figure 7.1: Activity diagram of the simplified vision video production and use process in requirements engineering; based on Creighton et al. [60], Creighton [61]

7.2 Research Process to Develop the Concept

Below, I present the three main steps of the research process shown in Figure 7.2.

7.2.1 Step 1: Analyze Generic Video Production Guidelines

The basic idea for this concept is to learn from the discipline video production (cf. section 2.3.1) how to visually communicate with videos to integrate videos into requirements engineering practices (cf. section 5.3). Although there are no universal rules for the production and use of

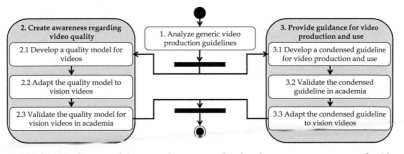

Figure 7.2: Activity diagram of the research process to develop the concept awareness and guidance

high-quality videos, the discipline of video production provides a variety of guiding recommendations [185]. These generic guidelines have been discovered through years of experience and represent best practices on how to produce a good video with specific characteristics [139].

The analysis of this existing know-how is the starting point of the research process to identify quality characteristics of videos with their relationships to the steps of the video production and use process (see section 7.3). I must emphasize that I do not want software professionals to become directors. It is necessary to understand the existing know-how of video production to transfer the essential knowledge into requirements engineering. I assume the necessity to focus on simplicity regarding the used process and technology as well as required knowledge and skills so that software professionals can apply videos more easily.

7.2.2   Step 2: Create Awareness Regarding Video Quality

For the awareness regarding video quality, I decided to develop a quality model for videos in analogy to the software quality model [26, 112] since video quality is rather ill-defined (cf. section 2.3.2). Following the ISO/IEC FDIS 25010:2010 for system and software quality models [112], the specification and evaluation of video quality requires the definition of the necessary and desired quality characteristics of a video associated with the producers' and viewers' goals and needs. This definition is made as a quality model that includes sensorial characteristics of the *representation* of a video, perceptual characteristics of the *content* of a video, as well as emotional characteristics regarding the *impact* of a video on its target audience [136, 139].

Based on the identified quality characteristics of videos with their relationships to the steps of the video production and use process (see section 7.3), I develop the quality model for videos (see section 7.4). This quality model is adapted to vision videos (see section 7.5) due to the specific context of this thesis (cf. Research Goal 1.1). Finally, I validate the quality model for vision videos in academia (see section 7.6) to ensure that this part of the concept is valid and sound to contribute to the fundamental relevance of the candidate solution (see Figure 1.1, (5)). The resulting quality model for vision videos serves a checklist for software professionals to ensure the comprehensive treatment of vision video quality over the entire vision video production and use process in requirements engineering (see Figure 7.1).

7.2.3   Step 3: Provide Guidance for Video Production and Use

Regarding the guidance for video production and use, I decided to develop a condensed guideline that summarizes the essential recommendations for video production and use to guide software professionals. According to *Cambridge Dictionary*[20], a guideline is a set of recommendations that advises a reader on how something should be done to achieve a particular result.

---

[20]https://dictionary.cambridge.org/de/worterbuch/englisch/guideline

The analysis of the generic video production guidelines provides a grounded and reflected body of knowledge consisting of a comprehensive set of recommendations on the production and use of generic videos. The reuse of these mutually supportive references enables the development of a condensed guideline for video production and use (see section 7.7). While vision videos are a very specific topic, there is a larger number of researchers and practitioners who are generally concerned with the application of videos in requirements engineering. For this reason, I first validate the developed condensed guideline in academia (see section 7.8) to achieve a greater added value for software professionals before adapting the condensed guideline to vision videos (see section 7.9). Software professionals can follow this adapted guideline to achieve the fundamental knowledge and skills to produce and use vision videos.

In the following sections, I present the details of the three main steps mentioned above. For a better orientation, I always refer to the section 7.2 and Figure 7.2 at appropriate point.

7.3 Step 1: Analyzing Generic Video Production Guidelines

This section presents the first main step of the research process (see section 7.2.1 and Figure 7.2) to develop the concept *awareness and guidance*. In this step, I conducted a literature review on generic video production guidelines to collect and analyze a set of mutually supportive references on video production and use. I must emphasize that this literature review is not a systematic literature review. I do not claim to provide a comprehensive overview. Nevertheless, the results of literature review lay the foundation for the further steps of the research process based on a grounded and reflected body of knowledge.

7.3.1 Literature Review Objective

The goal of the literature review is to collect recommendations that explain how to proceed in particular steps of the video production and use process to produce a video with specific characteristics. The analysis of these recommendations serves to identify the addressed video characteristics and their relationships to the steps of the video production and use process. For this purpose, I examine the following research goal by asking two research questions.

Research Goal 7.1

Analyze generic video production guidelines
for the purpose of collecting recommendations
with respect to how to proceed in particular steps of the video production and use process
to produce a video with specific characteristics
from the point of view of this researcher
in the context of a literature review.

On the one hand, it is necessary to identify the characteristics of videos that can be deduced from the recommendations of the generic video production guidelines. This topic is addressed in the first research question:

Research Question 7.1

What characteristics of videos can be deduced from the recommendations of generic video production guidelines?

On the other hand, one needs to know how the identified characteristics of videos relate to the steps of the video production and use process. Therefore, I ask the second research question:

Research Question 7.2

How do the identified characteristics of videos relate to the steps of the video production and use process?

7.3.2 Literature Review Design

The design of the literature review follows the guideline for performing systematic literature reviews in software engineering by Kitchenham and Charters [148]. Although this literature review is not a systematic one, I decided to follow the guideline as closely as possible to increase the quality and validity of the literature review. Therefore, I defined a search method, a search string, as well as exclusion and inclusion criteria.

7.3.2.1 Search Method

Generic video production guidelines belong to gray literature which can provide valuable insights for literature reviews [146, 166]. However, gray literature is often not included in scientific databases [33]. For this reason, I decided to perform a web search using the two popular web search engines *Google Scholar*[21] and *Google*[22] as proposed by Mahood et al. [166].

7.3.2.2 Search String

I developed the search string by using PICO (Population, Intervention, Comparison, and Outcomes) as suggested by Kitchenham and Charters [148]. PICO provides criteria whose consideration helps to identify keywords and formulate a search string from the research questions [190]. Table 7.1 shows the results from the consideration of the PICO criteria with the identified keywords and formulated search string.

---

[21]https://scholar.google.de/
[22]https://www.google.de/

Table 7.1: PICO criteria: Results, identified keywords, and search string

PICO criteria
(1) *Population*: The main topic of this literature review are video production guidelines.
(2) *Intervention*: I examine guidelines that belong to gray literature.
(3) *Comparison*: I do not compare the intervention with anything else, but I analyze the content of the intervention.
(4) *Outcomes*: I expect to collect recommendations on how to proceed in particular steps of the video production and use process to produce a video with specific characteristics.
Search string: video AND production AND guideline

7.3.2.3 Exclusion and Inclusion Criteria

For an objective selection of literature, I defined exclusion and inclusion criteria to identify those publications that provide direct evidence on the research questions [148]. These criteria help to reduce the likelihood of bias by supporting the classification of publications into selected and rejected ones. The criteria defined in Table 7.2 and Table 7.3 have been applied to each result of the search method. If none of the exclusion criteria E_i, $1 \leq i \leq 5$, and both inclusion criteria I_j, $j = 1, 2$, were met, the result was selected:

$$\text{Result selected} \Leftrightarrow \neg(E_1 \vee E_2 \vee E_3 \vee E_4 \vee E_5) \wedge (I_1 \wedge I_2)$$

Table 7.2: Exclusion criteria of the literature review

Exclusion criteria
E_1: The result does not provide a downloadable document, e.g., a PDF file, representing a publication that was consciously created.
E_2: The document is not written in English.
E_3: The document is not provided by an official institution or one or more authors experienced in video production.
E_4: The document focuses only on a specific type of video, e.g., tutorial videos.
E_5: The document is only partially accessible.

Table 7.3: Inclusion criteria of the literature review

Inclusion criteria
I_1: The document contains a statement that it is a guideline for video production and use.
I_2: The document contains a list of recommendations for video production and use.

7.3.2.4 Data Collection

I conducted the literature review in December 2017. I entered the search string "video AND production AND guideline" into both web search engines and investigated the results of each web search engine by applying the exclusion and inclusion criteria to each result. After the first 50 results in each search engine, I found no more results that met the exclusion and inclusion criteria. Another researcher with several years of experience reviewed my work and its results.

7.3.2.5 Data Analysis Methods

The selected publications are analyzed via manual coding [211]. Manual coding is a qualitative data analysis method consisting of two consecutive coding cycles each of which can be repeated iteratively. While the first coding cycle includes the initial coding of the data, the second cycle focuses on classifying, synthesizing, and conceptualizing (sub-)categories from the coded data. Figure 7.3 shows the manual coding process with two examples of extracted and coded text passages. I conducted this process with two researchers to increase the validity of the findings.

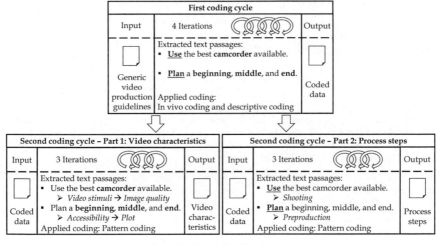

Figure 7.3: Manual coding process

In the first coding cycle, we applied a combination of *in vivo* and *descriptive* coding. These two methods assign a word or phrase as a code to a text passage in the qualitative data. While *in vivo* codes are words or phrases found in the actual data, *descriptive* codes are generated by the researcher. We coded the data regarding two aspects. On the one hand, we coded the text passages regarding their implication of video characteristics (see Figure 7.3, bold highlighting).

On the other hand, we coded the text passages regarding keywords, such as plan, record, edit, view, and similar words (see Figure 7.3, bold and underlined highlighting), that indicate one or more potential steps of the video production and use process. After four iterations, all three researchers agreed on the extracted and coded text passages. In the second coding cycle, we performed *pattern* coding which groups the coded data into a smaller number of themes to develop (sub-)categories (see Figure 7.3, italic highlighting). We applied the second coding cycle for both aspects: *video characteristics* and *process steps*. For both aspects, all three researchers agreed on the identified (sub-)categories after three iterations.

The results of the manual coding were validated by asking two other researchers to individually assign the identified (sub-)categories of *video characteristics* and *process steps* to the extracted text passages. Based on the assignments, I calculated the inter-rater reliability using *Cohen's κ* [55]. *Cohen's κ* is a robust measure of agreement between two raters on a certain topic since it takes into account the possibility of agreement occurring by chance.

7.3.3 Selected Publications, Extracted Text Passages, and Coding Results

The search method resulted in six generic video production guidelines [27, 57, 89, 105, 185, 242] which were analyzed according to the manual coding process. In the first coding cycle, all three researchers extracted a total of 307 text passages. We assigned at least one code regarding *video characteristics* and *process steps* to each extracted text passage resulting in 586 codes regarding *video characteristics* and 600 codes regarding *process steps*. In the second coding cycle, we grouped the codes into (sub-)categories for both aspects. For the *video characteristics*, we identified four categories and ten sub-categories. These (sub-)categories represent (sub-)characteristics of videos. For the *process steps*, we grouped the codes into four categories which correspond to the four steps of the video production and use process. Besides the three steps of the video production process (*preproduction*, *shooting*, and *postproduction*) (cf. section 2.3.1), we included the step *viewing* which represents the typical use of a video [185].

7.3.4 Results: Video Characteristics

Based on the results of the manual coding (cf. appendix E.1), I identified four characteristics and ten sub-characteristics of videos which I arranged by the three dimensions of a quality model (*representation*, *content*, and *impact*) [112, 139]. Below, I describe each dimension as well as the associated characteristics and sub-characteristics (see Table 7.4, Table 7.5, and Table 7.6).

Dimension: Representation. This dimension covers the sensorial characteristics of a video regarding its *representation*. The included characteristic *video stimuli* (see Table 7.4) considers the sensorial stimuli of a video. This characteristic aggregates the three sub-characteristics *image quality*, *sound quality*, and *video length* that a viewer perceives with his sensory organs.

Dimension: Representation – Video stimuli

Dimension:
Representation covers the sensorial characteristics of a video.

Characteristic:
Video stimuli considers the sensorial stimuli of a video.
Sub-characteristics:
Image quality considers the visual quality of the image of a video.
Sound quality considers the auditory quality of the sound of a video.
Video length considers the duration of a video.

Dimension: Content. This dimension covers the perceptual characteristics of a video regarding its *content*. The dimension includes the two characteristics *accessibility* and *relevance* (see Table 7.5). *Accessibility* focuses on the ease of access to the content of a video by containing the sub-characteristics *plot* and *prior knowledge*. A video is easier or harder to access for a viewer depending on the structuring of the content and the presupposed prior knowledge. *Relevance* considers the presentation of valuable information in a video. This characteristic includes the sub-characteristics *essence* and *clutter* that distinguish between important core elements, e.g., persons and locations, as well as disrupting and distracting elements, e.g., background actions or noises. While important core elements are deliberately recorded by a video producer since they shall be visible in a video, disrupting elements are inadvertently recorded and must be avoided since they may distract the viewer from the important core elements.

Table 7.5: Dimension: Content – Accessibility and relevance

Dimension:
Content covers the perceptual characteristics of a video.

Characteristic:
Accessibility considers the ease of access to the content of a video.
Sub-characteristics:
Plot considers the structured presentation of the content of a video.
Prior knowledge considers the presupposed prior knowledge to understand the content of a video.

Characteristic:
Relevance considers the presentation of valuable content in a video.
Sub-characteristics:
Essence considers the important core elements, e.g., persons, locations, and entities, which are to be presented in a video.
Clutter considers the disrupting and distracting elements, e.g., background actions and noises, that can be inadvertently recorded in a video.

Dimension: Impact. This dimension covers the emotional characteristics of a video regarding its emotional *impact* on its target audience. The included characteristic *attitude* (see Table 7.6) considers the humans' conception of a video. This characteristic aggregates the three sub-characteristics *pleasure, intention,* and *sense of responsibility*. *Pleasure* focuses on the enjoyment of watching a video. A video needs to be pleasant to watch to be interesting for its target audience. *Intention* considers the intended purpose of a video which has a strong influence on a video and its content since the purpose defines the reason why a video is necessary. In the context of video production and use, the *sense of responsibility* is a crucial concern. The production and use must comply with legal regulations to ensure legal reliability for all parties involved. Otherwise, a video producer or viewer may reject a video as a documentation option due to legal uncertainty.

Table 7.6: Dimension: Impact – Attitude

Dimension:
Impact covers the emotional characteristics of a video.
Characteristic:
Attitude considers the humans' conception of a video.
Sub-characteristics:
Pleasure considers the enjoyment of watching a video.
Intention considers the intended purpose of a video.
Sense of responsibility considers the compliance of a video with the legal regulations.

7.3.5 Results: Process Steps

For the relationships between the identified quality characteristics of videos and the steps of the video production and use process, I analyzed the results of the manual coding by determining the coding frequencies for each pair of video sub-characteristic and process step (see Table 7.7). These pairs indicate how often a particular video sub-characteristic is addressed in the respective process steps of the extracted and coded text passages. On the one hand, the results show that all video sub-characteristics can be affected in at least three different process steps. However, the individual coding frequencies reveal that some characteristics are addressed more frequently overall and in certain process steps than others. On the other hand, the overall coding frequencies of the process steps substantiate that the steps *shooting* (222 codes), *preproduction* (171 codes), and *postproduction* (139 codes) are frequently addressed in the generic video production guidelines while the step *viewing* (68 codes) tends to be less considered.

7.3.6 Validation of the Manual Coding Results

I validated the manual coding results by asking two raters to assign the identified sub-characteristics of videos and process steps to the extracted text passages on their own. The two raters

Table 7.7: Relationships between the identified video sub-characteristics and the steps of the video production and use process

Video sub-characteristics	Steps of the video production and use process			
	Preproduction	Shooting	Postproduction	Viewing
Image quality	13	65	23	4
Sound quality	8	30	15	2
Video length	15	7	8	0
Plot	32	7	19	1
Prior knowledge	15	0	1	4
Essence	28	45	12	6
Clutter	2	32	15	5
Pleasure	8	21	15	27
Intention	16	0	3	2
Sense of responsibility	34	15	28	17
In total	171	222	139	68

are computer science researchers who have both been working at the software engineering group at Leibniz Universität Hannover for more than three years. Both researchers are familiar with requirements engineering but do not have much experience in video production. In this way, I ensured that the raters had a comparable perspective as the initial coders when assigning the video sub-characteristics and process steps to the extracted text passages. I evaluated the reliability of the raters' classification by using *Cohen's* κ [55]. The calculated *Cohen's* κ value for the video sub-characteristics was 0.81 and for the process steps 0.83 which show an almost perfect raters' agreement according to Landis and Koch [155]. Therefore, I am confident that the identified sub-characteristics of videos and process steps emerge from the analyzed guidelines.

7.3.7 Threats to Validity

Below, I report the threats to construct, external, internal, and conclusion validity [257, 263].

Construct Validity. I performed a literature review which is probably one of the most simplified methods to fast and easily investigate literature compared to more complex methods such as a systematic literature review. Nevertheless, this type of literature review is still a systematic approach. Despite its weaknesses, this method allows a systematic reflection of literature which is a useful and proven means for developing a valid body of knowledge [92]. Due to the simplified investigation, I do not claim to present a comprehensive and systematic literature review on video production guidelines. Instead, the goal of this literature review was to lay the foundation for the development of a quality model for videos and a condensed guideline for video production and use. I validated the identified video characteristics and process steps by evaluating the reliability of two raters using *Cohen's κ*. The calculated *Cohen's κ* values show an almost perfect raters' agreement which substantiates that the identified characteristics and process steps emerge from the analyzed guidelines. However, the entire elaboration of quality characteristics of videos is based only on the literature review. This use of a single method causes a mono-method bias. There is a lack of extraction of information about video characteristics from humans producing and using videos. For example, other researchers and practitioners who are generally concerned with the application of videos in requirements engineering might be potential sources. Their experience in video production and use might help to verify the already known quality characteristics as well as to identify additional characteristics not yet considered in the literature. This kind of investigation requires the use of further methods such as questionnaires or focus groups which is future work.

External Validity. The selected method of literature review restricts the generalizability of the findings. I cannot guarantee that the identified quality characteristics of videos are complete since the literature review carried out is not a systematic literature review. However, to the best of my knowledge, this thesis provides the first comprehensive set of video characteristics for describing the rather ill-defined concept of *video quality* which is based on mutually supportive references. Although the identified characteristics are only an initial proposal, they provide a viable basis for future extensions and refinements.

Internal Validity. The results of the literature review are based on six generic video production guidelines. The selection of literature is probably the most crucial threat to internal validity since any bias in the selection affects the accuracy and quality of the final results. I mitigated this threat to validity by following a specified literature review design with a defined search method, search string, as well as exclusion and inclusion criteria. As a part of the data collection, a researcher with several years of experience reviewed my work to ensure the relevance and suitability of the literature used. In addition, the results of the manual coding process were validated by calculating the inter-rater reliability using *Cohen's κ*. The calculated values show an almost perfect raters' agreement. For these reasons, I am confident that the selected literature deals with video characteristics and their relationships to the steps of the video production and use process. However, the number of analyzed guidelines is rather small and thus restricts the validity of the findings. I focused on generic guidelines to deduce common characteristics of videos. I excluded guidance for certain kinds of videos, such as tutorials, to reduce any potential bias which might have been caused by a specific application context.

Conclusion Validity. The reproducibility of the literature review is limited due to its design. I found the generic video production guidelines by performing a web search using the web search engines *Google Scholar* and *Google*. Therefore, the search method can be hardly reproduced. However, I must emphasize that the literature review was not designed to identify all relevant literature in a reproducible manner as it would be the cases in a systematic literature review. A systematic literature review requires a more comprehensive and complex design. I decided to perform the simplified literature review since I was interested in a valid body of knowledge as a starting point to develop a grounded and reflected set of video characteristics with their relationships to the steps of the video production and use process. The results of the literature review are in turn based on the subjective interpretation of the coded text passages from the guidelines by three researchers. I cannot completely exclude the misinterpretation of the coded data. However, I mitigated this threat to validity with a clear strategy. Two researchers coded all data independently from each other and all three researchers cross-checked, discussed, and jointly agreed on the results after multiple iterations. Furthermore, I validated the manual coding results by calculating the inter-rater reliability using *Cohen's κ* whose results substantiate the validity of the findings due to the almost perfect raters' agreement.

7.3.8 Summary

This literature review lays the foundation for the further steps to develop a quality model for videos and a condensed guideline for video production and use. In particular, I extracted a set of coded text passages from generic video production guidelines that recommend how to proceed in particular steps of the video production and use process to produce a video with specific characteristics. Based on this set of coded text passages, I deduced characteristics of videos whose implementation affects the overall quality of videos. As an answer to Research Question 7.1, I can summarize:

Answer to Research Question 7.1

> *Based on the results of the literature review, I deduced the four video characteristics video stimuli, accessibility, relevance, and attitude, as well as the ten sub-characteristics image quality, sound quality, video length, plot, prior knowledge, essence, clutter, pleasure, intention, and sense of responsibility from the recommendations of generic video production guidelines.*

Furthermore, I examined how the identified video characteristics relate to the steps of the video production and use process. Based on the results of the manual coding process, I can answer Research Question 7.2 as follows:

Answer to Research Question 7.2

> *The identified characteristics of videos are related to almost every step of the video production and use process. However, the results show that particular video characteristics are addressed more frequently overall and in certain process steps. It is noticeable that the recommendations focus on the production while the use of a video tends to be less considered. Especially, 393 of the 600 codes regarding the process steps address the first two steps preproduction and shooting.*

The obtained insights and the set of coded text passages enable the development of the concept *awareness and guidance* according to the research process (see Figure 7.2). Thus, I can provide a dynamic perspective on video production and use by highlighting how the identified quality characteristics of videos can be affected in the individual process steps. For low-cost video production, this perspective provides awareness and guidance by answering the question: What are crucial quality characteristics in a particular process step and how can they be achieved?

7.4 Step 2.1: Developing a Quality Model for Videos

The following three sections present the second main step of the research process to create awareness regarding video quality (see section 7.2.2 and Figure 7.2). For this purpose, I subsequently develop a quality model for videos based on the identified quality characteristics of videos (see section 7.3). This quality model is adapted to vision videos (see section 7.5) which is validated in academia (see section 7.6).

Following the ISO/IEC FDIS 25010:2010 [112], the quality of a video is the degree to which the video satisfies the stated and implied needs of its video producer and target audience. These needs can be represented by a quality model that categorizes the quality of a video into characteristics which in some cases can be further divided into sub-characteristics [112]. A set of sub-characteristics associated with one characteristic needs to be representative of typical concerns regarding a video without necessarily being exhaustive. The benefit of such a quality model is its guidance for specifying requirements, establishing measurements, and performing quality evaluations of videos. Software professionals can use the defined characteristics as a checklist for ensuring the comprehensive treatment of video quality, thus providing a basis for estimating the consequent effort and activities needed during video production and use.

I present this quality model in two representation formats: (a) a hierarchical decomposition of the overall video quality into the individual quality characteristics and (b) a mapping of the quality characteristics to the steps of the video production and use process. The hierarchical decomposition provides a structured overview by breaking down video quality into individual quality characteristics that need to be assessed to evaluate the overall quality of a video. The mapping, in turn, shows how one upstream quality characteristic affects downstream characteristics along the video production and use process. While the first representation supports the evaluation of videos, the second representation serves as a checklist to ensure the comprehensive treatment of the video quality over the entire video production and use process.

7.4.1 Hierarchical Decomposition of Video Quality

Figure 7.4 shows the hierarchical decomposition of video quality. This quality model arranges the identified characteristics and sub-characteristics of videos by the three dimensions of a quality model, which cover the sensorial (*representation*), perceptual (*content*), and emotional (*impact*) characteristics. The labels used in Figure 7.4 follow the definitions in section 7.3.4.

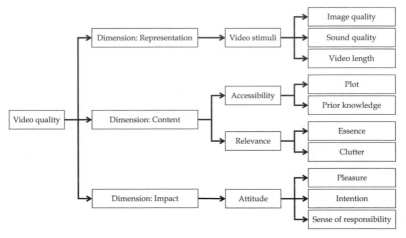

Figure 7.4: Hierarchical decomposition of video quality

7.4.2   Video Quality Along the Video Production and Use Process

Each step of the video production and use process is supposed to add value to a video. A poor implementation of quality characteristics in any step can reduce this value. The later a quality characteristic is addressed, the higher is the risk of diminishing the final value of a video. Therefore, any quality characteristic should be addressed as early as possible. Owens and Millerson support this conclusion by emphasizing that "*ninety percent of the work on a* [video] *production usually goes into the planning and preparation phase*" [185, p. 37]. For this purpose, it is necessary to know in which steps a particular quality characteristic can be more or less affected.

Based on the mean coding frequency of all pairs of video characteristic and process step ($M = 15$, cf. Table 7.7), I defined the *indicator of impact* (see Definition 7.1). This mapping returns a rough indicator of how strongly a video characteristic can be affected in a process step. I applied this mapping on each coding frequency of all pairs of video characteristic and process step (see Table 7.7). Figure 7.5 shows the final mapping of the quality characteristics to the steps of the video production and use process including the *indicators of impact*. I must remark that this mapping is discussible since the coding frequencies of the pairs show that all video characteristics can be affected in at least three different process steps. However, as explained above, quality characteristics should be addressed as early as possible. Below, I explain for each step why specific characteristics are strongly affected in the respective step.

Definition 7.1 (*Indicator of impact; according to Karras et al. [139, p. 14]*)

Let f be a mapping that assigns exactly one $y \in \{strong, medium, weak\}$ to each $x \in \mathbb{N}_0$:

$$f: \mathbb{N}_0 \to \{strong, medium, weak\},$$

$$x \mapsto \begin{cases} strong, & \text{if } x \geq 15 \\ medium, & \text{if } 7 < x < 15 \\ weak, & \text{else } x \leq 7 \end{cases}$$

f is the mapping and $f(x)$ is called the *indicator of impact*.

Video characteristic affected

X	strong ($X \geq 15$)
X	medium ($7 < X < 15$)
X	weak($X \leq 7$)

Dimension	Characteristic	Sub-characteristic	Preproduction	Shooting	Postproduction	Viewing
Represen-tation	Video stimuli	Image quality	13	65	23	4
		Sound quality	8	30	15	2
		Video length	15	7	8	0
Content	Accessibility	Plot	32	7	19	1
		Prior knowledge	15	0	1	4
	Relevance	Essence	28	45	12	6
		Clutter	2	32	15	5
Impact	Attitude	Pleasure	8	21	15	27
		Intention	16	0	3	2
		Sense of responsibility	34	15	28	17

Figure 7.5: Video quality along the video production and use process. Remark: The numbers are the coding frequencies of each pair of video characteristic and process step (cf. section 7.3.5).

In the preproduction, the purpose of a video (*intention*), its story (*plot*), the duration (*video length*), the necessary *prior knowledge*, and the relevant contents (*essence*) are defined so that the shooting can be done quickly and easily. During the shooting, the relevant contents (*essence*) of a video need to be captured pleasantly (*pleasure*) by avoiding any disrupting or distracting contents (*clutter*) such as background noise or actions. The video stimuli (*image quality* and *sound quality*) are mainly affected by the recording of the single video clips. In the postproduction, the whole video is produced by digitally postprocessing the image and sound of the video. Besides the video stimuli (*image quality* and *sound quality*), the *plot* of a video is mainly affected since the single video clips of each scene are combined and possibly rearranged to convey the planned story. One important task of the postproduction is to remove *clutter* from the video. During the entire postproduction, it must be ensured that the final video presents its content pleasantly and interestingly for the target audience (*pleasure*). The *pleasure* of the target audience is important to focus their attention on the conveyed content when viewing the video.

The characteristic *sense of responsibility* must be considered separately. The entire video production and use process requires to ensure legal reliability. In the preproduction, it has to be identified which permissions must be obtained, such as consent forms to record persons or places. During the shooting, compliance with the permissions must be ensured. In the postproduction, copyrights have to be fulfilled in case of used music or images by third parties. The postproduction also needs to ensure that the contents of the video are not falsified due to the editing. For viewing, it is important to ensure the right to share and distribute the video.

The resulting quality model for videos with its two representations is based on the subjective interpretation of the analyzed generic video production guidelines. Therefore, the quality model is a theoretical description of potentially relevant characteristics of videos. Thus, I do not claim that the proposed model is complete. Instead, this model is a starting point to better understand what constitutes a good video.

7.5 Step 2.2: Adapting the Quality Model for Videos to Vision Videos

The presented quality model is only based on the consideration of video as a representation format. Due to the specific context of this thesis (cf. Research Goal 1.1), it is necessary to adapt the quality model for videos to vision videos (see section 7.2.2 and Figure 7.2). For this purpose, I looked more closely at the content of a vision video, i.e., the vision, to substantiate the quality model for videos that is generic so far. In particular, I conducted a literature review to collect and analyze a set of mutually supportive references on software project vision in order to adapt the quality model to vision videos based on a grounded and reflected body of knowledge.

7.5.1 Literature Review Objective

The goal of this literature review is to identify characteristics regarding the quality of a software project vision according to literature. I examine the following research goal:

Research Goal 7.2

> *Analyze* publications on software project vision
> *for the purpose of* identifying characteristics
> *with respect to* the quality of a software project vision
> *from the point of view of* this researcher
> *in the context of* a literature review.

In consideration of Research Goal 7.2, I ask the following research question:

Research Question 7.3

> *What are the characteristics of a software project vision according to literature?*

7.5.2 Literature Review Design

The design of the literature review follows the guideline for performing systematic literature reviews in software engineering by Kitchenham and Charters [148]. I followed this guideline as closely as possible to increase the quality and validity of the literature review. Therefore, I defined a search method as well as exclusion and inclusion criteria.

7.5.2.1 Search Method

I performed a manual search in the internal library of the software engineering group at Leibniz Universität Hannover since the topic "software project vision" is established in literature for years. Different researchers [111, 145, 190] strongly advocated the use of manual search instead of electronic search due to the benefits of being more effective in identifying relevant literature.

7.5.2.2 Exclusion and Inclusion Criteria

For an objective selection of literature, I defined exclusion and inclusion criteria to identify those publications that provide direct evidence on the research question [148]. These criteria help to reduce the likelihood of bias by supporting the classification of publications into selected and rejected ones. The criteria in Table 7.8 and Table 7.9 have been applied to each result of the search method. If none of the exclusion criteria E_i, $1 \leq i \leq 3$, and at least one of the two inclusion criteria I_j, $j = 1, 2$, were met, the publication was selected:

$$\text{Publication selected} \Leftrightarrow \neg (E_1 \vee E_2 \vee E_3) \wedge (I_1 \vee I_2)$$

Table 7.8: Exclusion criteria of the literature review

Exclusion criteria
E_1: The publication is neither a book nor a journal article.
E_2: The publication is not written in English.
E_3: The publication is only partially accessible.

Table 7.9: Inclusion criteria of the literature review

Inclusion criteria
I_1: The publication contains an individual section on software project vision
I_2: The publication addresses the topic of vision and its influence, e.g., on a project.

7.5.2.3 Data Collection

In December 2017, I conducted the literature review by checking all 428 books, conference proceedings, and journal volumes in the internal library of the software engineering group by applying the exclusion and inclusion criteria. Another researcher with several years of experience reviewed my work and its results. This researcher extended the identified literature by proposing additional journal articles and books on software project vision which he knew due to his work on the book "Software Product Management: The ISPMA-Compliant Study Guide and Handbook" [149] in which he has contributed to a chapter on software project vision.

7.5.2.4 Data Analysis Methods

As in the literature review on generic video production guidelines (cf. section 7.3), the selected publications are analyzed by performing manual coding [211]. Figure 7.6 shows the manual coding process with two examples of extracted and coded text passages. I conducted this process with two researchers to increase the validity of the findings.

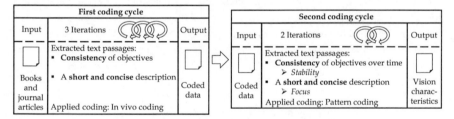

Figure 7.6: Manual coding process

In the first coding cycle, we applied *in vivo* coding to adhere to the terminology in the literature (see Figure 7.6, bold highlighting). After three iterations, all three researchers agreed on the extracted and coded text passages regarding the their implications of vision characteristics. In the second coding cycle, we used *pattern* coding to group the data into categories (see Figure 7.6, italic highlighting). After two iterations, all three researchers agreed on the identified categories. The results of the manual coding were also validated by asking two other researchers to individually assign the identified categories to the extracted text passages. I calculated the inter-rater reliability using *Cohen's* κ to assess the agreement of the two raters [55].

7.5.3 Selected Publications, Extracted Text Passages, and Coding Results

The search method resulted in four books [6, 195, 202, 251] from the internal library of the software engineering group. The researcher, who reviewed my work and its results (cf. section 7.5.2.3), proposed another nine journal articles [37, 67, 100, 142, 161, 162, 228, 231, 240] and six books [1, 51, 59, 149, 170, 176]. In total, these 19 publications were selected and analyzed according to the manual coding process. In the first coding cycle, 46 text passages were extracted and coded. Each extracted text passage had at least one code regarding *vision characteristics* resulting in a total of 55 codes. In the second coding cycle, these codes were grouped into five categories which represent quality characteristics of a vision.

7.5.4 Results: Vision Characteristics

Based on the results of the manual coding (cf. appendix E.2), I identified five characteristics of a vision which I arranged by the three dimensions of a quality model (*representation*, *content*, and *impact*) [112, 139]. Below, I describe each dimension and the associated characteristics (see Table 7.10, Table 7.11, and Table 7.12).

Dimension: Representation. This dimension covers the sensorial characteristics of a vision regarding its *representation*. The characteristic *focus* (see Table 7.10) considers the condensed and short description of a vision by presenting its essence compactly [170, 195, 251]. This description can either be a text with the length of a few sentences up to one page [149] or a picture [6]. Regardless of the representation format, the vision must show the conceptual image of the future product as a "big picture" [6, 149].

Table 7.10: Dimension: Representation – Focus

Dimension:
Representation covers the sensorial characteristics of a vision.
Characteristic:
Focus considers the compact representation of a vision.

Dimension: Content. This dimension covers the perceptual characteristics of a vision regarding its *content* by including the two characteristics *completeness* and *clarity* (see Table 7.11). *Completeness* deals with the coverage of the three contents of a vision: The addressed *problem*, the key idea of the *solution*, and how the solution *improves* the state-of-the-art [149, 176, 251]. A vision describes a business or stakeholder problem in a solution-neutral manner by explaining the pain-points addressed by the solution [149, 202]. The problem has to be anchored in the stakeholders' needs which offer the reasons for solving the problem [202, 251]. Robertson and Robertson suggest describing "*how the product will solve* [. . .] [the] *problem*" [202, p. 140]. A proposed solution needs to be different from the status quo, i.e., the essence of an aspired change [195]. Representing a change offers the option to present an argumentation that allows a person to decide whether the product proposed by the vision is worthwhile [202]. *Clarity* considers the intelligibility of the aspired goals of a vision by all parties involved. An under-

125

standable vision statement depends on the ability of a company to define clear objectives [240]. The inability to clearly define objectives greatly delays product development [67]. Ambiguous concepts of a product allow speculations and conflicts about what should be produced [142]. Instead of aspiring an unattainable goal, a clear and concise vision is associated with well-defined and verifiable goals that guide with explicit directions [161, 162, 195]. Specific goals are important since they make the advantages of a vision measurable and thus allow to determine whether a product meets its vision [149, 202, 240].

Table 7.11: Dimension: Content – Completeness and clarity

Dimension:
Content covers the perceptual characteristics of a vision.
Characteristic:
Completeness considers the coverage of the three contents of a vision, i.e., *problem, solution,* and *improvement.*
Clarity considers the intelligibility of the aspired goals of a vision by all parties involved.

Dimension: Impact. This dimension covers the emotional characteristics of a vision regarding its emotional *impact* on all parties involved. The dimension includes the two characteristics *support* and *stability* (see Table 7.12). *Support* focuses on the level of acceptance of a vision, i.e., whether all parties involved share and accept the same vision as their motivation and guidance of their actions and activities [149, 240]. A vision needs support in the development team [161] and has to reflect a balanced view that satisfies the needs of diverse stakeholders [251]. For this purpose, a vision tells a futuristic story that can be idealistic [6, 251] but needs to be achievable and grounded in the realities of existing or anticipated markets, enterprise architectures, corporate strategies, and resource limitations to be acceptable [149, 251]. *Stability* focuses in the consistency of a vision over time. A vision needs to be stable with consistent objectives over time to provide consistency to short-term actions while leaving room for reinterpretation as new opportunities emerge [100, 161]. In the case of dynamic goals, a stable vision helps to cope with a variety of uncertainties [1]. Thus, a vision helps to align a project by defining what needs to be done [161]. The stability of a vision enables an organization to learn and adapt to finish a project successfully [228].

Table 7.12: Dimension: Impact – Support and stability

Dimension:
Impact covers the emotional characteristics of a vision.
Characteristic:
Support considers the level of acceptance of a vision, i.e., whether all parties involved share and accept the vision.
Stability considers the consistency of a vision over time.

7.5.5 Validation of the Manual Coding Results

As in the literature review on generic video production guidelines (cf. section 7.3), I validated the manual coding results by asking the same two raters to assign the identified characteristics of a vision to the extracted text passages on their own. The reliability of the raters' classification was evaluated by using *Cohen's* κ [55]. The calculated *Cohen's* κ value was 0.84 which shows an almost perfect raters' agreement [155]. This result indicates that the identified categories represent major themes in terms of vision characteristics in the analyzed publications.

7.5.6 Threats to Validity

Below, I report the threats to construct, external, internal, and conclusion validity [257, 263].

Construct Validity. A literature review is one of the most simplified methods to fast and easily investigate literature. However, this method is a useful and proven means for developing a valid body of knowledge [92]. I do not claim to present a comprehensive and systematic literature review on software project vision. Instead, the literature review provides an initial overview of vision characteristics so that the quality model for videos can be adapted to vision videos. I validated the identified characteristics of a vision by calculating the inter-rater reliability using *Cohen's* κ [55]. The results substantiate that the identified characteristics emerge from the analyzed publications. The mere use of a literature review causes a mono-method bias since other methods such as interviews to collect the experience and knowledge of experts were neglected. I mitigated this threat to validity by selecting high-quality publications in the form of books and journal articles.

External Validity. The generalizability of the findings is restricted due to the selected method of literature review. I cannot guarantee that the proposed quality characteristics of a vision are complete since the literature review carried out is not a systematic literature review. For this reason, it is possible that not all relevant literature was found. However, I mitigated this threat to validity by having a researcher with several years of experience who reviewed my work and its results. This review improved the number of selected publications since the researcher proposed another six books and nine journal articles based on his expertise. Although the identified vision characteristics are only an initial proposal, they are based on mutually supportive references. Therefore, they provide a viable basis for future extensions and refinements.

Internal Validity. The results of the literature review are based on ten books and nine journal articles on software project vision. The search method for selecting the literature is probably the most crucial threat to internal validity since this method affected the number, accuracy, and quality of the final results. I mitigated this threat to validity by following a specified literature review design. A researcher with several years of experience reviewed my work to ensure the relevance and suitability of the literature used. This review improved the selected literature since the researcher recommended several books and journal articles dealing with software project vision to extend the set of selected publications. I validated the results of the manual coding process by calculating the inter-rater reliability using *Cohen's κ*. The calculated value shows an almost perfect raters' agreement. Thus, I am confident that I selected suitable literature that deals with vision characteristics. However, the number of analyzed publications is rather small which restricts the validity of the findings. For this reason, I decided that a characteristic of a vision should be supported by at least three different sources to increase the reliability of the findings. As a result of the analysis, each vision characteristic is even supported by at least five different sources.

Conclusion Validity. The selected publications on software project vision result from a manual search in an internal library as well as the recommendations of the researcher who reviewed my work and its results. Therefore, the search method can be hardly reproduced. However, the literature review was not designed to identify all relevant literature in a reproducible manner. I decided to perform the simplified literature review since I was interested in a valid body of knowledge as a starting point to develop a grounded and reflected set of vision characteristics for adapting the quality model for videos to vision videos. The results of the literature review are based on the subjective interpretation of the coded text passages from the publications by three researchers. I cannot exclude the misinterpretation of the coded data. However, this threat to validity was mitigated by a clear strategy. Two researchers coded all data independently from each other and all three researchers cross-checked, discussed, and jointly agreed on the results after multiple iterations. Furthermore, I validated the manual coding results by calculating the inter-rater reliability whose result substantiates the validity of the findings.

7.5.7   Summary

This literature review serves to identify characteristics of a vision to adapt the quality model for videos to vision videos. Based on the extracted set of coded text passages, I identified five characteristics of a vision whose implementation affect the overall vision quality. As an answer to Research Question 7.3, I can summarize:

Answer to Research Question 7.3

> Based on the results of the literature review, the characteristics of a vision according to literature are *focus, completeness, clarity, support,* and *stability*.

The obtained insights enable the adaption of the quality model for videos to vision videos. For this purpose, I integrate the identified vision characteristics into the quality model for videos based on the three dimensions of a quality model.

7.5.8 A Quality Model for Vision Videos

I present the quality model for vision videos, in both representation formats, to support, on the one hand, the evaluation of vision videos, and on the other hand, the production and use of vision videos (cf. section 7.4). This tailored quality model offers the essence of what constitutes a vision video to support requirements communication for shared understanding.

7.5.8.1 Hierarchical Decomposition of Vision Video Quality

A quality model is typically structured as a hierarchical decomposition [175]. This hierarchy shows how the overall quality of a product, i.e., a vision video, is composed of its quality characteristics that can be further divided into sub-characteristics. Figure 7.7 presents the hierarchical decomposition of vision video quality. I obtained this quality model by integrating the characteristics of a vision into the hierarchical decomposition of video quality by a simple merge of the three dimensions of a quality model. The labels in Figure 7.7 follow the previous explanations and definitions in section 7.3.4 and section 7.5.4.

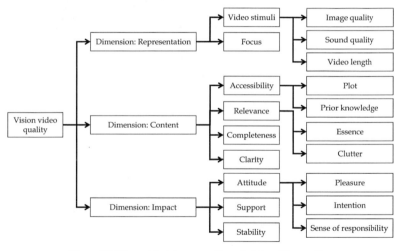

Figure 7.7: Hierarchical decomposition of vision video quality

7.5.8.2 Vision Video Quality Along the Video Production and Use Process

For the mapping of the vision characteristics to the steps of the video production and use process, I was not able to apply a similar procedure as for the video characteristics. The analyzed literature did not provide any information about the process steps of creating a vision that might have been mapped to the steps of the video production and use process. The assignment of the vision characteristics to the process steps is only based on the joint considerations of myself and the two researchers who supported me in both literature reviews. Figure 7.8 shows the resulting mapping based on our considerations. Below, I explain why we propose to address specific characteristics of a vision in particular steps of the video production and use process.

Vision characteristic affected	Video characteristic affected					
proposal	X	strong (X ≥ 15)				
unknown	X	medium (7 < X < 15)				
	X	weak(X ≤ 7)				

Dimension	Characteristic	Sub-characteristic	Preproduction	Shooting	Postproduction	Viewing
Representation	Video stimuli	Image quality	13	65	23	4
		Sound quality	8	30	15	2
		Video length	15	7	8	0
	Focus	-				
Content	Accessibility	Plot	32	7	19	1
		Prior knowledge	15	0	1	4
	Relevance	Essence	28	45	12	6
		Clutter	2	32	15	5
	Completeness	-				
	Clarity	-				
Impact	Attitude	Pleasure	8	21	15	27
		Intention	16	0	3	2
		Sense of responsibility	34	15	28	17
	Support	-				
	Stability	-				

Figure 7.8: Vision video quality along the video production and use process. Remark: The numbers are the coding frequencies of each pair of video characteristic and process step (cf. section 7.3.5).

The vision is the key content of a vision video. It represents the starting point for the video production. Furthermore, any poor quality in an early step constrains the quality in later steps. Therefore, we conclude that the vision characteristics should be addressed as early as possible and thus in the *preproduction*. It is important to specify clear goals of a vision (*clarity*) to define its essential parts (*completeness*) that need to be presented compactly (*focus*) in the vision video. The more stable a vision, the easier the *support* may be achieved since *stability* can contribute to acceptance. Nevertheless, we assume that the vision characteristics can and should be considered in later steps. We suggest addressing *focus*, *completeness*, and *clarity* in the *postproduction* to ensure that the final vision video fulfills these quality characteristics after editing and digital postprocessing. During the entire postprocessing, it must be ensured that the final video presents the complete vision to the target audience in a compact but understandable way. *Support* and *stability* are important to the *viewing* step since they mainly affect the target audience of a vision video. The stakeholders and development team need to support the vision by sharing and accepting the vision as their motivation and guidance to align their mental models, activities, and actions. It is important to clarify how stable the vision is. A vision video of a stable vision is suitable to be shared with the stakeholders and the development team as guidance. In contrast, a vision video of a unstable vision is unsuitable as guidance but beneficial for elicitation and validation since the vision has to adapt to changes and new insights.

I must emphasize that this mapping is only a first proposal and thus discussible. This mapping is a starting point for extensions and refinements which are part of my ongoing and future work.

7.6 Step 2.3: Validating of the Quality Model for Vision Videos

According to the research process (see section 7.2), the last step for creating awareness regarding video quality requires the validation of the quality model for vision videos (see section 7.2.2 and Figure 7.2). This validation is necessary to ensure that the quality model for vision videos is valid and sound to contribute to the fundamental relevance of the candidate solution (cf. section 1.3 and Figure 1.1, ⑤). For this purpose, I conducted a controlled experiment in academia to investigate whether the identified quality characteristics characterize the overall impression of a vision video.

7.6.1 Experimental Objective

For this characterization of the overall impression of a vision video, it is necessary to examine the overall quality of vision videos and its relationships with the quality characteristics. In the case of relationships, I assume that the quality model for vision videos is valid and sound. I formulated the corresponding research goal by applying the goal definition template [18].

Research Goal 7.3

Analyze the 15 characteristics at the lowest level of the quality model for vision videos
for the purpose of examining the characterization of the overall impression of a vision video
with respect to the relationships between the quality characteristics and the perceived overall quality of a vision video
from the point of view of students who actively develop software in the role of a developer
in the context of a controlled off-line setting of a software project course in academia.

The quality model for vision videos is a theoretical description of the potentially relevant characteristics of a vision video that needs to be validated [233]. According to Seshadrinathan and Bovik [221], subjective judgment of video quality collected by asking humans for their opinion is considered as the ultimate standard and right way to assess video quality. However, the wide variety and subjectivity of the characteristics impede the prediction of how different viewers assess the overall quality of a video [136]. Therefore, it is necessary to define who the viewers of a video are and to ensure that they belong to the target audience. For this reason, I focused the experiment on the point of view of developers who belong to the target audience of vision videos [139]. Based on the Research Goal 7.3, I ask the following research question:

Research Question 7.4

How do the individual quality characteristics relate to the overall quality of a vision video from a developer's point of view?

7.6.2 Experimental Design

I ensured that the experimental design is well-defined by following the recommendations and process for experimentation in software engineering by Wohlin et al. [257]. Below, I present the important details of the resulting experimental design.

7.6.2.1 Hypotheses

At first, it is necessary to specify the criteria for assessing whether the quality model for vision videos is valid and sound. I assume that the quality model is valid and sound, if:

(1) All three dimensions of the quality model for vision videos are related to the overall quality of a vision video.

(2) The related quality characteristics include both vision and video characteristics.

Based on the Research Goal 7.3, Research Question 7.4, and the criteria for assessing the validity and soundness, I formulated the following global null and alternative hypothesis:

gH_0: There are no quality characteristics that meet the criteria for the validity and soundness of the quality model for vision videos and relate to the overall quality of a vision video from a developer's point of view.

gH_1: There are quality characteristics that meet the criteria for the validity and soundness of the quality model for vision videos and relate to the overall quality of a vision video from a developer's point of view.

I concretized the global hypotheses for each of the 15 quality characteristics by considering a specific null and alternative hypothesis. Below, I present the generic pattern of the specific null hypothesis Hi_0 and alternative hypothesis Hi_1, $i \in \{1, \ldots, 15\}$. *NAME* has to be replaced with the quality characteristic. In appendix E.3.1, I formulated the specific null hypothesis.

Hi_0: The quality characteristic *NAME* does not relate to the overall quality of a vision video from a developer's point of view.

Hi_1: The quality characteristic *NAME* relates to the overall quality of a vision video from a developer's point of view.

7.6.2.2 Independent and Dependent Variables

The dependent variable is the overall quality of a vision video from a developer's point of view with two levels: *good* and *bad*. The independent variables are the 15 characteristics at the lowest level of the quality model for vision videos. While *video length* was measured in seconds, the subjects assessed all other 14 characteristics on a 5-point Likert scale (cf. appendix E.3.2) .

7.6.2.3 Context and Material

In a yearly academic course called *Software Project*, the software engineering group at Leibniz Universität Hannover conducts multiple software projects with real customers. The project course consists of a 4-week requirements analysis phase followed by the development phase divided into two 3-week iterations and one 2-week polish phase [150]. Each project team creates a vision video at the end of the second week of the requirements analysis phase. In these videos, the teams illustrate the given problem, their proposed solution, and the improvement of the problem due to the solution. These videos are intended to convey an integrated view of the future system and its use to validate the overall product goals with the customers. The teams produce their videos with simple equipment, i.e., smartphones and open-source software.

For the experiment, I used eight vision videos of eight projects from 2017. Each project covered a different domain with real customers, e.g., the Central Crime Service of the Police Administration Hannover who needed an investigation software for personal data in publicly available sources on the internet. The project teams who created the videos consisted of ten undergraduate students of computer science which were at least in their 5th academic semester. Apart from a maximum duration of 3 minutes, there were no further restrictions on the video production. On average, all eight vision videos had a duration of 103.4 seconds. The minimum and maximum duration of all videos were 69 respectively 155 seconds. I am not allowed to distribute these videos since I have to follow the guideline of the central ethics committee of our university to secure good scientific practice[23]. This committee regulates subjects' information and rights. I do not have the explicit consent of the actors to distribute the vision videos. For this reason, I have to archive the vision videos internally for future reference since recognizable persons shall not be visible on distributed videos without their explicit consent.

7.6.2.4 Subject Selection

Although experiments with students are often associated with a lack of realism [227], I consciously decided to select students as subjects for this experiment due to the following three reasons. First, students are often used as subjects for validation in academia since "*they are*

---

[23]https://www.uni-hannover.de/en/universitaet/profil/ziele/gute-wissenschaftli che-praxis/

more accessible and easier to organize [than professionals from the industry]" [227, p. 4]. Second, students form a more homogeneous group than professionals from the industry since they have comparable knowledge, experience, and skills. Despite reduced external validity, a more homogeneous group increases the conclusion validity since the risk of variation due to subjects' heterogeneity is mitigated. Third, there are only minor differences between students, which are close to their graduation, and software professionals concerning their ability to perform small but non-trivial assessment tasks [109]. Thus, students are suitable subjects for this experiment since the task to be performed only requires to subjectively assess vision videos.

Due to the subjective assessment of vision videos, I needed a larger number of subjects to draw grounded conclusions. The selection of subjects for the experiment was carried out using convenience sampling. In agreement with the lecturer of the *Software Project* course, I got the permission to conduct the experiment during the course in 2018, which was attended by 139 undergraduate students of computer science. In one appointment of the course, I invited the students to participate in the experiment. The participation was entirely voluntary and had no influence on passing the course. There was also no financial reward for participation.

7.6.2.5 Experimental Procedure

I conducted the experiment at the sixth of twelve one-hour appointments that were binding for all participants of the *Software Project* course. The experiment was conducted in a lecture hall with all 139 students at the same time. I presented the vision videos in a random presentation order via a projector with a resolution of 1920×1080 px and the sound was played through the sound system of the room. The whole experiment lasted 60 minutes. While all videos together had a duration of 13:47 minutes, the assessment of a single video took 5 to 6 minutes. The experiment has a within-subjects design. All subjects participated in all steps of the experimental procedure which was composed of the three steps: *introduction*, *viewing*, and *assessment*.

Before running the experiment, I explained to all students that their participation is voluntary, has no influence on passing the course, and that they can leave the lecture hall if they do not want to participate. All remaining subjects got an *introduction* to the experimental procedure with the task of assessing the presented vision videos and the provided assessment form. When explaining the assessment form, I also presented the quality characteristics. All subjects were asked to ask questions at any time if they needed clarification. Subsequently, the subjects read and signed the consent form for participation and completed a pre-questionnaire with which I collected each subject's demographic data (see appendix E.3.2).

For the experiment, each subject was put in the situation of joining an ongoing project in their familiar role as a developer. In this context, I showed each of the eight vision videos always for the purpose of sharing the vision of the project with the subjects. A defined context and purpose are important since the quality of any requirements engineering artifact is essentially influenced by them [74]. I repeated the following two steps for each vision video. First, I played the vision video once for all subjects at the same time (*viewing*). Second, each subject completed the assessment form (see appendix E.3.2) himself to rate the perceived overall quality of the vision video and the perceived level of each quality characteristic (*assessment*).

7.6.2.6 Data Analysis Methods

For the selection of suitable methods, it is necessary to consider the scales of the variables. While the *years of experience* and the *video length* have a ratio scale, all other variables such as *image quality* and *pleasure* have an ordinal scale (see appendix E.3.3). I use two different methods to investigate relationships in the collected data.

First, I investigate the relationships between the *years of experience* and each assessed variable to examine whether the *years of experience* as a developer had an impact on the assessments of each individual quality characteristics. For this analysis, I use *Spearman's* rank correlation [232] since the assessed variables have an ordinal scale. Such relationships would affect the procedure of the further analysis. Second, I apply *binary logistic regression* [15] to investigate the relationship between the 15 quality characteristics of vision videos (independent variables) and the overall quality of a vision video perceived by the subjects (dependent variable). I use *binary logistic regression* since I have more than two independent variables and the dependent variable is dichotomous with the two groups *good* and *bad*. This method examines the relationship between the likelihood that the dependent variable takes a certain value and the independent variables. Therefore, *binary logistic regression* does not predict the value of the dependent variable but the likelihood that the dependent variable has a certain value. In the case of this experiment, the *binary logistic regression* examines the relationship between the likelihood that the overall quality of a vision video perceived by the subjects is *good* and the 15 quality characteristics. This method enables to investigate whether the structures in the collected data match with the quality model for vision videos. Thus, I can determine a set of quality characteristics that correlate with the overall quality of vision videos from the subjects' point of view. The following four assumptions need to be fulfilled to perform *binary logistic regression* [15]:

(1) The investigated variable is dichotomous.

> The dependent variable *overall quality* is dichotomous with the two groups *good* and *bad*.

(2) The independent variables are metric or categorical.

> While *video length* is measured in seconds (metric), the other 14 characteristics are assessed on Likert scales (categorical).

(3) In the case of two or more metric independent variables, no multicollinearity is allowed to be present.

> This case is not fulfilled since *video length* is the only metric independent variable.

(4) Both groups of the dichotomous dependent variable contain at least 25 elements.

This assumption is fulfilled: Group *good* contains 671 elements and group *bad* contains 281 elements (see appendix E.3.3).

Remark. *The entire data set is published in "Karras, O. et al.: Experiment Data – 952 Assessments of 8 Vision Videos Regarding Overall Video Quality and 15 Individual Quality Characteristics. Zenodo, Version: 1, 2019" [138].*

7.6.3 Sample

In total, all 139 students participated in the experiment. However, after removing incomplete answers from the data set only the results of 119 subjects could be used. All subjects were undergraduate students of computer science which had the role of a developer and were actively developing software at the time of the experiment. The subjects were at least in their 5th academic semester and thus close to their graduation. The subjects formed a fairly homogeneous group. Table 7.13 shows the distribution of the subjects regarding their years of experience as a developer. While one-third of the subjects had less than one year of experience as a developer, two-third had at least one year of experience as a developer. On average, the subjects had 2.4 years of experience with a minimum of 0 and a maximum of 15 years of experience. The difference in the experience of up to 15 years increased the heterogeneity in the sample. This heterogeneity is representative of an industrial context since variations among software professionals are generally expected to be even greater than variations among students due to a more varied educational background and working experience [227]. In total, I expected the subjects to be suitable to assess the vision videos from a developer's point of view.

Table 7.13: Distribution of the subjects regarding years of experience as a developer

Classification	Inexperienced	Experienced											
Years of experience	0	1	2	3	4	5	6	7	8	9	10	12	15
Number of subjects	39	10	27	13	8	7	6	2	3	1	1	1	1
Proportion [%]	32.77	67.23											

7.6.4 Results: Spearman's Rank Correlation

Table 7.14 shows the *Spearman's* rank correlation coefficient ρ and p-value for each of the 15 pairs consisting of *years of experience* and assessed quality characteristic. Only one of the 15 analyses yielded a significant result. However, the resulting correlation coefficient ($\rho = 0.067 \approx 0$) indicates no correlation between the *years of experience* and the assessments of quality characteristics *stability* (see Table 7.14, bold cells). Based on these results, there are no relationships between the *years of experience* and the assessments of the quality characteristics. Therefore, I conclude that the *years of experience* and thus the increased heterogeneity of the sample had no major impact on the assessments. As a consequence, the collected data of the inexperienced and experienced subjects can be analyzed together using *binary logistic regression*.

Finding 7.1

According to the results of the Spearman's rank correlation analysis, there are no relationships between the years of experience and the assessments of the quality characteristics. Thus, all collected data of the inexperienced and experienced subjects can be analyzed together.

Table 7.14: Spearman's rank correlation coefficients between years of experience and each variable assessed by the subjects. Remark: The bold cells show the statistically significant result.

Assessed variable	Years of experience	
	ρ	p
Overall quality	−0.050	.125
Image quality	−0.047	.146
Sound quality	−0.053	.105
Focus	−0.036	.263
Plot	0.011	.742
Prior knowledge	0.010	.146
Essence	0.019	.551
Clutter	−0.032	.324
Completeness	−0.061	.060
Clarity	−0.008	.796
Pleasure	−0.054	.094
Intention	−0.047	.145
Sense of responsibility	0.037	.259
Support	−0.007	.841
Stability	**0.067**	**.038**

7.6.5 Results: Binary Logistic Regression

The report of the logistic regression analysis follows the recommendations by Peng et al. [187]. These recommendations provide a concise reporting format containing all necessary tables, figures, and explanations required to evaluate the results of the analysis. The procedure of *binary logistic regression* consists of two steps: (1) fitting a logistic model to the collected data and (2) evaluating the obtained model regarding its validity and soundness to draw conclusions.

7.6.5.1 Step 1: Fitting the Logistic Model to the Collected Data

After two iterations, I got a logistic model that fits the collected data and contains only quality characteristics of vision videos as predictors that are statistically significant. In the first iteration, I performed binary logistic regression with all 15 quality characteristics. As a result, I found that the nine characteristics *image quality, sound quality, plot, essence, clutter, completeness, intention, sense of responsibility*, and *support* do not affect the likelihood that the subjects perceive the overall quality of a vision video as *good*. Thus, I cannot reject the specific null hypotheses $Hi_0, i \in \{1, 2, 5, 7, 8, 9, 12, 13, 14\}$ (see Table E.7). I removed these nine characteristics from the 15 characteristics in the second iteration. The resulting logistic model contained all six remaining quality characteristics as significant predictors for the overall quality of a vision video (see Table 7.15). These six characteristics are *video length, focus, prior knowledge, clarity, pleasure*, and *stability*. Below, I report the identified relationships between the predicted probability of the logistic model and each predictor which are illustrated in Figure 7.9.

Based on the logistic model, *the likelihood that the subjects perceive the overall quality of a vision video as good from a developer's point of view is . . .*

Result 1: . . . *positively* related to the duration of a vision video ($p = .000, Exp(\beta) = 1.020 > 1$).
Interpretation: I can reject the specific null hypothesis $H3_0$ (see Figure 7.9a).
The closer the *video length* is to the given maximum duration of 3 minutes (cf. section 7.6.2.3), i.e., the longer the duration of a vision video, the higher the likelihood that the subjects perceive the overall quality of a vision video as *good*.

Result 2: . . . (a) *negatively* related to a non-compact ($p = .013, Exp(\beta) = .505 < 1$) and (b) *positively* related to a compact representation of a vision ($p = .018, Exp(\beta) = 1.599 > 1$).
Interpretation: I can reject the specific null hypothesis $H4_0$ (see Figure 7.9b).
(a): The lower the value for *focus*, i.e, the less compact a vision is represented, the lower the likelihood that the subjects perceive the overall quality of a vision video as *good*.
(b): The higher the value for *focus*, i.e., the more compact a vision is represented, the higher the likelihood that the subjects perceive the overall quality of a vision video as *good*.

Result 3: . . . (a) *positively* related to unnecessary ($p = .000, Exp(\beta) = 2.779 > 1$) and (b) *negatively* related to very necessary prior knowledge ($p = .000, Exp(\beta) = .331 < 1$).
Interpretation: I can reject the specific null hypothesis $H6_0$ (see Figure 7.9c).
(a): The lower the value for *prior knowledge*, i.e., the less prior knowledge is necessary to understand a vision video, the higher the likelihood that the subjects perceive the overall quality of a vision video as *good*.
(b): The higher the value for *prior knowledge*, i.e., the more prior knowledge is necessary to understand a vision video, the lower the likelihood that the subjects perceive the overall quality of a vision video as *good*.

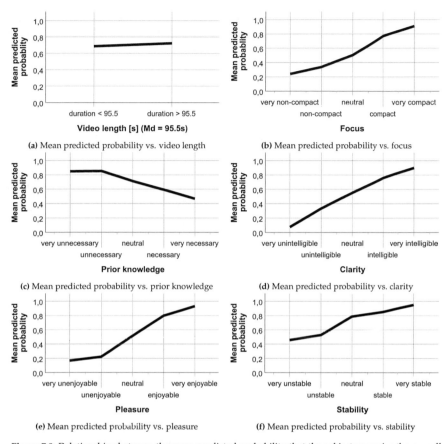

(a) Mean predicted probability vs. video length

(b) Mean predicted probability vs. focus

(c) Mean predicted probability vs. prior knowledge

(d) Mean predicted probability vs. clarity

(e) Mean predicted probability vs. pleasure

(f) Mean predicted probability vs. stability

Figure 7.9: Relationships between the mean predicted probability that the subjects perceive the overall quality of a vision video as good and each significant predictor

Result 4: ... (a) *positively* related to intelligible ($p = .001, Exp(\beta) = 2.043 > 1$) and (b) *positively* related to very intelligible aspired goals of a vision ($p = .000, Exp(\beta) = 3.831 > 1$).

Interpretation: I can reject the specific null hypothesis $H10_0$ (see Figure 7.9d).

(*a*) and (*b*): The higher the value for *clarity*, i.e., the more intelligible the aspired goals of a vision are represented, the higher the likelihood that the subjects perceive the overall quality of a vision video as *good*.

Result 5: ... (a) *negatively* related to an unenjoyable ($p = .000, Exp(\beta) = .245 < 1$), (b) *positively* related to an enjoyable ($p = .001, Exp(\beta) = 2.043 > 1$), and (c) *positively* related to a very enjoyable vision video ($p = .000, Exp(\beta) = 5.572 > 1$).

Interpretation: I can reject the specific null hypothesis $H11_0$ (see Figure 7.9e).

(a): The lower the value for *pleasure*, i.e., the less enjoyable a vision video is to watch, the lower the likelihood that the subjects perceive the overall quality of a vision video as *good*.

(b) and (c): The higher the value for *pleasure*, i.e., the more enjoyable a vision video is to watch, the higher the likelihood that the subjects perceive the overall quality of a vision video as *good*.

Result 6: ... (a) *negatively* related to an unstable ($p = .000, Exp(\beta) = .366 < 1$) and (b) *positively* related to a very stable vision ($p = .021, Exp(\beta) = 3.432 > 1$).

Interpretation: I can reject the specific null hypothesis $H15_0$ (see Figure 7.9f).

(a): The lower the value for *stability*, i.e., the less stable a vision is, the lower the likelihood that the subjects perceive the overall quality of a vision video as *good*.

(b): The higher the value for *stability*, i.e., the more stable a vision is, the higher the likelihood that the subjects perceive the overall quality of a vision video as *good*.

7.6.5.2 Step 2: Evaluating the Obtained Logistic Regression Model

The obtained logistic model must be evaluated to assess its validity and soundness. This assessment is necessary to draw a conclusion about the global null hypothesis gH_0. Below, I present the four required evaluations for a logistic model according to Peng et al. [187].

Overall Model Evaluation. The obtained model is compared with the intercept-only model, the so-called *null model*. The *null model* serves as the baseline since it contains no predictors. Therefore, the *null model* predicts all observations to belong to the largest outcome category. The obtained logistic model fits better to the collected data if it shows a significant improvement compared to the *null model*. I investigated whether there is such an improvement by using the *Likelihood Ratio* test (see Table 7.16). The test indicated that the obtained model is significantly better than the *null model* ($\chi^2(21) = 450.85, p = .000$).

Statistical Tests of Individual Predictors. A z-test is performed for each predictor to investigate the statistical significance of the individual predictors. According to Table 7.15 (bold cells), all six quality characteristics *video length, focus, prior knowledge, clarity, pleasure,* and *stability* are statistically significant predictors of the overall quality of a vision video.

Goodness-of-Fit Statistics. The goodness-of-fit statistics include the *Hosmer-Lemeshow* (H-L) test and the descriptive measure R^2 defined by Nagelkerke [179]. These statistics investigate the fit of the logistic model against the actual outcome, i.e., whether the perceived overall quality of a vision video is *good*. For the H-L test, the p-value should be greater than the significance level ($\alpha = .05$) since the null hypothesis of this test assumes that the model fits the data. The R^2 measure explains how much variation of the dependent variable is taken into account by the predictors of the model. R^2 ranges from 0 to 1. The closer the R^2 value is to 1,

Table 7.15: Details of the logistic model. Remark: The bold cells show that the respective quality characteristic is a statistically significant predictor.

Predictor	β	Standard error	Wald's χ^2	df	p	$Exp(\beta)$	95% CI Lower value	95% CI Upper value
Video length	.020	.004	**22.863**	1	**.000**	1.020	1.012	1.029
Focus			**16.282**	4	**.003**			
Non-compact	−.683	.276	6.109	1	.013	.505	.294	.868
Neutral	−.214	.205	1.086	1	.297	.807	.540	1.207
Compact	.469	.198	5.627	1	.018	1.599	1.085	2.357
Very compact	.515	.272	3.585	1	.058	1.673	.982	2.852
Prior knowledge			**38.838**	4	**.000**			
Unnecessary	1.022	.213	22.926	1	.000	2.779	1.829	4.223
Neutral	.203	.168	1.450	1	.229	1.225	.881	1.703
Necessary	−.216	.187	1.338	1	.247	.806	.559	1.162
Very necessary	−1.104	.227	23.714	1	.000	.331	.212	.517
Clarity			**36.644**	4	**.000**			
Unintelligible	−.446	.265	2.829	1	.093	.640	.381	1.076
Neutral	.113	.230	.239	1	.625	1.119	.713	1.757
Intelligible	.714	.223	10.247	1	.001	2.043	1.319	3.164
Very intelligible	1.343	.259	26.876	1	.000	3.831	2.306	6.367
Pleasure			**72.749**	4	**.000**			
Unenjoyable	−1.408	.285	24.431	1	.000	.245	.140	.428
Neutral	−.147	.219	.453	1	.501	.863	.562	1.325
Enjoyable	.914	.216	17.828	1	.000	2.493	1.631	3.810
Very enjoyable	1.718	.302	32.248	1	.000	5.572	3.080	10.081
Stability			**39.391**	4	**.000**			
Unstable	−1.006	.200	25.231	1	.000	.366	.247	.542
Neutral	.181	.214	.717	1	.397	1.199	.788	1.823
Stable	.270	.255	1.118	1	.290	1.309	.795	2.158
Very stable	1.233	.536	5.287	1	.021	3.432	1.200	9.816
Constant	−.048	.253	.035	1	.851	.954		

the more variability in the collected data set can be explained by the model. The R^2 value can be converted to the effect size η^2 to assess the practical relevance of the findings. According to Table 7.16, the *Hosmer-Lemeshow* test showed that the obtained model fits the data well ($\chi^2(8) = 13.17, p = .106$). The R^2 value is 0.54. Thus, all six predictors in the model explained 54.0% of the variability of the perceived overall quality of a vision video. The effect size value ($\eta^2 = 0.54 > 0.20$) indicates a large practical relevance of the logistic model [56].

Table 7.16: Significance and quality of the logistic model

Model	χ^2	df	p
Overall model evaluation			
Likelihood ratio test	450.851	21	.000
Goodness-of-fits test			
Hosmer-Lemeshow test	13.169	8	.106
Note. Nagelkerke's $R^2 = 0.54$, effect size $\eta^2 = 0.54$			

Validation of Predicted Probabilities. A logistic model can be used to predict the probability that the dependent variable belongs to the desired group of its two possible groups. Based on the predicted probabilities, the model classifies each entry in the analyzed data set into one of the two groups. In general, the desired group is associated with a higher probability and the other group with a lower probability. However, the exact distinction between high and low depends on the individual data set. The resulting classification of the model is compared with the actual classification in the analyzed data set to determine the accuracy of the logistic model. This accuracy can be expressed as a measure of association and a classification table. In the case of this experiment, the logistic model predicts the probability that the subjects perceive the overall quality of a vision video as *good* based on the six significant predictors.

An established measure of association is the *c*-statistic [108]. The *c*-statistic represents the proportion of pairs with different observed groups for which the logistic model correctly predicts a higher probability for observations with the desired group (perceived overall quality is *good*) than for observations without the desired group (perceived overall quality is *bad*). This measure ranges from 0.5 to 1. While 0.5 means that the model is not better than assigning observations randomly to groups, 1 means that the model always assigns higher probabilities to observations with the desired group than to observations without the desired group.

The *c*-statistic of the logistic model is 0.89 (see Table 7.17) indicating a strong model [108]. This value means that for 89.0% of all possible pairs of assessments of vision videos – one with an overall quality rated as *good* and one with an overall quality rated as *bad* – the model correctly assigned a higher probability to those assessments which rated a vision video as *good*.

Besides the measure of association, a classification table illustrates the validity of the predicted probabilities (see Table 7.17). The classification shows the practical results of applying the logistic model on the collected data set. For each entry in the data set, the model calculates the predicted probability and classifies each entry into one of the two groups of the dependent variable. The classification depends on a defined cutoff value. This cutoff value typically corresponds to the proportion of entries in the analyzed data set that rated the dependent variable according to the desired group which is the *null model*. In the case of this experiment, the cutoff value is 0.705 corresponding to the proportion of entries that rated the overall quality as *good*. Thus, the obtained model classifies an entry as *good* if the predicted probability is greater than the cutoff value and otherwise as *bad*. A classification table presents three important proportions: *specificity*, *sensitivity*, and *overall correct prediction rate*. The *specificity* measures the proportion of correctly classified observations without the desired group, i.e., perceived overall quality is *bad*. The *sensitivity* measures the proportion of correctly classified observations with the desired group, i.e., perceived overall quality is *good*. The *overall correct prediction rate* measures the proportion of all correctly classified observations.

The *specificity* (82.2%) and the *sensitivity* (81.1%) show that the prediction of entries that rated the overall quality as *bad* was slightly more accurate than the prediction of entries which rated the overall quality as *good*. However, in both cases, the accuracy of correct predictions is high. This observation is supported by the *overall correct prediction rate* which is 81.4%. This result is an improvement of 10.9 percentage points compared to the *null model* that has an overall correct prediction rate of 70.5% which corresponds to the cutoff value. Based on the c-statistic and the results of the classification table, I conclude that the obtained logistic model has high accuracy in predicting whether the subjects perceive a vision video as good.

7.6.5.3 Summary

The binary logistic regression resulted in a significant model ($\chi^2(21) = 450.85, p = .000$) that contains the six quality characteristics (*video length, focus, prior knowledge, clarity, pleasure,* and *stability*) as significant predictors of the perceived overall quality of a vision video. The other nine characteristics of the quality model for vision videos (*image quality, sound quality, plot, essence, clutter, completeness, intention, sense of responsibility,* and *support*) are not significant and thus do not affect the likelihood that the subjects perceive the overall quality of a vision video as *good*. All predictors of the obtained model explain 54.0% of the variability of the perceived overall quality of a vision video. The effect size $\eta^2 = 0.54$ indicates a large practical relevance of the obtained model. The model correctly classifies 81.1% of the entries in the collected data set

Table 7.17: Specificity, sensitivity, and overall correct prediction rate of the logistic model. Remark: The cutoff value of the logistic model is 0.705.

Observed overall quality	Predicted overall quality		Correct prediction [%]
	Bad	Good	
Bad	231	50	82.2 (Specificity)
Good	127	544	81.1 (Sensitivity)
Overall correct prediction rate			81.4
Note. c-statistic $= 0.89$			

where the overall quality was assessed as *good* and 82.2% of entries where the overall quality was assessed as *bad*, resulting in an *overall correct prediction rate* of 81.4%. These findings allow rejecting the global null hypothesis gH_0 and accepting the global alternative hypothesis gH_1. According to the binary logistic regression results, six characteristics (concretely three vision and three video characteristics) covering all three dimensions of the quality model for vision videos affect the likelihood that the subjects perceive the overall quality of a vision video as *good* from a developer's point of view. Based on these results, I conclude that the obtained logistic model is valid and sound. I reached this conclusion with multiple evidence:

(1) The logistic model is significantly better than the *null model*.

(2) The six quality characteristics in the logistic model are significant predictors of the perceived overall quality of a vision video.

(3) The logistic model fits the data well and has a large practical relevance.

(4) The logistic model has high accuracy in predicting whether a vision video is perceived as good or not.

Finding 7.2

> *The binary logistic regression resulted in a valid and sound logistic model which substantiates that six out of 15 quality characteristics (video length, focus, prior knowledge, clarity, pleasure, and stability) relate to the perceived overall quality of a vision video from a developer's point of view. These six quality characteristics, in turn, meet the criteria for the validity and soundness of the quality model for vision videos.*

7.6.6 Threats to Validity

Construct Validity. Although I used eight vision videos of projects with real customers, I had a mono-operation bias. All vision videos were created in the context of the *Software Project* course at Leibniz Universität Hannover. Thus, the videos did not convey a comprehensive overview of the complexity in practice. Nevertheless, the videos were from real projects. Therefore, I expect a sufficient realistic complexity for the first experiment. Apart from the duration of the videos, all data were collected by using only an assessment form which caused a mono-method bias. This use of a single subjective method allows only restricted explanations of the findings. However, I focused on the use of subjective assessments since asking humans for their opinion is considered as the ultimate standard and right way to assess video quality [221]. Conducting the experiment with all subjects at the same time caused an interaction of different treatments. Although I instructed the subjects to assess each vision video for itself without any comparison with the other ones, I cannot exclude that later assessments of videos were influenced by previous ones. I had to conduct the experiment with all subjects at the same time since there was no other option to handle the assessment of all eight vision videos by all 139 subjects during the course. The given task of assessing the overall quality and individual quality characteristics of vision videos implied to analyze the relationship between both aspects. This implication caused an interaction of testing and treatment. I could not exclude that the subjects tried to guess the potential outcome of the experiment what might have affected their assessments. I did not expect any notable impact on the overall results due to the assessment of 14 characteristics by over 100 subjects. This threat to validity might have been mitigated by two separate groups. While the first group only assesses the overall quality, the second group assesses the individual quality characteristics. However, this type of design has several disadvantages. First, two separate groups require spatial separation. Otherwise, the subjects notice that they evaluate different aspects. Second, the subjects who only assess the overall quality would be much faster than the other ones which may affect the other group who assess the 14 quality characteristics. I had only the permission to carry to the experiment in one 60-minute appointment of the *Software Project* course. Thus, I did not have the time to perform one session with each of the two groups since watching and assessing all eight vision videos already required the entire 60 minutes (see section 7.6.2.5). Another option would have been the use of a second lecture hall which accommodates 70 people (half of the subjects). However, this lecture hall would have to be equipped with the same projector and sound system as the lecture hall of the *Software Project* course since the display devices have a major impact on the perceived video quality [252]. Such a lecture hall was not available since the experiment took place during the lecture period. For these reasons, the chosen experimental design was the only possible one.

External Validity. The selected subjects and eight vision videos of real projects produced a good level of realism. The undergraduate students were close to their graduation, actively developed software at the time of the experiment, and had on average 2.4 years of experience as a developer. Thus, they were suitable to assess the vision videos from a developer's point of view. However, in contrast to professionals, the subjects formed a more homogeneous group which restricts the generalizability of the results. Furthermore, not only the point of view of a developer is important since other stakeholders and team members also belong to the target audience of vision videos. The presented findings are restricted to the point of view of a developer and do not need to hold for other roles, such as stakeholders or video producers. The controlled off-line setting caused an interaction of setting and treatment. Watching a vision video in a lecture hall with over 100 people is not a typical setting compared to an industrial environment. I had to accept this threat to validity to conduct the experiment. The given task of sharing the vision of the particular project had also no pragmatic value for the subjects. As the next step, future experiments need to be conducted in real projects with different roles.

Internal Validity. Maturation is one crucial threat to internal validity. The whole experiment lasted 60 minutes which might have affected the subjects negatively by getting tired or bored. I had to accept this threat to validity since the constraints of the *Software Project* course did not allow any other setting to conduct the experiment. However, I only lost 20 out of 139 subjects due to incomplete answers. Thus, I assume that the duration of the experiment was still acceptable for most of the subjects. The way of testing presents a further threat to validity since there might have been a learning effect. The subjects repeated the same assessment for eight videos one after the other. The later assessments might have been affected by the previous ones. The used assessment form is another threat to validity. In the case of a bad design or wording, the experiment might have been affected negatively. I tested and refined the assessment form in a pilot study with 18 subjects to improve the instrumentation. In addition, I explained the assessment form and quality characteristics to all subjects, asking the subjects to ask questions at any time. I restricted the selection of subjects on computer science students who were active participants in the *Software Project* course. In this way, I ensured that the subjects actively develop software and thus have the point of view of a developer. All subjects participated voluntarily in the experiment. There was no financial reward and the participation did not influence the success of passing the course. Thus, there was little incentive to participate without being self-motivated. However, even self-motivated subjects are a threat to validity since they might be more motivated and suited for the experiment than the entire target population [257].

Conclusion Validity. The validity of any scientific evaluation highly depends on the reliability of measures. Most of the collected data is based on subjective assessments which reduce the reliability and reproducibility. However, I consciously decided on this kind of assessment since the subjective assessment of video quality is the ultimate and right way [221]. In contrast to typical video quality assessments with 15-30 subjects, I had 139 subjects to increase the reliability of the measurements. I ensured the reliability of the treatment implementation by conducting the experiment in a lecture hall with all 139 subjects at the same time. Thus, all subjects watched the eight vision videos under the same conditions which mitigated the risk that the implementation was not similar for all subjects. The subject formed a more homogeneous group than professionals from the industry. This counteracted the threat of erroneous conclusions. A more homogeneous group mitigates the risk that the variation due to the subjects' random heterogeneity was larger than due to the investigated treatments. The increased homogeneity of the subjects, in turn, restricts the external validity since a group of professionals is rarely homogeneous due to their different backgrounds.

7.6.7 Discussion

The findings of the experiment provide important insights into the characterization of the overall impression of a vision video. These insights substantiate that there are relationships between individual quality characteristics and the perceived overall quality of vision videos. Thus, the quality model contains at least a subset of relevant characteristics of a vision video.

*The quality model for vision videos is a valid and sound description of potentially relevant charac-
teristics that allow the characterization of the overall impression of a vision video.* The results of the
statistical analysis show that there are six out of the 15 quality characteristics that relate to the
likelihood that the overall quality of a vision video is perceived as *good* (see Finding 7.2). The
findings validate obvious and logical relationships. It is not surprising that a vision video is
more likely to be perceived as *good* if the target audience enjoys watching the video (*pleasure*).
Furthermore, it is obvious that the less *prior knowledge* is necessary to understand a vision video,
the higher is the likelihood that the video is perceived as *good* since the video can be understood
more easily. For the vision characteristics *focus*, *clarity*, and *stability* the conclusions are similar.
The more compact, clearer, and more stable a vision video is, the more consistently the essence
and aspired goals of the vision are presented. The relationship between a longer *video length*
and the likelihood that the overall quality is perceived as *good* seems surprising at first. According to Broll et al. [34], a three-minute video appears as short but should still be presented
in shorter clips to avoid that the viewers become mentally inactive. This recommendation corresponds to the findings for Guo et al. [97] which yielded that videos of massive open online
courses are watched at most six minutes, regardless of the total *video length*. For longer videos,
viewers watch less than half of a video. In consideration of these findings, the identified relationship between *video length* and overall quality seems plausible. The used vision videos had
a mean duration of 1:43 minutes and a minimum and maximum duration of 1:09 minutes and
2:35 minutes. All used vision videos are shorter than the recommended upper limits. I assume
that the videos with a duration closer to the given maximum of three minutes are perceived
as better since they may provide more information and time to understand the information
than shorter videos. This assumption is supported by Owens and Millerson [185, p. 143] who
stated: *"If the shots [and thus the video] are too brief, they may flick past the viewer's eyes without
entering the brain"*. However, I must remark that depending on the content of a vision video
even a longer duration may have a negative impact on its perceived overall quality. According
to Owens and Millerson [185], if longer videos contain too many topics, they cannot address
these contents adequately. In contrast, if longer videos cover too few topics, they appear to be
slow and labored. Both cases negatively affect the target audience and their perception of the
overall video quality either since they do not understand the video or get bored.

Although I found no relationships between the likelihood that the overall quality of a vision video is perceived as *good* and the nine characteristics *image quality*, *sound quality*, *plot*,
essence, *clutter*, *completeness*, *intention*, *sense of responsibility*, and *support*, I cannot exclude that
there are relationships. In contrast, I assume that there are specific reasons why I could not find
these relationships. First of all, the teams produced the used vision videos with similar simple
equipment, i.e., smartphones. Thus, all assessed vision videos have a comparable *image quality*
and *sound quality* resulting in barely noticeable differences. One could argue that professional

equipment might have caused a better quality and thus clearer differences. However, on the one hand, I assume the necessity to focus on simplicity regarding the equipment used as well as knowledge and skills required to simplify the production and use of vision videos by software professionals. On the other hand, different researchers [32, 34, 217] showed that vision videos with a lower *image quality* and *sound quality* due to the use of simple equipment such as smartphones, tablets, and digital camcorders are completely sufficient for the purposes in requirements engineering. Owens and Millerson [185] support these views by emphasizing that it is important to know how to communicate visually no matter how professional the equipment is. Nevertheless, I presume that a vision video with a very poor *image quality* and *sound quality* affects its perceived overall quality negatively. Furthermore, I assume that the experimental design and the chosen point of view of developers have led to difficulties to adequately assess the other seven quality characteristics. All videos were only watched once. Therefore, I suppose that the subjects might not be able to directly recognize and assess the structured presentation (*plot*), the important core elements (*essence*), potentially disrupting and distracting elements (*clutter*) as well as whether the vision is complete or not (*completeness*). The subjects might also be confused about why I ask them whether the video is suitable for the given task (*intention*) since the experiment implied that this aspect is fulfilled. The given task also had no pragmatic value for the subjects why there was no need for them to support the vision (*support*). In contrast to the subjects who only watched the video, a video producer might be more concerned whether the legal regulations are fulfilled (*sense of responsibility*) since this role is responsible and legally liable.

Nevertheless, the key finding of this experiment is not the individual relationships. Instead, the more important insight is that the experiment resulted in significant relationships between individual quality characteristics and the likelihood that the subjects perceive the overall quality of a vision video as *good*. Based on the results of analysis, I can reject the global null hypothesis gH_0. This rejection, in turn, substantiates that the quality model for vision videos is valid and sound. Therefore, I am confident that the quality model for vision videos is a viable basis that contributes to the fundamental relevance of the candidate solution. As an answer to the Research Question 7.4, I can summarize:

Answer to Research Question 7.4

> *The obtained findings show that six out of the 15 individual characteristics of the quality model are statistically significantly related to the overall quality of vision videos. In particular, the better each of the six characteristics is fulfilled the higher is the likelihood that the overall quality of a vision video was perceived as good. These relationships meet the specified criteria for the validity and soundness of the quality model for vision videos. Therefore, this quality model represents a viable description of potentially relevant characteristics of vision videos that enable to characterize the overall impression of a vision video.*

7.6.8 Conclusion

This experiment validated the quality model for vision videos which is one of the key results of the second main step of the research process (cf. section 7.2.2) to create awareness regarding (vision) video quality. The developed quality model for vision videos with its two representation formats (cf. section 7.5.8) serves as a checklist for software professionals to ensure the comprehensive treatment of vision video quality by providing orientation and guidance over the entire vision video production and use process in requirements engineering (see Figure 7.1). In the experiment, I investigated whether the 15 quality characteristics are related to the overall quality of vision videos and thus characterize its overall impression. According to the findings, there are significant relationships between individual quality characteristics and the likelihood that the subjects perceive the overall quality of a vision video as good. These relationships substantiate the validity and soundness of the quality model for vision videos. Therefore, I am confident that the quality model for vision videos contributes to the fundamental relevance of the candidate solution by providing a clearer definition of the hitherto ill-defined concept of video quality in the context of representing a software project vision. The quality model is intended to engage the awareness of software professionals on quality characteristics of vision videos. The benefit of the quality model is its support of software professionals to identify and specify the quality characteristics that they believe are relevant for their particular vision video. When software professionals know which characteristics are relevant for their vision video, they can more easily establish requirements, satisfaction criteria, and measures to guide the video production and use as well as the evaluation of the resulting vision video.

The quality model is a validated but theoretical description of relevant quality characteristics. It is necessary to provide guidance for software professionals on how to proceed in the video production and use to achieve a video with specific characteristics. For this purpose, I enhance the practical utility of the quality model by developing a condensed guideline for video production and use. This guideline reveals how the individual quality characteristics can be affected in the particular steps of the video production and use process.

7.7 Step 3.1: Developing a Condensed Guideline

Besides the awareness regarding video quality, the concept *awareness and guidance* focuses on guiding software professionals in the production and use of videos. This guidance is developed in the third main step of the research process (see section 7.2.3 and Figure 7.2) that is presented in the following three sections. Based on the analysis of the generic video production guidelines (cf. section 7.3), I subsequently develop a condensed guideline that summarizes essential recommendations for video production and use. For the development of the condensed guideline, I conducted a workshop whose details are reported below. This condensed guideline is validated in academia (see section 7.8) and adapted to vision videos (see section 7.9).

7.7.1 Workshop Objective

I ensured that the workshop is well-defined by formulating its underlying research goal:

Research Goal 7.4

> *Analyze* the extracted and coded text passages from the analyzed generic video production guidelines (cf. section 7.3.3)
> *for the purpose of* developing a condensed guideline for video production and use
> *with respect to* the essential knowledge on how something in video production and use should be done (HOW) to achieve a particular result (WHAT) by emphasizing the motivation, reason, or purpose for following the given advice (WHY)
> *from the point of view of* active video producers in requirements engineering
> *in the context of* a workshop.

The basic idea is to reuse the extracted and coded text passages from the different generic video production guidelines that are related to the identified quality characteristics and steps of the video production and use process. However, these text passages differ in their structure and details on how something in the video production and use should be done to achieve a particular result. For this reason, I discussed each text passage with two active video producers in requirements engineering regarding its potential to be an essential recommendation that should be included in a condensed guideline. In this way, I ensured that the selection of recommendations and the development of the condensed guideline is based on the experience and knowledge of persons who produce and use videos in requirements engineering.

7.7.2 Workshop Design

I designed the workshop in consideration of the recommendations for planning and conducting workshops by Pohl [195]. Below, I present the important details of the workshop design.

7.7.2.1 Criteria for Discussing and Selecting Recommendations

For the discussion and selection of the extracted and coded text passages as essential recommendations, I specified three criteria in consideration of the *Golden Circle* by Sinek [226]. The *Golden Circle* is a concept for finding order and predictability in human behavior by helping to understand *"why we do what we do"* [226, p. 42]. In particular, this concept argues that inspirational guidance is more powerful and sustainable than manipulative guidance to influence human behavior. For this purpose, inspirational guidance must explain how something should

150

be done (HOW) to achieve a particular result (WHAT) by emphasizing the motivation, reason, or purpose for following the given advice (WHY) [226]. Based on these three aspects, I specified the following three criteria that were used in the workshop:

(1) HOW: The text passage explains how something in video production and use should be done by describing the process or method used.

(2) WHAT: The text passage explains what result is achieved by the process or method used.

(3) WHY: The text passage explains the motivation, reason, or purpose for following the given advice.

7.7.2.2 Participants of the Workshop

Besides myself as moderator, scribe, and participant, the workshop was attended by two participants who are active video producers. These participants have been producing and using videos in requirements engineering for several years. Both participants are computer science researchers who have both been working in the software engineering group at Leibniz Universität Hannover for more than two years. The first participant and I had four years of experience in producing and using videos in requirements engineering and the second participant had two years of experience. The years of experience were important for my selection of the participants to ensure that the discussion and selection of the text passages as essential recommendations were made in consideration to practical and theoretical experience and knowledge.

7.7.2.3 Workshop Procedure

The workshop was carried out in December 2019 with an overall duration of five hours. The workshop had a fixed agenda consisting of four main activities (see Figure 7.10).

In a short introduction, I explained to the two participants the research goal of the workshop and the three specified criteria. Afterward, the first activity took part in which we discussed each extracted and coded text passage regarding its potential to be an essential recommendation based on the three criteria. The respective text passage was only selected as an essential recommendation if all participants agreed that all three criteria were met. In the second activity, we edited the selected recommendations by grouping and merging them to structure the results and remove duplicates. Based on these results, we manually extracted the HOW, WHAT, and WHY information from the edited recommendations. This third activity was necessary to enable the last activity in which we reformulated the edited recommendation according to the defined pattern (see Figure 7.10). The purpose of this reformulation was to standardize the different representation formats of the edited recommendations by providing their information in a uniform structure similar to the templates for requirement by Rupp et al. [208].

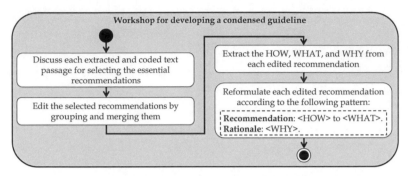

Figure 7.10: Activity diagram of the workshop procedure

7.7.3 Results

Below, I present the results of the individual activities of the workshop. Based on the 307 extracted and coded text passages (cf. section 7.3.3), the discussion of the participants resulted in 105 selected recommendations. After grouping and merging these recommendations, we obtained 63 edited recommendations from which we extracted the HOW, WHAT, and WHY information. Based on the extracted information, we reformulated the 63 recommendations according to the defined pattern (see Figure 7.10). Thus, all recommendations have a uniform structure by summarizing how someone should proceed in the video production and use (HOW) to achieve a particular result (WHAT) by emphasizing the motivation, reason, or purpose for following the given advice (WHY). Table 7.18 shows one exemplary structured recommendations. All structured recommendations are related to the affected quality characteristics of videos and the affected steps of the video production and use process since they are based on the coded text passages. These 63 recommendations form the condensed guideline for video production and use that summarizes the essential recommendations to guide software professionals. The complete condensed guideline can be found in appendix E.4.

Table 7.18: Exemplary structured recommendation of the condensed guideline

ID	Recommendation
03.	Create a list of topics that you want to address in your video to define the final number of topics addressed in your video.
	Rationale: If you have too many topics, the audience rarely remembers more than a fraction of them. If you have too few topics, the audience perceives the video as slow and labored.
	Steps: Preproduction, Viewing
	Characteristics: Essence, Pleasure

7.7.4 Threats to Validity

The results of the workshop are based on the participants' practical and theoretical experience and knowledge regarding the application of videos in requirements engineering. Therefore, the entire discussion and the selection of the extracted and coded text passages as essential recommendations are purely subjective. However, this subjective assessment was necessary to obtain a pragmatic perspective on the recommendations. For this reason, the personal experience and knowledge of active video producers in requirements engineering were substantial for the development of the condensed guideline for video production and use. Nevertheless, the developed guideline is only based on the assessments of three persons. Thus, the validation of the condensed guideline is necessary which is presented in section 7.8.

7.7.5 Summary

The workshop resulted in a condensed guideline for video production and use consisting of 63 structured recommendations. On the one hand, each recommendation is related to the affected quality characteristics of videos and the affected steps of the video production and use process. Thus, these recommendations enhance the practical utility of the quality model for videos. On the other hand, each recommendation explains how something should be done in the video production and use to achieve a particular result by emphasizing the motivation, reason, or purpose for following the given advice. Therefore, the condensed guideline provides inspirational guidance that helps software professionals to understand why they should do what the recommendations suggest by guiding their human behavior in a balanced way throughout all steps of the video production and use process in requirements engineering.

7.8 Step 3.2: Validating the Condensed Guideline

The condensed guideline and its structured recommendations have to be validated (see section 7.2.3 and Figure 7.2) since they are only based on the assessments of three persons. The validation is required to ensure that the developed artifact (guideline) and its contained items (recommendations) are valid and sound to contribute to the fundamental relevance of the candidate solution (cf. section 1.3 and Figure 1.1, ⑤). For this purpose, I conducted a content validation study in which experts assess whether the items of a developed artifact and thus the entire artifact are valid by providing the content that they are supposed to provide [261].

7.8.1 Study Objective

The underlying research goal of the content validation study of the condensed guideline and its recommendations is formulated as follows:

Research Goal 7.5

Analyze the 63 *structured recommendations and thus the condensed guideline*
for the purpose of evaluating their content validity
with respect to providing essential knowledge (RELEVANCE) on how something in video
production and use should be done (HOW) to achieve a particular result (WHAT) by em-
phasizing the motivation, reason, or purpose for following the given advice (WHY)
from the point of view of active video producers in requirements engineering
in the context of a content validation study conducted in academia and industry.

I developed the condensed guideline with the intent to summarize the essential recommendations (RELEVANCE) that explain how something in video production and use should be
done (HOW) to achieve a particular result (WHAT) by emphasizing the motivation, reason, or
purpose for following the given advice (WHY). Therefore, if the structured recommendations
and thus the guideline are valid in terms of content, these four aspects (RELEVANCE, HOW,
WHAT, and WHY) must be met. Thus, I asked the following research question:

Research Question 7.5

How valid is the content of the individual structured recommendations and thus of the
condensed guideline regarding the four aspects RELEVANCE, HOW, WHAT, and WHY?

7.8.2 Study Design

The design of the study is based on the content validation process by Yusoff [261]. This process
comprises three main steps: Development of the content validation form, data collection, and
data analysis. In the following three sections, I explain the details of the individual steps.

7.8.2.1 Development of the Content Validation Form

In the first step, it is necessary to develop the content validation form which contains the items
to be assessed and a defined rating scale for each aspect to be examined (cf. appendix E.5.1). In
the case of this study, the items are the individual structured recommendations. For the ratings
of the four aspects RELEVANCE, HOW, WHAT, and WHY, I used four 4-point Likert scales to
obtain the level of agreement of the experts on a defined statement regarding the respective
aspect. The four defined statements are the following ones:

(1) RELEVANCE: The structured recommendation provides essential knowledge that is relevant for an inexperienced software professional who wants to produce and use videos
in requirements engineering.

(2) HOW: The structured recommendation explains how something in video production and
use should be done by describing the process or method used.

(3) WHAT: The structured recommendation explains what result is achieved by the process or method used.

(4) WHY: The structured recommendation explains the motivation, reason, or purpose for following the given advice.

7.8.2.2 Data Collection

In the second step, the experts are selected and the study is conducted. For the sampling, I applied *purposive sampling* which is a non-probabilistic sampling technique that is most effective when experts are needed as subjects [241]. For purposive sampling, I directly contacted five persons from my network who are active video producers in requirements engineering. Two persons are from the industry and three persons are from academia. All of them have already produced and used videos in requirements engineering in their previous work. For this reason, I consider them as experts due to their practical and theoretical experience and knowledge.

In December 2019, all five experts accepted my invitation. They received an email with detailed explanations of the study and the required materials. I also personally explained the study process and the materials to each subject. I received all completed forms one week later.

7.8.2.3 Data Analysis

For the data analysis, I selected the *content validity index* (CVI) according to the approach by Polit et al. [197]. This method allows the subjective opinion of experts on the contained items of an artifact to be quantified by ratings to draw conclusions about the content validity of the individual items and the entire artifact. Thus, developers of an artifact obtain the information whether their developed artifact and its contained items provide the content that they are supposed to provide. The approach of Polit et al. [197] is widely used since it fulfills the following important criteria: Finding consensus rather than consistency estimates, ease of computation, comprehensibility, ease of communication, provision of both item and artifact validity information, and adjustments for chance agreement [197]. The approach of Polit et al. [197] comprises three metrics: item-level CVI (I-CVI), modified kappa (κ^*), and scale-level CVI (S-CVI/Ave). The I-CVI describes the proportion of experts who agree that a respective statement applies to an evaluated item. The calculation of the I-CVI is necessary to calculate κ^* that is the adapted I-CVI taking into account chance agreement. Based on the value of κ^*, I can determine the content validity of each item regarding the aspect examined. Table 7.19 summarizes the value range of κ^*, its interpretation for the level of agreement, and its meaning for the content validity of an item for each of the four aspects under investigation. The S CVI/Ave describes the average I-CVI over all evaluated items of an artifact for one examined aspect and thus the content validity of the entire artifact regarding the respective aspect.

Table 7.19: Interpretation of the κ^* and its meaning for the content validity of an item

κ^*	Interpretation; according to Landis and Koch [155]	Meaning for content validity regarding			
		HOW	WHAT	WHY	RELEVANCE
< 0	Poor agreement	Invalid, exclude item.			Invalid, exclude item.
0 – 0.2	Slight agreement				
0.21 – 0.4	Fair agreement	Revise item.			Valid, include item.
0.41 – 0.6	Moderate agreement				
0.61 – 0.8	Substantial agreement	Valid, include item.			
0.81 – 1	Almost perfect agreement				

7.8.3 Results

Based on the assessments of the five experts, I calculated the I-CVI and κ^* for each item regarding each of the four aspects. The detailed results of the analysis can be found in appendix E.5.2. Table 7.20 summarizes the detailed results of data analysis. According to these results, all 63 structured recommendations are valid in terms of content regarding all four examined aspects HOW, WHAT, WHY, and RELEVANCE. With regard to the aspects HOW, WHAT, and WHY, the experts' assessments show a substantial to an almost perfect agreement that the respective recommendation explains how something in video production and use should be done by describing the process or method used, what result is achieved by the process or method used, and why the given advice should be followed. With regard to the aspect RELEVANCE, the experts' assessments show a moderate to an almost perfect agreement that the respective recommendation provides essential knowledge that is relevant for an inexperienced software professional who wants to produce and use videos in requirements engineering. Therefore, all 63 structured recommendations are valid in terms of content and thus should be included in the condensed guideline. Each S-CVI/Ave value (HOW: 0.96, WHAT: 0.97, WHY: 0.97, and RELE-VANCE: 0.94) is larger than the defined threshold of 0.9 that must be fulfilled to ensure that the entire artifact is valid in terms of content [197]. Thus, the S-CVI/Ave values substantiate that the condensed guideline is valid in terms of content regarding all four aspects.

Finding 7.3

According to the results of the content validation study, all 63 structured recommendations and thus the condensed guideline are valid in terms of content regarding all four examined aspects RELEVANCE, HOW, WHAT, and WHY.

7.8.4 Threats to Validity

Below, I report the threats to construct, external, internal, and conclusion validity [141, 257].

Table 7.20: Summarized results of the data analysis using the content validity index

Agreement	Number of items						S-CVI/Ave ($\geq 0.9?$)
	Poor	Slight	Fair	Moderate	Substantial	Almost perfect	
Interpretation	Invalid		Revise		Valid		Valid
HOW	0	0	0	0	14	49	0.96
WHAT	0	0	0	0	11	52	0.97
WHY	0	0	0	0	11	52	0.97
Interpretation	Invalid			Valid			Valid
RELEVANCE	0	0	0	5	10	48	0.94

Construct Validity. The content validity of any artifact must be assessed regarding one or more defined aspects to clarify the context of the study. An inadequate preoperational explication of the examined aspects is a crucial threat to construct validity. I mitigated this threat to validity by reusing the defined criteria of the workshop (cf. section 7.7.2.1) to specify the aspects assessed by the subjects of this study. The subjects assessed the defined aspects by using only a content validation form which caused a mono-method bias. The use of one single subjective method to collect the opinions of the subjects only allows restricted explanations of the findings. However, the mere use of a content validation form follows exactly the defined and established process for content validation studies by Yusoff [261]. The focus on subjective data that is quantified by ratings serves to compensate for lack of objective measures for content validity [183]. This quantification also counteracts the risk of researcher bias since the subjects quantified the data themselves. Thus, I did not have to code and interpret the data myself.

External Validity. All invited subjects had already produced and used videos in requirements engineering in their previous work. For this reason, I consider them as experts on video production and use in requirements engineering due to their practical and theoretical experience and knowledge. Although these subjects are experts and thus belong to the target population of a content validation study, they do not represent the target population of the condensed guideline that consists of inexperienced software professionals who want to produce and use videos in requirements engineering. Therefore, the generalizability of the findings is restricted since they do not necessarily apply to the target population of the condensed guideline. However, it does not make sense to ask novices in a content validation study since they do not have the required practical experience and knowledge to make such assessments. For this reason, it is necessary to ask experts. As future work, I want to ask inexperienced software professionals for their opinions regarding the content validity of the condensed guideline and its contained recommendations to compare their assessments with those of the experts. This procedure is also recommended by Keeney et al. [141] to clarify and strengthen the findings.

Internal Validity. Probably one of the most crucial threats to internal validity is the selection of the experts who participate in the study. The selected experts have the main influence on the results. For the selection, I relied on my own judgment when inviting persons as experts to participate. This technique is called *purposive sampling* which is most effective when experts are needed as subjects [241]. For my judgment, I had two defined criteria. First, I only contacted persons from my network who I knew were active video producers at the time of the study. Second, these person have also already produced and used videos in requirements engineering in their previous work. Thus, I ensured that an expert has practical and theoretical experience and knowledge about video production and use in requirements engineering. Despite this concise selection criteria, the risk remains that the results of the study are specific to this particular group of experts. However, this is a limitation of every content validation study using experts as subjects [212]. Besides the selection, the number of experts is also crucial. Polit et al. [197] suggest that three experts should be the minimal acceptable number for content validation studies. However, the recommended and maximum number of experts is unclear and discussible since the number of experts is not as important as their expertise and representativity [52]. I invited each selected person individually by email and ask to keep the content of the study confidential. In this way, I followed the defined process for content validation studies to ensure the anonymity of the experts among each other [261]. The experts should not know about each other to ensure that they do not influence each other in their assessments. According to the explanations of Keeney et al. [141], anonymous assessment methods have the distinct advantage of a higher accuracy of the results compared to interactive group processes such as workshops or brainstorming. Despite my actions to preserve the subjects' anonymity, I cannot exclude that the subjects did not exchange information with each other about the study.

Conclusion Validity. The validity of any scientific study highly depends on the reliability of measures. In this study, the content validity regarding all four aspects were assessed subjectively using an content validation form. A good wording, instrumentation, and instrumentation layout were crucial for the validity of the findings. For this reason, I followed the explanations, recommendations, and examples of Yusoff [261] and Polit et al. [197] for the design of the content validation form and its instrumentation. Although the content validation form quantifies the experts' opinions on Likert scales the data is based on subjective assessments which reduce the reliability and reproducibility. All subjects got the same documents (content validation form and condensed guideline) for the study and I personally explained to each subject how to use the documents. I conducted the different conversations as similar as possible to ensure the reliability of treatment implementation. Despite this standardized procedure, the reproducibility of the study is low. The results are not necessarily repeatable with other groups of similarly qualified experts due to the heterogeneity of the subjects caused by their individual experiences and educational backgrounds [212].

7.8.5 Discussion

The findings of this study provide important insights into the content validity of the condensed guideline for video production and use. These findings substantiate that all 63 structured recommendations provide essential knowledge (RELEVANCE) on how something in the video production and use should be done (HOW) to achieve a particular result (WHAT) by emphasizing the motivation, purpose, or reason for following the given advice (WHY).

The condensed guideline is a valid artifact in terms of content by summarizing essential recommendations for video production and use to guide software professionals. The results of the study show that all recommendations are valid in terms of content regarding all four examined aspects (see Finding 7.3). However, these findings should not be overgeneralized. Content validation studies are not strict scientific methods. These methods are intended to find consensus among experts to compensate for the lack of objective measures for content validity. For this purpose, these methods serve as a theory-building process to make the best use of subjective data such as practical and theoretical experience and knowledge of experts [177]. The results of this study show that experienced and active video producers agree very well in their individual opinions. On the one hand, the experts confirm that the structured recommendations address the three aspects HOW, WHAT, and WHY that are necessary for inspirational guidance to guide human behavior [226]. On the other hand, the experts agree that the recommendations provide essential knowledge that inexperienced software professionals should know if they want to produce and use videos in requirements engineering. I must remark that my decision to include recommendations as relevant in the case of a moderate agreement is discussible (cf. Table 7.19). In general, one could argue to exclude these items due to the lower agreement. However, I consciously decided to include even recommendations as relevant with a moderate agreement since all recommendations are valid in terms of content regarding the HOW, WHAT, and WHY. I justify this decision by preferring to include more potentially relevant recommendations in the guideline rather than excluding recommendations too early since this is the first version of the condensed guideline for video production and use. When including the recommendations assessed with a moderate agreement, I checked that the scale-level CVI of RELEVANCE is at least as large as the threshold defined by Polit et al. [197] (S-CVI/Ave(RELEVANCE) = 0.94 $\geq$ 0.9). In this way, I ensured that the inclusion of these recommendations does not compromise the content validity of the entire artifact.

Based on these insights, I am confident that the condensed guideline for video production and use is valid and sound and thus contributes to the fundamental relevance of the candidate solution. As an answer to the Research Question 7.5, I can summarize:

Answer to Research Question 7.5

> *All 63 structured recommendations and thus the condensed guideline for video production and use are valid in terms of content regarding the four aspects RELEVANCE, HOW, WHAT, and WHY. The scale-level CVI (S-CVI/Ave) of all four aspects yield an almost perfect experts' agreement that the condensed guideline and its contained recommendations are relevant for inexperienced software professionals who want to produce and use videos in requirements engineering (RELEVANCE). The experts almost perfectly agree that the individual structured recommendations provide essential knowledge on how something the video production and use should be done (HOW) to achieve a particular result (WHAT) by emphasizing the motivation, purpose, or reason for following the given advice (WHY).*

7.8.6 Conclusion

This study validated the condensed guideline for video production and use which is one of the key results of the third main step of the research process (cf. section 7.2.3 and Figure 7.2) to provide software professionals with guidance for applying videos in requirements engineering. The condensed guideline and its structured recommendations serve to enhance the practical utility of the developed quality model for videos by summarizing the essential knowledge on the video production and use (RELEVANCE). Each recommendation is related to the affected quality characteristics of videos and the affected steps of the video production and use process. In this way, the recommendations show how (HOW) individual quality characteristics can be achieved (WHAT) in certain process steps, whereby the rationale is given (WHY). In the content validation study, I examine whether the recommendations are valid in terms of content regarding RELEVANCE, HOW, WHAT, and WHY. According to results, the surveyed experts agreed very well that the recommendations and thus the condensed guideline meet all four aspects. Therefore, I am confident that the condensed guideline contributes to the fundamental relevance of the candidate solution by providing inspirational guidance for software professionals who want to produce and use videos in requirements engineering. This inspirational guidance is the benefit of the condensed guideline since this kind of guidance is an effective means to influence human behavior [226]. As a consequence, the condensed guideline helps software professionals to guide their actions in video production and use to produce videos that are more consistent with their understanding of video quality.

7.9 Step 3.3: Adapting the Condensed Guideline to Vision Videos

The condensed guideline addresses the production and use of generic videos. Although the structured recommendations are valid, they are unspecific regarding the context of this thesis (cf. Research Goal 1.1). It is necessary to adapt the condensed guideline to vision videos to pro-vide more specific guidance for software professionals to apply vision videos in requirements engineering (see section 7.2.3 and Figure 7.2)). For the adaption, I conducted a review of all 63 structured recommendations regarding their relevance for vision videos with one active video producer experienced in the production and use of vision videos in requirements engineering.

7.9.1 Review Objective

The objective of the review was to analyze the 63 restructured recommendations of the con-densed guideline (see appendix E.4) regarding their relevance for the production and use of vision videos. I formulated the research goal by applying the goal definition template [18].

Research Goal 7.6

> **Analyze** all 63 *structured recommendations of the condensed guideline*
> **for the purpose of** *adapting the structured recommendations to vision videos*
> **with respect to** *their relevance for the production and use of vision videos*
> **from the point of view of** *active video producers experienced in the production and use of*
> *vision videos in requirements engineering*
> **in the context of** *a review.*

Although I validated the condensed guideline and its structured recommendations (cf. sec-tion 7.8), it is possible that not all recommendations are directly applicable to vision videos and must either be adapted or even omitted. Besides myself, one active and experienced video producer of vision videos has reviewed the 63 structured recommendations. Based on our joint feedback, I either adapted or omitted the respective recommendation. Thus, I ensured that the adapted guideline for vision video production and use is based on experience and knowledge of different persons who produce and use vision videos in requirements engineering.

7.9.2 Review Design

Below, I report the details of the review design that is based on the recommendations for plan-ning and conducting reviews by Frühauf et al. [87].

7.9.2.1 Questions for Reviewing the Structured Recommendations

For the review, I specified the following two questions that were applied to each recommen-dation. While the first question filters the recommendations regarding their relevance for the production and use of vision videos in requirements engineering, the second question collects feedback on how a recommendation can be adapted to better fit the production and use of vision videos.

(1) RELEVANCE: Is the structured recommendation relevant for the production and use a vision videos in requirements engineering?

(2) ADAPTION: In the case of a relevant structured recommendation, how would you adapt the recommendation to vision videos?

7.9.2.2 Reviewers

Besides myself, one computer science researcher participated in the review process. We are both active video producers of vision videos in requirements engineering, having worked together for the last two and a half years on the research project "Assessing the Potential of Interactive Vision Videos for Requirements Engineering (ViViReq)". In this project-specific context, we gained a lot of practical and theoretical experience and knowledge of the production and use of vision videos [124, 126, 129–131, 136, 139, 144, 216–218]. Based on this experience and knowledge, we independently reviewed the recommendations and provided feedback regarding their relevance for the production and use of vision videos in requirements engineering.

7.9.2.3 Review Procedure

The two reviews were carried out in January 2020. The other reviewer received an email with an explanation of the research goal, the previously mentioned questions, and the condensed guideline for video production and use (cf. appendix E.4). I also personally explained the review process to the other reviewer. I received the commented guideline one week later from the reviewer. Based on our joint feedback, I adapted the guideline to vision videos. Finally, I distributed the resulting adapted guideline for vision video production and use to the other reviewer to verify that I had addressed his feedback correctly.

7.9.3 Results

Out of the 63 structured recommendations, both reviewers confirmed 55 recommendations as relevant for the production and use of vision videos in requirements engineering. I obtained 47 recommendations for vision videos by revising the 55 relevant recommendations according to the feedback given. Eight times, the reviewers suggested that two structured recommendations should be combined into one recommendation so that the related information is not separated over different recommendations. Based on the feedback, I adapted the recommendations so that they better fit the production and use of vision videos. Furthermore, I added five new recommendations that the reviewers proposed themselves to be relevant for the production and use of vision videos. Thus, the resulting guideline consists of 52 structured recommendations. Table 7.21 shows one exemplary structured recommendation for vision videos. All 52 recommendations refer to the affected quality characteristics of vision videos and the affected steps of the vision video production and use process. In the case of more than one affected process step, I highlighted the step in italics for which both reviewers have agreed that the recommendation provides the most benefit. I also indicated whether the recommendation is based on other reviewed recommendations or the reviewers' experience. The adapted guideline for vision video production and use can be found in appendix E.6.

Table 7.21: Exemplary structured recommendation of the adapted guideline

ID	Recommendation
03.	Define the topics of a vision (addressed problem, key idea of the solution, and improvement of the problem by the solution) that you want to address in your vision video to clarify the content addressed in your vision video.
	Rationale: These topics are crucial for a vision video since a vision video is a video that presents a vision or parts of it.
	Steps: *Preproduction*, Viewing
	Characteristics: Essence, Pleasure, Completeness
	Based on: Recommendation 03

7.9.4 Threats to Validity

The results of the reviews are based on the reviewers' practical and theoretical experience and knowledge regarding the application of vision videos in requirements engineering. Therefore, the entire adaption of the restructured recommendations to vision videos is purely subjective. However, the subjective consideration of the recommendations was required to obtain a pragmatic perspective on them. For this reason, the personal experience and knowledge of two active and experienced video producers of vision videos in requirements engineering were substantial for adapting the guideline to vision videos. Nevertheless, the adapted guideline is only based on the reviews of two persons. Thus, further research is necessary that applies the adapted guideline for producing and using vision videos.

7.9.5 Summary

The review resulted in an adapted guideline for vision video production and use consisting of 52 structured recommendations. These recommendations are based either on the validated recommendations of the condensed guideline for video production and use or on the practical and theoretical experience and knowledge of the reviewers. The adapted recommendations provide more specific guidance for software professionals who want to apply vision videos in requirements engineering. Thus, they enhance the practical utility of the quality model for vision videos since each recommendation refers to the affected quality characteristics of vision videos and the affected steps of the video production and use process. I must remark that I only included recommendations which the reviewer and I could confirm based on our experience and knowledge. The unconfirmed recommendations were omitted. This omission does not mean that the respective recommendations cannot be useful for the production and use of vision videos. However, we were not able to assess their relevance for the production and use of vision videos based on our experience and knowledge.

7.10   Summary of the Chapter

This chapter presents the concept *awareness and guidance* of the candidate solution for reducing variability in human behavior by supporting awareness and guidance of software professionals. Based on a defined research process (see section 7.2 and Figure 7.2), I developed a quality model for videos to create awareness regarding video quality and a condensed guideline for video production and use to provide guidance for software professionals. Due to the specific context of this thesis (cf. Research Goal 1.1), I adapted the quality model and the condensed guideline to vision videos to better support software professionals who want to produce and use vision videos in requirements engineering. The results were validated in academia to ensure the validity and soundness of this concept, which thus contributes to the fundamental relevance of the candidate solution.

Regarding Research Goal 5.2, I can summarize that I developed an approach to reduce the variability in the human behavior of software professionals when they produce and use videos in requirements engineering. On the one hand, the findings and insights of the controlled experiment show that the adapted quality model is a viable description of potentially relevant characteristics of vision videos that enable to characterize the overall impression of a vision video. Therefore, the quality model provides a clearer definition of the hitherto ill-defined concept of video quality in the context of representing a software project vision and thus creates awareness. On the other hand, the results of the workshop and the review indicate that the adapted guideline for vision video production and use contains structured recommendations that provide essential knowledge on how something in the video production and use should be done to achieve a particular result by emphasizing the motivation, purpose or reason for following the given advice. As a consequence, this guideline provides inspirational guidance that is essential to reduce variability in human behavior. Overall, I am confident that the concept *awareness and guidance* is also valid and sound like the concept *video as a by-product*. For this reason, I conclude that the candidate solution is of fundamental relevance to be applied and validated in a real industrial context. This transfer of the entire candidate solution from academia to industry is the last step of the scientific approach of this thesis (cf. section 1.3 and Figure 1.1, ⑥). I present this last step in the following chapter.

8

Case Study for Validation of the Candidate Solution in the Industry

After validating the two concepts in academia to ensure the fundamental relevance of the candidate solution, it is necessary to transfer and investigate the candidate solution in an industrial context (cf. section 1.3 and Figure 1.1, ⑥). For this transfer, I conducted a case study in a real project to obtain a deeper understanding of how the application of the candidate solution affects the work of software professionals who want to produce and use videos as a communication mechanism in requirements engineering. This case study has a descriptive and explorative nature since it portrays the situation when software professionals apply the candidate solution.

Related Publication. *The case study is based on "Karras, O. et al.: Using Vision Videos in a Virtual Focus Group: Experiences and Recommendations. Softwaretechnik-Trends 41 (2021), No. 1" [133].*

8.1   Case Study Objective

I ensured that the case study is well-defined by formulating its underlying research goal:

Research Goal 8.1

Analyze the candidate solution (cf. chapter 5)

for the purpose of supporting software professionals in the production and use of videos as a communication mechanism in requirements engineering

with respect to (1) creating awareness regarding video quality as well as sharing knowledge about the production and use of videos to enable the production and use of videos at (2) moderate costs and with (3) sufficient quality

from the point of view of software professionals from the industry

in the context of an on-line setting of a real project in the industry.

According to Research Goal 8.1, I analyze on the one hand how the candidate solution affects software professionals' awareness and knowledge regarding the quality of videos and their production and use. On the other hand, I investigate how the candidate solution affects software professionals' effort to produce and use videos in requirements engineering as well as the quality of the produced videos. Thus, I examine the application of the candidate solution throughout the entire video production and use process to draw conclusions on the issues addressed by the concepts (cf. chapter 5), that emerged in the survey as main problems of software professionals when producing and using videos as a documentation option in requirements engineering (cf. chapter 4). In particular, I ask the following three research questions:

Research Question 8.1

How does the application of the candidate solution affect software professionals' awareness regarding video quality as well as knowledge about the production and use of videos?

Research Question 8.2

How does the application of the candidate solution affect software professionals' effort for the production and use of videos?

Research Question 8.3

How does the application of the candidate solution affect the quality of the videos produced by software professionals?

8.2 Case Study Design

I developed the design of the case study by following the guideline and process for conducting and reporting case study research in software engineering by Runeson and Höst [207].

8.2.1 The Case and Unit of Analysis

In the joint project[24] "Transparente und selbstbestimmte Ausgestaltung der Datennutzung im Unternehmen (TrUSD)", the consortium consisting of the partners *HK Business Solutions GmbH*[25], *Fraunhofer IESE*[26], *Institut für Technologie und Arbeit*[27], *Technology Arts Science TH Köln*[28], *Universität des Saarlandes*[29], and *Hochschule Bonn-Rhein-Sieg*[30] develops a practical and legally compliant approach to technology-supported employee data protection. In the context of growing

---

[24]https://www.trusd-projekt.de
[25]https://www.hk-bs.de
[26]https://www.iese.fraunhofer.de
[27]https://www.ita-kl.de
[28]https://www.th-koeln.de
[29]https://www.uni-saarland.de
[30]https://das.h-brs.de/

digitalization, companies have several options for collecting and using extensive data of its employees in various working processes. Although digitalization lays the foundation for process improvements using data analysis, it presents companies with new challenges in terms of employee data protection and data security. The goal of the TrUSD project is to create more transparency for employees in the collection, storage, dissemination, and use of their personal data in their company to offer them opportunities to exercise their rights of self determination and co-determination. As one of the key results of the TrUSD project, the consortium develops a software application, the so-called *Privacy Dashboard*. The *Privacy Dashboard* offers every employee of a company an overview of and access to the personal data collected and processed by the company. As part of the development of the *Privacy Dashboard*, two staff members of the *Fraunhofer IESE* validate the graphical user interface and its usage scenarios by applying *prototyping of scenarios* using image sets of static mockups.

This prototyping of scenarios is the unit of analysis in this case study. The two staff members were interested in changing the previous prototyping process by applying videos as a by-product instead of using image sets of static mockups as before. This interest resulted from the benefits of using videos to support requirements communication which I have shown and validated (cf. Karras et al. [129, 130, 140]). In particular, the two staff members focused on the second use case of the *Mockup Recorder* for validating scenarios (cf. section 6.3.3). They wanted to produce and use a video to specify and illustrate an interaction process between a user and the future *Privacy Dashboard* based on the existing mockups. This video, in turn, was presented to future users in a virtual focus group to validate the scenario and collect feedback.

8.2.2 Subject Selection

First of all, the selection of subjects is based on the availability of persons who participate in the prototyping. The two staff members of the *Fraunhofer IESE* are the main subjects of the case study since they carried out the prototyping and thus applied the candidate solution. At the time of the case study, further persons of the other partners in the consortium were not involved in the prototyping. Besides the staff members, I considered the participants of the virtual focus group as an important source of information since they can provide feedback on the use of videos and assess the quality of the videos from the viewers' point of view.

8.2.3 Data Collection

The case study and the data collection were carried out in the period from June 30th, 2020 to 05th August, 2020. In total, the case study consists of the four activities *kick-off meeting*, *preproduction*, *production*, and *virtual focus group*. Figure 8.1 shows an FLOW diagram [236] to provide an overview of the activities, documents, and parties involved in these phases.

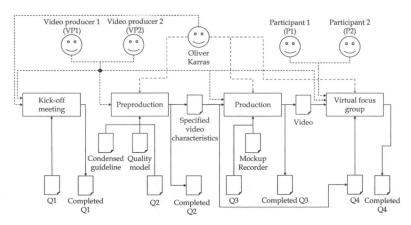

Figure 8.1: Information flow diagram of the case study process

In the *kick-off meeting*, I clarified the context and research goal of the case study with the two staff members of the *Fraunhofer IESE*, hereinafter referred to as video producer 1 (VP1) and video producer 2 (VP2). In addition, each video producer completed the questionnaire Q1 (see appendix F.1). I used this questionnaire collect the video producers' demographics and their initial subjective assessments of their awareness regarding video quality and knowledge about video production and use. Subsequently, the two video producers received the quality model for vision videos as well as the condensed guideline for video production and use for planning their video production. I assisted them with my experience and knowledge in case of problems, questions, and uncertainties during the *preproduction*. One key result of the *preproduction* activity was a specified set of relevant video characteristics from the point of view of the video producers. These specified video characteristics served as a basis for assessing the quality of the produced video. At the end of the *preproduction*, each video producer complete the questionnaire Q2 (see appendix F.2). In this questionnaire, I collected the subjective assessments of the video producers on their awareness regarding video quality and knowledge on video production and use after working with the quality model and the condensed guideline. In consideration of the specified video characteristics, video producer 1 mainly used the *Mockup Recorder* to produce a video illustrating a scenario of using the *Privacy Dashboard* as an administrative staff member to request personal information from four employees for disclosure to third parties. Video producer 2 was partly on vacation at that time. I assisted video producer 1 during the entire *production* with my experience and knowledge since the *Mockup Recorder* is only a prototypical implementation developed in less than three weeks. At the end of the *production*, video producer 1 completed the entire questionnaire Q3 (see appendix F.3) regarding various aspects, such as the achievement of the values of the *video as a by-product* approach to reduce the effort for video production and use, the perceived usability of the *Mockup Recorder*, the time needed for video production, and again the video producer's awareness and knowledge. Due to the vacation, video producer 2 completed the questionnaire Q3 as far as possible. The *virtual focus group* took place on August 05th, 2020. In this meeting, the two video producers first explained the vision of the TrUSD project to the two participants (P1 and P2) who are administrative staff members at the *Fraunhofer IESE*. Afterward, the video producers introduced the participants to the produced video in its entirety and commented on the scenario shown. In a subsequent in-depth discussion, the video producers and participants viewed excerpts of the video to validate whether the developed interaction sequences fit the workflows of the administrative staff members. Finally, each of the parties involved completed the questionnaire Q4 (see appendix F.4 and appendix F.5). In this questionnaire, I collected data from each subject's point of view regarding the perceived video quality. Although I participated in the entire *virtual focus group*, I did not have the permission to collect any of the given feedback. This information is confidential since it relates to the internal processes of the *Fraunhofer IESE*.

8.2.4 Data Analysis Methods

The data analysis consists of a qualitative analysis of the collected data since the sample size is too small for quantitative analysis, including descriptive or even inferential statistics. Besides a chain of evidence to follow the derivations of results and conclusions from the collected data, a qualitative analysis is characterized by being carried out in parallel with the data collection. In this way, the data collection can be adapted to the flexible research method of a case study and new insights found during the case study [207]. I adapted the questionnaires according to the new insights after each activity. I regularly consulted with the subjects to ensure that the drawn conclusions are correct.

8.3 Sample

Four subjects participated in the case study. The two video producers are staff members of the *Fraunhofer IESE*. While video producer 1 is a requirements engineer with three to four years of experience in this role, video producer 2 is a user experience designer with one to two years of experience. Both work for three to four years in the industry. The two participants are administrative staff members of the *Fraunhofer IESE*. Participant 1 has three to four years of experience in this role, and participant 2 has more than ten years of experience. While participant 1 works in the industry for five to ten years, participant 2 works for more than ten years in the industry. All four subjects have several years of practical experience in the industry. For this reason, the subjects are a suitable sample for the case study.

8.4 Results

8.4.1 Awareness and Knowledge of the Video Producers

Throughout the entire case study process, I repeatedly collected the video producers' subjective assessments of their awareness regarding video quality and their knowledge about video production and use to answer Research Question 8.1. In this way, I examined whether working with the candidate solution helped them to understand better what constitutes a good video and how to produce and use it. For this purpose, the video producers assessed the same three statements on a 7-point Likert scale after each activity in the case study process. Figure 8.2 shows the results that I explain below.

First, I need to emphasize that the assessments of video producer 2 are higher than the assessments of video producer 1. This higher assessments results from the education of video producer 2 as a user experience designer. Video producer 2 explained to be more familiar with the production and use of videos since she applies videos more often in her work.

Overall, there is a trend for both video producers to better understand what constitutes a good video and how to produce and use it. Although this trend is rather small for video producer 2, due to her educational background, the trend is well visible by video producer 1. In particular, all assessments of video producer 1 show an increase in the awareness regarding video quality (Figure 8.2a) as well as the knowledge to produce (see Figure 8.2b) and use (see Figure 8.2c) a good video for effective communication. This result is particularly noteworthy since video producer 1 is a requirements engineer. I primarily developed the candidate solution to provide this role with the necessary awareness and knowledge to produce and use videos for effective requirements communication in requirements engineering.

Finding 8.1

The subjective assessments of the two video producers show a positive trend that working with the candidate solution helped them to understand better what constitutes a good video and how to produce and use a video for effective requirements communication. Therefore, the candidate solution helped to positively affect software professionals' awareness regarding video quality and knowledge about the production and use of videos in requirements engineering.

8.4.2 Effort

The alleged high effort for producing and using videos is the most crucial issue that I identified in the survey (cf. chapter 4). I addressed this issue by developing the *video as a by-product* approach (cf. section 6.1.2) with the underlying objective to keep the effort for producing and using a video low. The concepts of the *Mockup Recorder* implement the principles of the *video as*

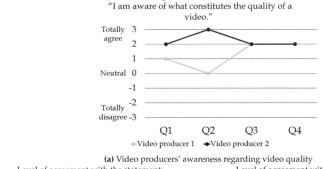

Level of agreement with the statement: "I am aware of what constitutes the quality of a video."

(a) Video producers' awareness regarding video quality

Level of agreement with the statement: "I have the knowledge to produce a good video."

Level of agreement with the statement: "I have the knowledge to use a video for effective communication with the parties involved."

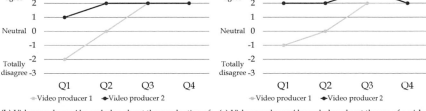

(b) Video producers' knowledge about the production of a good video

(c) Video producers' knowledge about the use of a video for effective communication

Figure 8.2: Video producers' subjective assessments of their awareness regarding video quality and knowledge about video production and use

a by-product approach to achieve the corresponding values (see Table 6.1), and thus the aspired objective. I examined whether the *Mockup Recorder* has satisfied the values by formulating the values as statements (see appendix F.3) and asking the video producers to indicate their level of agreement with the respective statement. I divided the values *involvement* and *simplicity* into several statements since these values combine different aspects that I wanted to analyze in more detail by their separate assessment. In this way, I can answer Research Question 8.2. Figure 8.3 shows the results for each video producer in detail.

I consider a value as satisfied if the two video producers at least agreed with the given statement. Overall, there is a positive trend. The values *integration, involvement,* and *supplementation* are satisfied. Thus, the production and use of a video as additional material (*supplementation*) is integrated into the practice of prototyping (*integration*), involving only the parties who are already involved and being as little intrusive as possible to those involved (*involvement*).

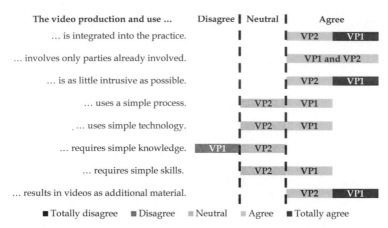

Figure 8.3: Video producers' agreement with the achievement of the values of the *video as a by-product* approach (cf. section 6.1.2). Remark: The exact statements can be found in appendix F.3.

However, it is noticeable that the value *simplicity* is not satisfied. Especially, this value is insufficiently implemented regarding the knowledge required to produce and use a video with *Mockup Recorder*. Video producer 1, who intensively worked with the *Mockup Recorder*, stated: *"The Mockup Recorder is not intuitive to use, but once you know what to do, it is easy to use. You do not need to learn a lot of things before you can use the Mockup Recorder, but you need an introduction"*. This statement emphasizes that the *Mockup Recorder* has the potential to be easy to use but its prototypical implementation impedes its usability and thus affects the entire *simplicity*. I examined the usability of the *Mockup Recorder* by determining its *System Usability Scale* (SUS) score. This score is an established measure of the perceived usability of software from the user's point of view [35]. The *Mockup Recorder* achieved a SUS score of 60.0 which indicates only a moderate usability [16]. In comparison, software with excellent usability has a SUS score of at least 85.5 or higher [16]. Therefore, the usability of the *Mockup Recorder* is insufficient and needs to be improved in the future.

Besides the achievement of the values as an indicator for reaching the aspired objective of a low effort, I quantified the effort for the video production by asking the video producers to report the duration for the video production. The video producers needed approximately 90 minutes to produce the video with a length of 2 minutes. Video producer 1 explained: *"The production itself did not last long. The problem was the usage of the Scene Builder[31] and learning to use it. [...] Next time, I will be much faster. I estimate for the future maybe 30 - 40 minutes for a video of about 2 minutes"*. This duration for the production of the video with the *Mockup Recorder* seems

---

[31]The Gluon Scene Builder is a user interface builder that is used to add responsive controls to the mockups (cf. section 6.3.1.1).

to be short, especially compared to the regular production of a video. For example, Schneider et al. [217] reported that just shooting the individual shots without producing a video already took three hours of a single working day. Busch et al. [45] even reported that their production of an animated video using the software *CrazyTalk Animator*[32] took one and a half days.

Finding 8.2

> *From the video producers' point of view, the concepts of the Mockup Recorder satisfy three out of the four values of the video as a by-product approach. However, the prototypical implementation makes the Mockup Recorder difficult to use which is indicated by the moderate SUS score. This insufficient usability prevents the achievement of the value simplicity, especially regarding the knowledge required to use the Mockup Recorder.*
>
> *Nevertheless, the results show that the candidate solution provides a software tool, i.e., the Mockup Recorder, that integrates the production and use of videos (integration) as supplementary material in the practice of scenario prototyping (supplementation), involving only the parties who are already involved and being as little intrusive as possible to those involved (involvement). The quantified effort shows that inexperienced video producers can produce a 2-minute video in 90 minutes from scratch. According to the video producers, it is possible to shorten this time significantly with some practice in using the Mockup Recorder.*

8.4.3 Video Quality

The video producers created the video in consideration of the set of relevant video characteristics specified in the *preproduction* activity (see Figure 8.1). Before the production began, the video producers had selected these characteristics according to their objectives for the video. For each characteristic, they specified the aspired level of fulfillment as a statement. The specification of the statements is based on the 5-point Likert scales used in the experiment for validating the quality model for vision videos (cf. section 7.6 and appendix E.3.2). The selected video characteristics and their specified statements are shown in Table 8.1. I used these statements to assess the quality of the produced video to answer Research Question 8.3. I asked the video producers and participants to indicate their level of agreement with the respective statement at the end of the *virtual focus group*. Besides the statements, I also asked all four subjects to assess whether they perceive the overall quality of the video as good.

Figure 8.4 shows the detailed results for each subject in the case study. First, I consider the overall quality of the video and the individual video characteristics as good enough if the majority of the subjects agree with the respective statement. According to the results, all subjects agreed that the *overall video quality* and *image quality* are good as well as that the video is suitable for the intended purpose (*intention*). Furthermore, three out of the four subjects agreed that the

---

[32]https://www.reallusion.com/de/crazytalk

Table 8.1: Set of relevant video characteristics specified by the two video producers in the preproduction

Characteristic	Specified statements
Image quality	The image of the produced vision video has a *good* visual quality.
Focus	The vision video presents the visionary scenario of the prototype and its use in a *compact* way.
Pleasure	The vision video is *enjoyable* to watch.
Intention	The vision video is *suitable* for presenting a scenario of an interaction process between a user and the prototype to validate the scenario and collect feedback.

video presents the scenario of the prototype and its use in a compact way (*focus*). The same three subjects also agreed that the video is enjoyable to watch (*pleasure*). Only participant 1 has a neutral opinion regarding the video characteristics *focus* and *pleasure*. However, no subject disagreed with any of the statements. Based on these results, I conclude that the aspired levels of fulfillment of the specified video characteristics are achieved and the overall quality of the video is perceived as good enough by the subjects. Therefore, the candidate solution enabled the video producers to produce a video whose overall quality and individual characteristics are good enough for its intended purpose.

Finding 8.3

> *From the subjects' point of view, the overall quality of the produced video and its characteristics are good enough. All subjects agreed that the video has a good overall quality, shows the prototype and its use with good image quality, and is suitable for the intended purpose of validating the scenario and collecting feedback. With slight concerns from participant 1, the video shows the scenario compactly and enjoyably. Therefore, the candidate solution helped the video producers to create a video with a good enough quality that is suitable for its intended purpose.*

8.5 Threats to Validity

Construct Validity. There is a mono-operation bias since the case study is based on one case that does not represent the complexity in reality. Thus, the generalizability of the results is limited. There is also a mono-method bias since I only used questionnaires to collect the qualitative data. This subjective data only enables limited explanations of the results since the subjects' rationales and thoughts remain unknown. I mitigated this threat to validity by having several talks with the subjects to validate the results and their interpretation. The questionnaires focused on collecting the subjects' level of agreement with the respective statements. This type of data collection may have caused an interaction of testing and treatment since the subjects were

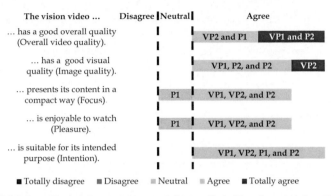

Figure 8.4: Subjective video quality assessments of the specified video characteristics. Remark: The exact statements can be found in appendix F.4 and F.5.

more aware of the topic of the case study. The subjects might have tried to guess the purpose and intended results that might have affected their behavior and answers. However, this threat to validity is small since there are also negative results, e.g., regarding the value *simplicity* of the *video as a by-product* approach. In the talks, the subjects provided crucial feedback, i.a., to improve the *Mockup Recorder*, the resulting video, and thus the candidate solution.

External Validity. The single case in this study limits the generalization of the results. However, this generalization was not the focus of the case study. Instead, the case study served to portray the application of the candidate solution by software professionals in a descriptive and explorative way. The results show a positive tendency regarding the applicability and usefulness of the candidate solution from the subjects' point of view. A crucial threat to external validity is the COVID-19 pandemic. The pandemic caused an interaction of setting and treatment since the focus group had to be conducted virtually. The streaming of the video was partly affected by delays. I mitigated this threat by making the video available for download so that the subjects could watch the video locally on their computers. Another problem that arose from the virtual setting was that all subjects had different technical equipment. The two participants (P1 and P2) only used small laptops. Both participants emphasized that their small screens impeded participating in the focus group and watching the video. This circumstance had a negative influence on the presentation of the video since various aspects such as texts were difficult to read. Second, the COVID-19 pandemic caused an interaction of history and treatment. The COVID-19 pandemic led to more home office. As a result, all subjects were more aware of remote work and video conferences. This increased awareness may have had an impact on the subjects' behavior and answers. However, the virtual setting was the only possible solution due to the work restrictions that the *Fraunhofer IESE* imposed on its employees.

Internal Validity. In this case study, maturation is a critical threat to internal validity. The case study lasted over five weeks, and the virtual focus group lasted two hours. Therefore, all subjects may have been negatively and positively influenced during the course of the case study that, in turn, may have affected the results. This threat to validity could not be mitigated since the case study focused on the application of the entire candidate solution whose implementation required this amount of time due to the flexible design of a case study. The flexible design is the strength and weakness of case studies at the same time. While a flexible design allows for changes to respond to new insights during the case study, the impact of the changes must be fully considered to ensure good instrumentation. For this reason, I followed the guidelines and process for conducting and reporting case study research in software engineering by Runeson and Höst [207]. Despite this guideline and the comprehensive design of the process, the virtual setting was new to all involved parties. As a consequence, the video producers and I were not aware of various problems during the focus group, such as the different technical equipment by the subjects. The participants (P1 and P2) also provided valuable feedback to improve the process of the virtual focus group, e.g., explaining the context and topic more comprehensively or considering the accessibility of the video for visually impaired persons. The subjects and their selection represent a further threat to validity. All selected subjects belong to the respective target populations of software professionals as video producers and future users of the system as participants in the focus group. However, all of them participated voluntarily, which may have influenced the results since volunteers are often more motivated to participate than the whole target population [257].

Conclusion Validity. The virtual setting of the case study and especially the focus group caused random irrelevancies in the experimental setting. During the focus group, the subjects often drifted away from the topic and the video by focusing on how to improve the virtual experience of the focus group. Although this feedback was valuable for the video producers and me, it was out of the scope of this case study. The results of the case study are mainly based on subjective data representing the opinions and perceptions of the subjects. This focus on subjective data is a threat to validity since this data limits the reliability and reproducibility of the findings. However, the case study was designed with a clear descriptive and explorative nature to portray the situation of applying the entire candidate solution for the first time in a real project context. For this reason, the case study was not intended to allow the generalization of the results. Instead, I wanted to understand better what happens when software professionals apply the candidate solution. I analyzed the collected data alone. Therefore, there is a threat to validity of potential researcher bias in the interpretation of the data. I mitigated this threat to validity by having several talks with the subjects to validate the results and their interpretation. The subjects confirmed the interpretations. In this way, I ensured that my interpretations, findings, and conclusion result from the statements and answers of the subjects.

8.6 Discussion

The case study revealed important insights about the first application of the entire candidate solution in a real project context. These insights show that software professionals can obtain a better understanding of video quality and how to produce and use a video with good enough quality at low effort. Thus, the candidate solution and its application throughout the entire video production and use process helped to address the three identified issues (cf. chapter 5).

The candidate solution enabled the software professionals to produce and use a vision video at moderate costs and with sufficient quality that is suitable for supporting requirements communication for shared understanding. The key to any successful video production is knowing how to produce and use a good video for visual communication [185]. For this purpose, it is necessary to be aware of what constitutes a good video and to know how to achieve these quality characteristics. This awareness and knowledge help to counteract unsafe decisions (in planning activities) and actions (in execution activities) of humans by reducing variability in their behavior. In this way, the risk of human errors can be managed and prevented according to the person approach of the human errors model [199, 200] (cf. section 5.1). According to Finding 8.1, the software professionals agreed that they obtained this awareness and knowledge while working with the candidate solution. For this reason, I am confident that the candidate solution helps to address software professionals' lack of knowledge and skills to produce and use videos for visual communication (cf. chapter 5, Issue (2)). As an answer to Research Question 8.1, I can summarize:

Answer to Research Question 8.1

The application of the candidate solution helped the software professionals to achieve a better understanding of what constitutes the quality of a video (awareness) and the knowledge to be able to produce and use a good video for effective communication with the involved parties (guidance). Therefore, I am confident that the candidate solution reduced the variability in the human behavior of the software professionals by creating awareness regarding video quality and providing inspirational guidance for video production and use.

The most crucial step in this case study was the video production since software professionals associate this step with high effort (cf. chapter 5, Issue (1)). The candidate solution addresses this issue based on the system approach of the human errors model [199,200] (cf. section 5.1). In particular, I revised the practice of *scenario prototyping* according to the developed *video as a by-product* approach. The software professionals used the *Mockup Recorder* to produce their video. The concepts of *Mockup Recorder* implement the principles of *video as a by-product* approach to achieve the corresponding values and thus the aspired objective of a low effort for producing and using videos. From the software professionals' point of view, the *Mockup Recorder* integrates the production and use of videos (*integration*) as supplementary material (*supplementation*) in the corresponding practice, involving only the parties who are already involved and being as little intrusive as possible to those involved (*involvement*). Thus, I satisfied three out of the four targeted values. Even the quantified effort shows that the software professionals were able to produce their video in only 90 minutes (see Finding 8.2). However, although these results indicate a low effort, there is still potential for improvement. One crucial problem is the lack of the value *simplicity*. As I explained in the conclusion of the survey (cf. section 4.8), I assume the necessity to focus on simplicity regarding the used process, technology, knowledge, and skills due to the alleged high effort. The prototypical implementation of the *Mockup Recorder* lacks this simplicity due to insufficient usability. As a part of the future work, I need to revise the implementation of the *Mockup Recorder* to improve its usability and thus achieve the value *simplicity*. As answer to Research Question 8.2, I can summarize:

Answer to Research Question 8.2

Despite certain limitations in the value simplicity, the candidate solution satisfied the other three values (integration, involvement, and supplementation) of the video as a by-product approach that shape a practice to focus on the production and use of videos as a by-product. The application of the candidate solution allowed the software professionals to produce their video in only 90 minutes. This temporal effort is relatively low compared to other approaches (cf. Schneider et al. [217] or Busch et al. [45]). Therefore, the candidate solution kept the software professionals' effort for video production and use at moderate costs.

The above mentioned results on enabling software professionals to produce and use videos for communication are only relevant if the resulting video has sufficient quality. The low quality of videos produced by software professionals is the third identified issue (cf. chapter 5, Issue (3)). According to Finding 8.3, the majority of the subjects agreed that the video has a good overall quality and that the individual specified quality characteristics are also met. I must emphasize that no subject disagreed with any of the specified statements regarding the aspired levels of fulfillment of the individual video characteristics (see Table 8.1). Although this finding is based on the subjects' subjective assessments, these insights are of high relevance since the subjective video quality assessment is the ultimate standard and right way to assess video quality [221]. For this reason, I am confident that the candidate solution enabled the software professionals to produce and use a video with sufficient quality that is suitable for its intended purpose. As an answer to Research Question 8.3, I can summarize:

Answer to Research Question 8.3

The application of the candidate solution helped the software professionals to produce a video with a good enough overall quality whose individual specified characteristics are also sufficiently well met. Therefore, the candidate solution enabled the software professionals to produce and use a video at moderate costs and with sufficient quality suitable for supporting requirements communication for shared understanding.

8.7 Conclusion

This case study is the final step of the scientific approach of this thesis (cf. section 1.3 and Figure 1.1, ⑥). This step serves the application of the entire candidate solution for validation in a real project context in the industry. With my assistance, two software professionals applied the candidate solution to produce and use a vision video for validating their planned scenario of an interaction process between a user and their future software tool. According to the findings, the candidate solution helped the software professionals to obtain the necessary awareness and knowledge to produce and use a video at moderate costs and with sufficient quality. This video was suitable for its intended purpose of validating the scenario and collecting feedback. Video producer 1 supports this conclusion: *"In my opinion, the* [candidate] *solution is helpful. This* [candidate] *solution addresses aspects that I would not have thought of. With the* [candidate] *solution, I am now confident to produce a good video on my own. Although the* [candidate] *solution is not sufficient to produce a high-end video, it is sufficient to produce a good enough video"*.

Overall, I cannot generalize the findings since they are based on this single case only. However, the positive tendencies in the results strengthen my confidence that the candidate solution I developed helps to integrate videos in requirements engineering practices to support requirements communication for shared understanding.

9

Summary of the Thesis

9.1 Conclusion

Effective requirements communication about the stakeholders' needs among all parties involved is a prerequisite for establishing the system vision in the relevant system context. This establishment of the system vision is the overall goal of the requirements engineering process. For this goal, it is necessary to achieve *shared understanding* and a *clear scope* by aligning the mental models of the stakeholders and the development team. This alignment requires that the parties involved disclose and discuss their mental models. For this purpose, a documentation option with sufficient *specification quality* for externalizing the mental models is necessary to provide a rich communication mechanism for effective requirements communication.

Stakeholders and the development team can communicate more effectively if they use requirements engineering practices that enable synchronous, proximate, and proportionate interaction for proactive information exchange. However, requirements engineering practices mainly rely on the use of written documentation, including textual and pictorial representations. This documentation option is in conflict with the required type of interaction since written documentation reinforces asynchronous and distant communication that is often disproportionate to develop and negotiate shared understanding. In contrast to written documentation, videos convey information more richly and effectively since they are more concrete due to the visualization of their content. Although videos are known as a promising communication mechanism for shared understanding, software professionals neglected this medium as a documentation option for effective requirements communication.

According to Research Goal 1.1, this thesis analyzes the application of videos as a documentation option in requirements engineering to integrate them into requirements engineering practices to support effective requirements communication for shared understanding.

181

For this purpose, I investigated the reasons why software professionals neglect videos as a documentation option for coordinating and communicating stakeholders' needs in requirement engineering (cf. Research Question 1.1). The survey showed that software professionals do not fundamentally reject videos as a documentation option and are even aware of their strengths and opportunities for requirements engineering. However, there are several weaknesses and threats of videos that prevent software professionals form applying them in requirements engineering. The insights of the survey substantiate three main issues of software professionals: (1) An alleged high effort for video production and use, (2) a lack of knowledge and skills for video production and use, and (3) a lack of videos with sufficient quality. In summary, I can answer Research Question 1.1 as follows:

Answer to Research Question 1.1

> *Despite strengths and opportunities, several weaknesses and threats of videos impede their application as a communication mechanism in requirements engineering. In particular, three main issues explain why software professionals neglect videos as a documentation option for coordinating and communicating stakeholders' needs between stakeholders and a development team in requirements engineering.*
>
> *Issue (1): Software professionals associate the production and use of videos as a communication mechanism in requirements engineering with a high effort.*
>
> *Issue (2): Software professionals lack knowledge and skills to produce and use good videos for visual communication.*
>
> *Issue (3): Software professionals either lack videos that could be used at all or they produce and use videos that are likely to have frequent flaws and thus insufficient quality.*

Based on these issues, I developed a candidate solution for integrating videos into requirements engineering practices to support effective requirements communication for shared understanding (cf. Research Question 1.2). The candidate solution consists of two concepts that are based on a fundamental human information processing model, the so-called *human errors model*. Both concepts counteract unsafe decisions and actions by software professionals in video production and use by integrating videos into requirements engineering practices at moderate costs and with sufficient quality. The concept *video as a by-product* is based on the *system approach* of the *human errors model*. This concept addresses potential error traps in requirements engineering practices by revising a practice to produce and use videos as a by-product at low effort. The concept *awareness and guidance* is based on the *person approach* of the *human errors model*. This concept addresses the variability in the behavior of software professionals when they produce and use videos by creating awareness regarding video quality and providing guidance with a condensed guideline for video production and use.

According to the scientific approach of this thesis (see section 1.3), I first validated each concept in academia to ensure that it is valid and sound to contribute to the fundamental relevance of the candidate solution. This fundamental relevance must be ensured to transfer the candidate solution to the industry. Due to the positive results in academia, I conducted a case study with two software professionals who applied the entire candidate solution in a real project context with my support. The findings of the case study indicate that the candidate solution helps software professionals to obtain the necessary awareness, knowledge, and ability to produce and use a vision video at moderate costs and with sufficient quality. This vision video is suitable for their intended purpose of supporting requirements communication for shared understanding. As an answer to Research Question 1.2, I can summarize:

Answer to Research Question 1.2

The integration of videos into requirements engineering practices to support the coordination and communication of stakeholders' needs among stakeholders and a development team requires that software professionals are able to produce and use videos at moderate cost and with sufficient quality. This thesis provides a corresponding candidate solution consisting of the two concepts video as a by-product and awareness and guidance. Both concepts counteract unsafe decisions and actions of software professionals in video production and use to apply videos at moderate costs and with sufficient quality in requirements engineering practices.

The concept video as a by-product counteracts unsafe decisions and actions of software professionals when producing and using videos during their normal work. For this purpose, the concept supports the revision of requirements engineering practices by integrating videos as a by-product to keep the effort low and to counteract potential error traps in the revised practice for the production and use of videos.

The concept awareness and guidance counteracts unsafe decisions and actions of software professionals due to a lack of awareness and knowledge about what constitutes a good video and how to achieve a sufficient video quality. For this purpose, the concept provides a quality model for videos to create awareness regarding video quality and a condensed guideline for video production and use to guide software professionals. In this way, software professionals can reduce the variability in their human behavior, resulting in videos with good enough quality. Due to the specific application context in this thesis, I also adapted the generic quality model and condensed guideline to vision videos.

9.2 Limitations of the Thesis

As any scientific work, the candidate solution of this thesis is subject to limitations that restrict its applicability and reliability.

The concept *video as a by-product* is based on the *rationale as a by-product* approach which has already been evaluated and adopted several times. However, the concept itself is limited in its applicability and reliability since I have only applied the concept to two requirements engineering practices and corresponding techniques so far. Each instantiation of the *video as a by-product* approach has been validated in academia and one instantiation has also been applied in a real project context in the industry. Nevertheless, the open question for future research remains how the concept can be successfully and reliably applied to other requirements engineering practices and corresponding techniques.

The concept *awareness and guidance* is essentially based on a literature review of generic video production guidelines. These guidelines have been discovered through years of experience and thus represent best practice on how to produce a good video with specific characteristics. However, the resulting quality model and condensed guideline are only theoretical constructs of potentially relevant video characteristics and recommendations. Despite the validations in academia and the application in the case study, the current version of the concept is only a starting point for future research. In particular, the practical application of the concept is necessary to strengthen and verify its applicability and reliability.

Overall, the findings of this thesis substantiate that the current version of the candidate solution is a viable and stable basis for future extensions and refinements. However, dealing with the above mentioned limitations is subject to future work.

9.3 Future Work

The limitations of this thesis mentioned above offer several starting points for future work. Below, I provide an overview of these starting points, some of which are already underway to further explore the topic of applying videos in requirements engineering and beyond.

The concept *video as a by-product* has so far been applied only to two requirements engineering practices and corresponding techniques. There are two options to revise and refine this concept for future improvements. On the one hand, the concept must be applied to further requirements practices and techniques to produce and use videos as a by-product. The further application of the concept may contribute to a better understanding of the weaknesses and shortcomings of the current version of the concept that may require to revise the defined values and principles based on new insights. On the other hand, the current instantiation of each of the two revised practices and corresponding techniques must be applied. In this way, each instantiation itself can be improved, and the insights gained from the application allow conclusions to be drawn to improve the concept *video as a by-product*.

Based on the shown and validated benefits of applying vision videos in requirements engineering, each instantiation of the concept *video as a by-product* has already been used by one of two different organizations, resulting in two active collaborations. The first collaboration is with the *SOPHIST GmbH*. Staff members of the *SOPHIST GmbH* used *ReqVidA* (cf. section 6.5.2) to analyze videos of interviews. Based on their positive experiences with *ReqVidA*, they started an innovation project on the application of videos for knowledge transfer [77] in which I collaborate closely with them. The second collaboration is with the *Fraunhofer IESE*. Based on the positive findings of the case study (cf. chapter 8), the two staff members and I plan the application of vision videos to validate scenarios of the *Privacy Dashboard* in further focus groups.

The concept *awareness and guidance* is a theoretical construct based on the analysis of literature. I cannot guarantee that the quality models and condensed guidelines are complete. So far, these artifacts have only been applied to a limited extent in practice. It is now necessary to actively apply the concept to further investigate its practical application in order to extend and refine the individual artifacts. Despite the recommendations on how to produce and use a video, it remains unclear how specific implementations of video characteristics exactly affect the viewers' quality assessments. I developed the concepts for a software tool that enables the continuous collection of the assessment data of generic video characteristics during video playback and their immediate analysis with the viewer afterward [131]. This detailed video analysis provides fine-grained insights into the interrelationships of the implementation of a video characteristic and its impact on the viewer's quality assessments. Based on these insights, I expect to be able to concretize the recommendations on how the respective video characteristic should be implemented in a video. Arulmani Sankaranarayanan [12] implemented these concepts in a software tool, the so-called *Feedback Recorder*. In her bachelor thesis, Rohde [205] used the *Feedback Recorder* in a first experiment. The detailed video analysis identified several implementations of different video characteristics that meet respectively contradict the recommendations of the condensed guideline for video production and use [205]. These results are promising to concretize the recommendations regarding the implementation of video characteristics.

The candidate solution of this thesis and the related work (cf. chapter 3) focus on the short-term application of videos in requirements engineering activities. Despite some starting points for the use of videos in later activities of the software development process [60,191,213], future research is required to investigate this mid-term application of videos. For this purpose, the use of videos must be integrated into the overall development process of a project and its underlying development approach depending on a plan-driven, agile, or hybrid development context. In addition to the use of videos in a project, videos are documentation whose long-term application beyond a project must also be considered, especially due to increasing awareness of personal data protection in the context of the *General Data Protection Regulation* (GDPR) [72].

Future work on the short-, mid-, and long-term application of videos offers the potential to extend the support of effective requirements communication for shared understanding in requirements engineering and beyond.

Supplementary Materials of the Related Work

In the following, I present the supplementary materials of the related work on the application of vision videos in requirements engineering.

This appendix includes the two tables with the extracted information from the presented approaches on the application of vision videos in requirements engineering.

Table A.1: Application of vision videos in requirements engineering – Part 1

Paper	Supported activities	Parts of a vision	Video content	Audience	Producer	Guidance
[60]	Elicitation, Validation	Problem, Solution	Work practice, Scenario	Customer, User, Analyst	Video producer	No
[32]	Elicitation, Validation	Solution	Scenario	Customer, Analyst	Analyst	No
[28]	Elicitation, Validation	Solution	Prototype	User	Designer	No
[192]	Elicitation, Validation, Documentation	Solution	Vision, Scenario	Stake-holder	Analyst	No
[204]	Elicitation, Validation	Problem, Solution	Vision	User	Analyst	Yes
[140]	Elicitation, Validation, Documentation	Solution	Prototype, Scenario	User, Developer	Analyst	No
[64]	Elicitation, Validation	Problem, Solution	Prototype, Vision, Scenario	Stake-holder	Analyst	No
[217]	Elicitation, Validation	Problem, Solution	Vision, Scenario	Stake-holder	Analyst	No
[45]	Elicitation	Problem, Solution	Vision	Stake-holder	Analyst	No
[258]	Elicitation, Validation	Problem, Solution	Work practice, Scenario, Software	Stake-holder, Team member	Team member	Yes
[259]	Elicitation, Validation	Problem, Solution	Work practice, Scenario, Software	Stake-holder, Team member	Team member	Yes
[86]	Documentation	Problem, Solution	Meeting, Vision	Developer	Video producer	Yes
[36]	Elicitation, Documentation	Problem	Environment	Decision maker	Analyst	No
[40]	Elicitation, Documentation	Problem	Work practice, Meeting	Developer, User	Team member	No

Table A.2: Application of vision videos in requirements engineering – Part 2

Paper	Supported activities	Parts of a vision	Video content	Audience	Producer	Guidance
[103]	Elicitation, Validation	Problem	Work practice	Team member, Stakeholder	Analyst	No
[164]	Elicitation, Validation	Problem, Solution	Work practice, Scenario	User, Manager, Designer	Designer	Yes
[262]	Elicitation, Documentation	Problem	Environment	Stakeholder	Analyst	No
[118]	Elicitation, Documentation	Problem	Work practice	Analyst	Analyst	Yes
[198]	Elicitation, Documentation	Problem	Work practice, Meeting	Analyst, User	Analyst, User	No
[34]	Elicitation	Problem, Solution	Vision, Scenario	Stakeholder	Video producer	Yes
[223]	Elicitation	Problem	Environment, Meeting	Domain expert	Unknown	No
[38]	Elicitation, Validation	Problem, Solution	Vision, Scenario	Customer, Supplier	Video producer	No
[39]	Elicitation, Validation	Solution	Scenario	Customer, Developer	Video producer	No
[167]	Elicitation	Problem, Solution	Vision	Analyst	Video producer	No
[215]	Elicitation	Problem	Environment, Work practice	Analyst	User	No
[234]	Elicitation, Validation	Solution	Prototype, Scenario	Stakeholder	Analyst	No
[21]	Elicitation	Problem, Solution	Vision	User	Analyst	No
[130]	Elicitation, Documentation	Problem, Solution	Vision, Meeting	Analyst, Developer	Analyst	No
[129]	Documentation	Problem, Solution	Vision	Developer	Team member	No
[216]	Elicitation	Problem, Solution	Vision	Stakeholder	Analyst	Yes

Supplementary Materials of the Survey

In the following, I present the supplementary materials of the survey on videos as a documentation option for communication in requirements engineering.

This appendix includes:

B.1 The questionnaire of the survey

B.2 An activity diagram of question order of questionnaire

B.3 The results of the manual coding process

B.1 Questionnaire of the Survey

1 Welcome

Welcome to our survey!

Thank you for taking the time to participate. This survey will be gathering thoughts and opinions in order to explore the current attitudes of software professionals from industry and academia towards videos as a documentation option for communication (medium) in requirements engineering (RE).

The survey covers the following topics:

- Demographics
- Your attitude towards videos as a medium in RE including its strengths, weaknesses, opportunities and threats
- Your current production and use of videos as a medium in RE

This survey should take 10 – 15 minutes to complete.

2 Demographics

A1: Are you a software professional from academia or industry in the field of computer science?

( ) Yes, I am a researcher.   ( ) Yes, I am a practitioner.

( ) No, I am neither of them.

2.1 Demographics – Software professional from academia

AR1.1: What is your primary research area?

( ) Requirements Engineering   ( ) Software Engineering

( ) other: _____

AR1.2: How many years of experience do you have in your primary research area?

Years of experience: ____

2.2 Demographics – Software professional from industry

AP1.1: What is your primary business role?

( ) Project manager   ( ) Requirements Engineer   ( ) Software architect

( ) Developer   ( ) Tester   ( ) Administrator

( ) IT-Operator   ( ) Quality manager

( ) other: _____

AP1.2: How many years of experience do you have in your primary business role?

Years of experience: _____

2.3 Demographics – Country

A2: In which county is your workspace?

_____

3 Attitude towards videos as a medium in RE

B1: What is your overall attitude towards videos as a medium in RE?
( ) Positive   ( ) Neutral   ( ) Negative

B2: What are the strengths of videos as a medium in RE?
1. _____
2. _____
3. _____

B3: What are the weaknesses of videos as a medium in RE?
1. _____
2. _____
3. _____

B4: Do you think the medium video has the potential (opportunities) to improve a requirements engineering context?
() Yes.   () No.

B5: Do you have any concerns (threats) about the application of the medium video in a requirements engineering context?
( ) Yes.   ( ) No.

3.1 Attitude towards videos as a medium in RE – Opportunities and threats

B4.1: What are the opportunities of videos as a medium in RE?

_____
_____
_____
_____

B5.1: What are the threats of videos as a medium in RE?

_____
_____
_____
_____

4 Application of videos – Production

C1: Have you produced at least one video in a requirements engineering context?
( ) Yes.   ( ) No.

4.1 Production of videos

CY1.1: How many videos have you produced so far in total in any requirements engineering context?
Number of videos: _____

CY1.2: For which of the following purposes do you produce videos in a requirements engineering context?

Purpose		Definition
[ ]	Information	Convey knowledge and/or new information (declarative knowledge)
[ ]	Experience: Learning	Convey skills or something practically by experience (procedural knowledge)
[ ]	Experience: Exposure	Convey particular experiences. The video serves as a replacement of an actual person, place, entity, or event
[ ]	Affect	Convey a mood or affective state. The video serves for relaxation or entertainment purposes.

CY1.3: From your experience, have you encountered frequent flaws when producing videos in a requirements engineering context?
( ) Yes.   ( ) No.

4.2 Production of videos – Frequent flaws

CY1.3.1:   What are the most frequent flaws you encountered when producing videos in a requirements engineering context?

_____

_____

_____

_____

4.3 Production of videos – Obstacles

CN1.1: What are the reasons that prevent you from producing videos in a requirements engineering context?

_____

_____

_____

_____

5 Application of videos – Use

D1:   Have you used at least one video in a requirements engineering context?
( ) Yes.   ( ) No.

5.1 Use of videos

DY1.1: How many videos have you used so far in total in any requirements engineering context?
Number of videos: _____

DY1.2: For which of the following purposes do you use videos in a requirements engineering context?

	Purpose	Definition
[ ]	Information	Convey knowledge and/or new information (declarative knowledge)
[ ]	Experience: Learning	Convey skills or something practically by experience (procedural knowledge)
[ ]	Experience: Exposure	Convey particular experiences. The video serves as a replacement of an actual person, place, entity, or event
[ ]	Affect	Convey a mood or affective state. The video serves for relaxation or entertainment purposes.

DY1.3: From your experience, have you encountered frequent flaws when using videos in a requirements engineering context?
( ) Yes.   ( ) No.

5.2 Use of videos – Frequent flaws

DY1.3.1:   What are the most frequent flaws you encountered when using videos in a requirements engineering context?

_____
_____
_____
_____

5.3 Use of videos – Obstacles

DN1.1: What are the reasons that prevent you from using videos in a requirements engineering context?

_____
_____
_____

We thank you for your efforts and time to support our research.

B.2 Question Order of the Questionnaire

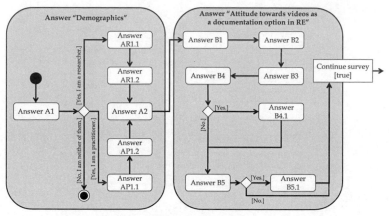

(a) Question order – Part 1

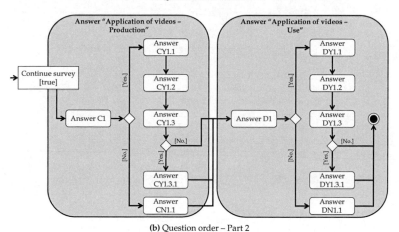

(b) Question order – Part 2

Figure B.1: Activity diagram of the question order

B.3 Manual Coding Results

		Coding frequency		
		Total	Industry	Academia
Categories	**1. Richness** means that videos provide detailed and comprehensive information. Codes: rich, gestics & mimic, information, knowledge, lots of information, context, document decisions and rationales, rich context, a lot of context information, context behavior, put all requirements related things together, visual and audio, details, rich data, larger amount of data, more contextual information, comprehensive information, all details, real-world and additional data (AR), catch what you want, determine who was more involved, mood, high density of information, gesture and facial expressions, how-to knowledge, rich array of information, audible, "feel" of environment, richer information, comments, little information loss, body language, system and its context, entire scenario, a lot of diverse/multimedia information	42	22	20
	2. Simplicity means that videos are suitable for fast, easy use and understanding. Codes: faster, simpler, analyse fast processes, easy understanding, better to understand, 1 picture says more than 1000 words, easy to understand, understandable manner, better understanding, fast, quick, easy communication, quickly receive information, easier and faster way, straightforward, fast overview, fast communication, easier, entry level is very low, easy, intuitive, efficient, easy tracking, easy to understand, efficient way, easy-to-use, easy-to-distribute, comfortable, good to use, easily extracted, cost effective, easier to comprehend, simple	32	19	13
	3. Accuracy means that videos are more accurate in what they show and describe. Codes: exact words, live coding, how things work, showcase, precise, statements, customer's requirements, visualize the usage flow, tracking activities, dynamic aspects of a system, workflows in the optimal way, quickly and more efficient then documents, illustrate complex issues, in motion, how a potential solution could look like, describe things better, tell more accurately how people mean something, show interactions, requirements could become much clearer, activities and interactions, lowers possibility to misunderstand, make problems and handicaps visual, interactive, processes, visualize relations, less ambiguity	27	15	12
	4. Reusability means that videos are persistent and can be reused in later activities. Codes: detailed analysis afterwards, reused, reproduce bugs, sorting out conflicting situations, persistence, later analysis, facts can be looked up, viewed/studied asynchronously, reuse, longterm accessability, playback, replay, multiple access, distributable form, ask follow up questions, shared among others, help later to make right decisions, suitable for management, repeatedly available, start and stop it where I want, rewatch videos, multiple access, share videos everywhere, reviewed by all participants, self evaluation and reflection, watched multiple times	26	13	13
	5. Appealing means that videos are an appealing medium due to their visualizations. Codes: appealing for learners, high acceptance, learning effect, prefer videos, visualization, it's visual, proper visualization, people usually like watching videos, more interesting, better connection to the author, appealing, some people learn new things quicker, prefer watching, enjoyable, entertainment, accommodate user's willingness to read, more tangible, experience with this medium, appealing, it's tangible, more entertaining, more enjoyable, fun and "convincing", more fun	23	11	12

Figure B.2: Manual coding: Strengths – Categories and codes

Categories		Coding frequency		
		Total	Industry	Academia
1. Effort means that videos cause high effort in terms of costs and time for production and use. Codes: time consuming, more time to watch, often need to pause/rewind, hard to analyze, effort to produce, information can be hard to find, hard to scan, wasting time, hard to create, additional workload, difficult to find contents, high effort, lots of effort and resources, time it takes to create, high costs, time to learn how to make an effective video, time, higher costs and time and additional equipment cost, higher overall cost and time, production costs, long time to re-view, unlikely to change…means creating the video again, handling, speed and accessibility, more time consuming, time required to look up, hard to search / process, difficult to search, watching a video takes time, retrieval of content, harder to edit, only sequential access, cost, need to be planned, not suited for quick look ups under time pressure, outdated an would need to be recreated, difficult to update, expensive, intense resource consuming task, take (so much) time, effort to guarantee up-to-date, scripting is more important than most people think, extensive and time consuming, searching distinct information without knowing the time, lack of guidelines, don't have much explanation on how to do it, difficult to edit, weeks to analyze, summery…is not easy, costly to transfer, hard to edit, corrections are too expensive, might be costly, hard to index, additional reviewing, assure reliability, often not reviewed, production time		63	33	30
2. Constraints means that videos have restrictive constraints such as proper file format and size, need for equipment or no direct feedback options. Codes: no direct feedback, storage capability, more technical equipment, size of the files, not easy to make comments, file format issues, large amount of data, proper video format, disk space, good internet connection, no search, large file size, size, can't copy… from video, not searchable, data management, links to special features are not easy, no direct comment options, storing, video format, hard to link, more difficult to search a video, tracing to videos is hard, file size is large, big to store, commenting sequences is difficult, difficult to search, bad video quality may be worthless, quality of images and sound		29	17	12
3. Impact means that videos have different influences such as too high expectation, low acceptance, or unprofessional appearance. Codes: does not look like "business professional", prevents thinking about a problem, low acceptance, be afraid of being recorded, intimidate, high-quality expectation, prefer, hawthorne effect, address the viewer directly, don't like being filmed, not good for conservative people, missing acceptance, pretend, take care of whatever they say, suppressed, illusion of completeness, feel observed and therefore change their behavior, make a mistake that can be a bit difficult for them, negative impact, behave different / unnaturally, shy in front of a camera, do not talk as much as we need, lead to a less focused attitude, user expectations… may be far too high, make you confused, easier to think that you have understand it and skip parts		25	11	14
4. Applicability means that videos are difficult to apply due to legal and privacy issues as well as a doubtful suitability for specific different contexts. Codes: disagreement of work council, over imposed than its real helpful limit, personal user rights/privacy, privacy, legal restricted, legal issues, informal, not ideal for shorter and simple workflows, hard to apply it to agile development, slower than real hands on, cannot replace additional / complete / comprehensive documentation, data a security / enterprise secrets, only work well in some context, a video should not be the "the sole" instrument, not suitable in all "RE-Cases"		22	12	10
5. Content means that videos are difficult in terms of their information content, such as precision, amount of details, or relevant and irrelevant parts. Codes: all information… no matte if relevant or irrelavant, no details, precision, too much freedom, different people mind different details… distracted from important aspects, could be tedious and slow to watch, too high level, and details are lost, can't see which parts are the most relevant, distinguishing between important and non-important information can be hard, capture wrong or misleading content information, ove complicated examples, more work … graphical aspects than to the content, not good for too much content, content may not be understandable, short overview and not more		14	6	8

Figure B.3: Manual coding: Weaknesses – Categories and codes

198

Categories	Coding frequency		
	Total	Industry	Academia
1. Support of RE means that videos can support specific RE activities (elicitation, interpretation, documentation, and validation) and techniques (interview, workshop, focus group, observation).			
Codes: requirements elicitation meetings, more efficient capturing of requirements, recording of real work processes for later analysis, recording of discussion and meetings, support interview phase, improve recording of interviews/workshops, create table o contents (specification), tracking meetings / changes / details, extract requirements ... to make elicitation process faster, video can be a strong tool, capture and elicit risks / roles / responsibilities and needs for systems / security or software requirements engineering / design / development, source of requirements with some traceability, help to elicit and document requirements, faster introduce the source, excellent initial information gathering tool, mainly provide validation support, analyzed to determine as-is situations, observed several times, more time to detect special aspects, requirements specification can be improved, long-term and repeatedly accessible, retrospective source of information, rewatch, documentation of elicitation sessions, present to potential users a demo, save time for creating documentation, after a meeting it its comprehensibly to understand, viewed again and again for mining details, good starting point in e.g. focus groups, later analyzing requirements and human interactions, people would be more careful when making decisions, turn the requirements engineering activities more productive	27	12	15
2. Communication means that videos can support, improve, and simplify communication between all involved parties.			
Codes: communicate, reduce the effort of explaining multiple times, help for communication, better communication, support communication between stakeholders, convey, communication improved, more potential user could be reached, a perfect communication medium, very helpful medium to clearly communicate elicit requirements, conveying relevant information to other stakeholders, easy communication between all stakeholders, helps communication, information on complex subjects... can be conveyed easily, show the customer that you understood his vision of the product, shared amonf other relevant people, aid the "learning" aspect of communication to new people	22	10	12
3. Understanding means that videos allow a better understanding of their contents by all involved parties.			
Codes: increase understanding of users, understand the requirements better, better business understanding, make it easy to understand, get a better understanding of the problem domain, easy to understand, verify for yourself/team, better understanding of what they are supposed to build, better understanding of what potential edge cases are, better understanding, better understanding the context, learn better, improve to picture the environment or complex action chains, express the "feeling", people... can understand a good prepared video very easily, straightforward way to learn, what and how it should be made, helps to understand complex things better, easily understood by different people, easier to follow, valuable since you see how the person works, necessary to fulfill perhaps otherwise confusing requirements, avoid misunderstanding, comprehensibly to understand, help developers to understand the product vision, a customer can better understand and assess user interactions, shared understanding	22	14	8
4. Richer content means that videos have an increased information content due to more detailed and comprehensive information.			
Codes: more context and domain knowledge, exact words spoken, more details, opinions / decisions / rationales, providing primary detailed evidence about requirements, requirements sources, and stakeholder agreement, video shows how, more complex workflows can be demoed, capturing the information exactly, provides enough details, concrete scenarios and comprehensive information, catch emotions, whole picture, a rich medium, combining visual and audio, richness of information, it is rich in a better way, usage of the product under development in the real context, great detail depth	17	7	10
5. Representation means that videos are a good documentation option due to a better visualization.			
Codes: describe things better, visualize concrete examples, visualization of planned/implemented product features, show the vision and interplay of a system in a dynamic manner, clear cut examples, visualization of requirements or future system usage scenarios, show click dummies in an easy way, more accurate recording, this is a much more reliable than the immature prototype directly, by having a visual representation, sees them in the video instead of just seeing a use case, when seeing in a video, videos of the business process, serve as the documentation, avoid misunderstandings or even missing, incorrect requirements as they are visualized ir a manner, present concrete scenarios	17	11	6

Figure B.4: Manual coding: Opportunities – Categories and codes

199

Categories	Coding frequency		
	Total	Industry	Academia
1. Confusion means that videos can be confusing due to the large amount of data. Codes: rewatch all videos, big heap of unstructured data, too costly and hard to use / process, difficult to produce it in an ambiguous way, source of misunderstandings and communication errors, what is part of reality-to-come and what are decorative accessories, the video can be too noisy with dialogs, know that the viewer watched everything? assimilated everything?, make development really confusing, bad/unrelated/vague visuals can then confuse text/audio, no additional explanation...so there might be misunderstandings, finding the right or meaningful information, huge amount of data, it gets more difficult to find and figure out what the important parts are, build the wrong impression he watched an out of date video without knowing, they might get the wrong impression of the software if the video is out of date, time-consuming nature	13	6	7
2. Misuse means that videos need to be used properly since they cannot be the only documentation option. Codes: no replacement for additional/complete/comprehensive documentation, videos must not be overused, when a video is suitable, a poorly conceived video can have a detrimental effect in RE, it should not be the sole medium, it might not be clear how to use videos the right way, a video should only be seen as a supporting tool, video cannot replace another documentation, bias development results to be too similar to the visual, influence customers and distract them from the main problems, they may rely to much on the video source and spend less time with other information sources, how to handle with different kinds of methods	Total	Industry	Academia
	10	5	5
3. Intimidation means that videos can intimidate people whereby they feel uncomfortable which in turn affects their behavior. Codes: people do not like to be filmed, might not feel comfortable, may act different with a camera in front, will not speak about enterprise senstive aspects and dissatisfaction with the current work situation, not able to speak freely, might hesistate to tell critical opinions or talk about delicate topics, recognize your face, your words might be used against you, resistance of people supposed to appear in a video, being filmed makes people uncomfortable, easy tracability to a real person, creepy to imagine some random person watching a video of you, some will not be comfortable, may act differently or not offer up information, they will not react naturally, maybe someone disagrees and you will not be able to apply the method, stakeholders behaving differently while being taped	Total	Industry	Academia
	10	2	8
4. Outdated means that videos are quickly out of date since they are difficult to update. Codes: hard to modify, making changes quickly is crucial, management of different videos is not easy, mark changes in different versions, become out of date due to changes, things which get said may be withdrawn later, can be quickly outdated, difficult to update videos, even harder is adjustment after a requirements negotiation session...videos has to be modified,	Total	Industry	Academia
	10	6	4
5. Privacy means that videos cause concerns in terms of privacy and copyright issues. Codes: privacy concerns, privacy of employees, privacy issues, protection is needed for the video material, privacy and copyright issues	5	3	2

Figure B.5: Manual coding: Threats – Categories and codes

Categories	Coding frequency		
	Total	Industry	Academia
1. **Content** means that video producers often fail to produce a video including an adequate amount of information.	7	4	3
Codes: amount of information can be a problem; too much stuff; information in video is hard to identify; not focusing; users get lost in all of the points; difficult to determine the relevant content[...] what needs to be in the video			
2. **Image quality** means that video producers often fail to produce a video with sufficient visual quality of its image.	5	3	2
Codes: Problems with image quality; lack of focus on video [...] quality; poor image quality; recording only from one single perspective; shaky picture			
3. **Sound quality** means that video producers often fail to produce a video with sufficient auditory quality of its sound.	5	4	1
Codes: Problems with audio quality (too loud surroundings); lack of focus on [...] audio quality; overuse of distracting background music; poor [...] sound; quality of audio recording; poor audio, background music taking over			
4. **Plot** means that video producers often fail to produce a video with a clear structured presentation of its content.	5	3	2
Codes: no clear structure; not following a clear structure; script for capture of the image, action sequence (storyboard); to fast shifts between content making it hard to follow, not enough "space" to reflect on what is said; difficult to determine [...] a good structure			
5. **Prior knowledge** means that video producers often produce a video that lacks information since the producer presupposed specific prior knowledge by the viewer.	4	2	2
Codes: Assumption that the things that you want to show are completely recognizable to the people; used language/terminology unclear; it is faily easy to omit relevant tacit knowledge; what is contextual knowledge a viewer should have			
6. **Preparation** means that video producers often fail to prepare the video production sufficiently.	4	2	2
Codes: Preparation for video is mandatory; technical problems; inadequate preparation: technical problems; not recording, low battery and memory			
7. **Video length** means that video producers often fail to produce a video with an adequate duration.	3	2	1
Codes: video too long; video is too long; [video] too long capture the attention of the viewer			

Figure B.6: Manual coding: Frequent flaws of produced videos – Categories and codes

201

Categories	Coding frequency		
	Total	Industry	Academia
1. **Effort** means that potential video producers stated that video production causes high effort in terms of costs and time. Codes: no time to cut; time expensive; a lot of effort, time consuming; effort seems to be too high; a lot of time and effort; time / budget reasons; hard to create videos; time, resource and budget are usual constraints; take a lot of time; the effort; equipment handling was too complicated; spent time on it; easier to use other artifacts	14	6	8
2. **Lack of knowledge** means that potential video producers stated that video production requires specific knowledge to produce videos. Codes: not common practice; untrained; lack the required know-how; I do not know how to do it; you tipically just dont do it; (missing) knowledge to create the video; no clue when to use videos and for what; don't understand how to make videos; I am not a director	9	5	4
3. **No equipment** means that potential video producers stated that video production requires equipment (camera, software) which they is often do not have. Codes: No (good) camera; no tools available; do not have cameras and other technical equipment; not available technical preconditions; no availability of such software; no actual software to generate videos; lack of automation for processing the video and extract the information; missing equipment	8	6	2
4. **Low added value** means that potential video producers stated that video production is not considered necessary due to a limited added value. Codes: not see that much added value to written notes; no need for additional medium to illustrate the product. Usually, creating screenshots / photos with live-talking supports [...] well enough; video would not add much content; expected benefit is not large enough; no need; never [...] feel the need; not yet seen the need	8	4	4
5. **Antipathy of others** means that potential video producers stated that video production is refused by other persons (participants, customers). Codes: missing understand [...] and antipathy of participants; most customers are used to exchanging letters/mails; make participants more uncomfortable; the aversion of other people to see the advantage of a video	4	2	2
6. **Limited applicability** means that potential video producers stated that video production is not suitable for their context. Codes: missing context; no suitable opportunity; no appropriate project, not part of my work	4	1	3

Figure B.7: Manual coding: Obstacles to the production of videos – Categories and codes

		Coding frequency		
		Total	Industry	Academia
Categories	1. **Representation** means that videos used often had an insufficient visualization of their content.	9	8	1
	Codes: bad realization of the content; too low effort [...] on presenting clear content; clarity [...] lacks; unclear video content; unclear structure; implemented feature without explaining the use case/context first; present content either too complex or easy; bad structure; slow presentation			
	2. **Sound quality** means that videos used often had insufficient auditory quality of their sound.	8	6	2
	Codes: quality of audio [...] too low, too loud surroundings; bad quality ([...]sound); sound [...] quality is sometimes not good enough; poor audio; low audio quality; poor audio; low audio quality; bad [...] sound quality			
	3. **Content** means that videos used often did not provide an adequate amount of information.	7	4	3
	Codes: essence lacks; rambling about irrelevant stuff before getting to the actually interesting point; too much irrelevant information included, no focus on essence; too much information; terminology [...] a gap in language [...] consider this issue and be simple to understand by a broad audience; too much irrelevant stuff; information not much condensed			
	4. **Video length** means that videos used often did not have an adequate duration.	7	5	2
	Codes: too long; video too long; it's too long; video too long; video was too long; a good video length is really difficult			
	5. **Image quality** means that videos used often had insufficient visual quality of their image.	6	4	2
	Codes: Quality of [...] image too low, light problem; bad quality (image[...]); video quality is sometimes not good enough; no steady iamge; inadequate perspective of the image; video had bad picture [...] quality			
	6. **Impact** means that videos used often had a negative influence on the target audience.	5	3	2
	Codes: boring; boring; over-estimating the willingness of the intended audience to view the video; feel a bit boring; difficult to hold viewers' interest, viewing a video can easily lead to inactivity and thus tediousness			

Figure B.8: Manual coding: Frequent flaws of used videos – Categories and codes

Categories	Coding frequency		
	Total	Industry	Academia
1. No video means that videos were not used since there were no videos that could be used.	Total	Industry	Academia
Codes: no usable videos; no sources; there wasn't any videos that could have been used; no one produces videos so they do not exist; never produced videos; Where do I get videos?; never had a video; no requirements video be offered; project situation in the past didn't provide me yet with such mattrial; no videos available; not use it beause nobody created it; nobody created it; i have never seen one [video]	13	5	8
2. Low added value means that videos were not used since videos were not considered necessary due to a limited added value.	Total	Industry	Academia
Codes: no use/need for it; video would not add much in terms of content; no need; lack of about the usefulness; value of video is not large enough; not know why I neeed videos; benefit of video [...] seems too low; when a video shows a content that could have been explained in a few sentences; not seen the need; what is the added value of a video?; no need	11	6	5
3. Limited applicability means that videos were not used since videos were not considered suitable for every context.	Total	Industry	Academia
Codes: no opportunity; do kot know where and when to use it; no opportunity; missing opportunity; pure lack of opportunity; I haven't had the opportunity to use videos; no suitable opportunity; no appropriate project in the past; had no opportunity to use one yet	9	4	5
4. Effort means that videos were not used since the effort to use them was too high.	Total	Industry	Academia
Codes: effort to use it; time is often a problem; watching videos requires a lot of time; often times time is an issue	4	3	1

Figure B.9: Manual coding: Obstacles to the use of videos – Categories and codes

C

Supplementary Materials of the Prototyping Experiment

In the following, I present the supplementary materials of the experiment for validating the benefits of videos as a by-product of prototyping.

This appendix includes:

C.1 The textual description of the scenarios

C.2 The image set of the static mockups

C.3 The questionnaire of the experiment

C.4 The data set of the experimental results

C.1 Textual Description of the Scenario

Experiment: Understandability of Documentation Options for Interaction Processes

Webshop Scenario: Purchase of a product

1. In the beginning, the system displays the login view **(Mockup 01 – Login)**.
2. The user enters his email address and password. Subsequently, the user clicks on "Sign in" to confirm the process.
3. The login is successful and the system displays the homepage **(Mockup 02 – Homepage)**.
4. The user enters "usb stick" in the search bar and clicks on "Search".
5. The system displays products, matching the search term, with the name product name, a preview image, and the user rating **(Mockup 03 – Search)**.
6. The user filters the search results by clicking on the filter option "64 GB".
7. The system only displays the corresponding products **(Mockup 04 – Filtering)**.
8. The user is interested in the product "SanDisk Ultra Fit 64GB" and clicks on its preview image.
9. The system displays the product page with more details of the product **(Mockup 05 – Details of the product)**.
10. The user clicks on "Add to Basket".
11. The system adds the product to the "basket" and displays a confirmation **(Mockup 06 – Basket)**.
12. The user finishes shopping and clicks on "To Checkout".
13. The system displays the first view of the ordering process **(Mockup 07 – Ordering process 1)**.
14. The user enters the first name, last name, street, house number, city, and post code and clicks on "Next".
15. The system displays the second view of the ordering process **(Mockup 08 – Ordering process 2)**.
16. The user enters the BIC, IBAN, and account owner and confirms his input by clicking on "Next".
17. The system displays the summary of the order **(Mockup 09 – Summary of the order)**.
18. The user selects the "FREE Premium shipping" and confirms his order by clicking on "Order now".
19. The order is completed and the system displays a confirmation **(Mockup 10 – Confirmation)**.

C.2 Image Set of the Static Mockups

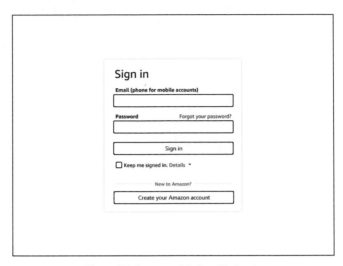

Figure C.1: Image set: Mockup 01 – Login

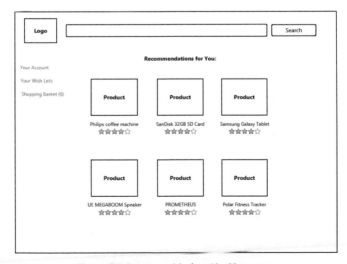

Figure C.2: Image set: Mockup 02 – Homepage

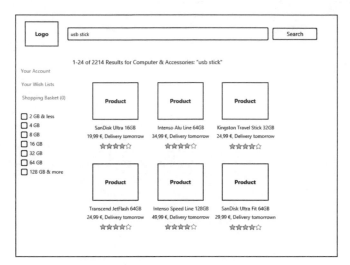

Figure C.3: Image set: Mockup 03 – Search

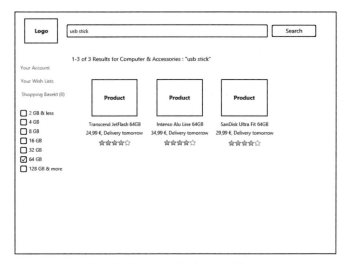

Figure C.4: Image set: Mockup 04 – Filtering

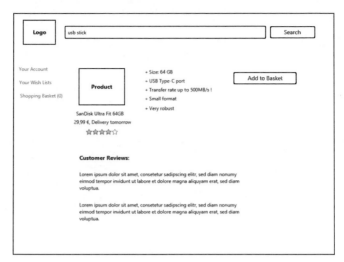

Figure C.5: Image set: Mockup 05 – Details of the product

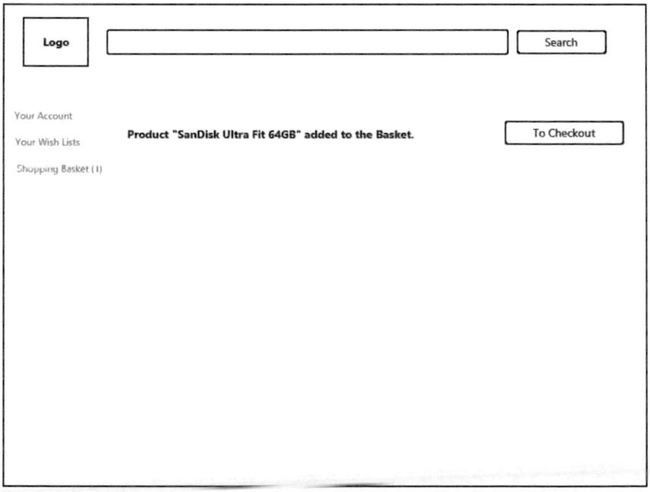

Logo		Search

Your Account

Your Wish Lists

Shopping Basket (1)

Product "SanDisk Ultra Fit 64GB" added to the Basket.

To Checkout

Figure C.6: Image set: Mockup 06 – Basket

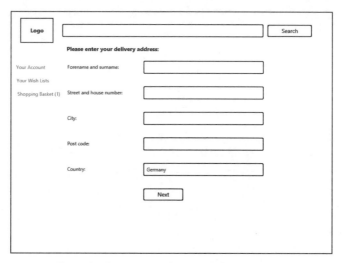

Figure C.7: Image set: Mockup 07 – Ordering process 1

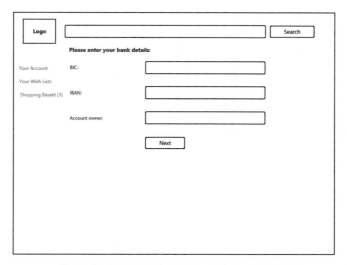

Figure C.8: Image set: Mockup 08 – Ordering process 2

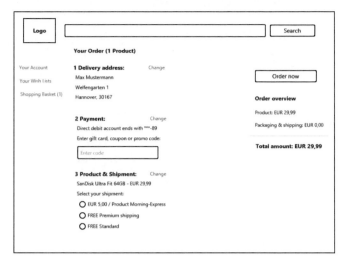

Figure C.9: Image set: Mockup 09 – Summary of the order

Figure C.10: Image set: Mockup 10 – Confirmation

Experiment: Understandability of Documentation Options for Interaction Processes

Consent Form

Please, read this consent form carefully before you decide whether you participate in this experiment.

Description of the experiment:

The experiment investigates the understandability of different documentation media for interaction processes (scenarios) between a user and a software system. The goal of this experiment is to investigate which documentation option is most suitable to support requirements communication for shared understanding. The duration of the experiment is limited to 30 minutes.

Risk and benefits:

Participation in the experiment is not associated with any risks or benefits.

Costs and rewards:

Apart from your investment of time, there are no other costs. Furthermore, no reward is paid for participation in the experiment.

Confidentiality:

All data collected during the experiment will be anonymous and only accessible for the software engineering group at Leibniz Universität Hannover. A random ID is assigned to each subject to ensure that the real person cannot be identified. The subject undertakes to keep the experiment contents confidential.

Cancellation of the experiment:

The subject can finish or cancel the experiment at any time. This decision does not result in any advantage or disadvantage for the subject.

Voluntary consent:

The above-listed points were explained to me and my questions were answered. Before, during, and after the experiment the experimenter answers my further questions. I confirm with my signature that I participate voluntarily in the described experiment.

(First name, last name)

(Place, date, and signature)

Questionnaire

ID: _____

Demographics

Course of study: ( ) Undergraduate student　　　　　( ) Graduate student

　　　　　　　　　　　( ) _____

Semester: _____

I have visited the following lectures:

( ) Introduction to software engineering

( ) Software quality

( ) Software project

( ) _____

Do you have at least one year of experience as a developer?

( ) Yes　　　　( ) No

Scenario of the Experiment

You are a developer of a software project that develops a webshop. You have the task to understand the scenario of how a customer of the webshop wants to purchase a product to implement the corresponding software. You receive a textual description of the webshop scenario supplemented by additional material.

Task 1 – Familiarization

Familiarize yourself with the material provided to understand the webshop scenario. Please, state explicitly when you start the familiarization and when you think you have understood the scenario.

Start time: _____　　　　　　**End time:** _____

Task 2 – Extraction

Answer the following questions regarding your understanding of the scenario. Please, state explicitly when you start the extraction and when you have answered all questions.

Start time: _____   End time: _____

1) **Which product is purchased?**
   ( ) Charging cable   ( ) USB stick   ( ) SD card

2) **What is the maximum price difference of the displayed products after filtering?**
   ( ) 5€   ( ) 10€   ( ) 15€

3) **What color is the product?**
   ( ) Blue   ( ) Green   ( ) Red   ( ) Not specified

4) **When will the product be delivered?**
   ( ) Tomorrow   ( ) In three days   ( ) Not specified

5) **How much does the shipping by Morning-Express cost?**
   ( ) 5€   ( ) 6€   ( ) Not specified

6) **Which data is queried?**
   ( ) Street, user name, email
   ( ) Account owner, post code, country
   ( ) Mobile phone number, gender, Street and house number

7) **Is the bank data or the shipping address asked first?**
   ( ) Bank data   ( ) Shipping address

8) **Is the salutation of the buyer queried (Mr. or Mrs.)?**
   ( ) Yes   ( ) No

9) **How many different shipping options are there?**
   ( ) 2   ( ) 3   ( ) 4

10) **What can be entered as an alternative to the email address for the login?**
   ( ) User name   ( ) Mobile phone number

C.4 Data Set of the Experimental Results

Table C.1: Experimental results of the group G_{Video}

Subject	Familiarization time [s]	Extraction time [s]	Number of correct answers
P1	124	160	6
P2	154	333	9
P3	140	190	8
P4	133	165	9
P5	85	180	9
P6	144	251	9
P7	90	204	8
P8	90	175	10
Boxplot values			
Max	154	251	10
Q3	141	215.75	9
Mdn	128.5	185	9
Q1	90	172.5	8
Min	85	160	8

Table C.2: Experimental results of the group $G_{Image\ set}$

Subject	Familiarization time [s]	Extraction time [s]	Number of correct answers
P9	225	245	9
P10	160	175	10
P11	171	160	9
P12	150	188	10
P13	96	232	8
P14	128	228	10
P15	273	250	9
P16	237	173	10
Boxplot values			
Max	273	250	10
Q3	228	235.25	10
Mdn	165.5	208	9.5
Q1	144.5	174.5	9
Min	96	160	8

Supplementary Materials of the Workshop Experiment

In the following, I present the supplementary materials of the experiment for validating the benefits of videos as a by-product of workshops.

This appendix includes:

D.1 The questionnaire of the experiment for the subjects who use ReqVidA

D.2 The questionnaire of the experiment for the subjects who use a text editor

D.3 The data set of the experimental results

D.1 Questionnaire of the Experiment for Subjects Using ReqVidA

Experiment: Writing the Textual Minutes of a Facilitated Workshop

Consent Form

Please, read this consent form carefully before you decide whether you participate in this experiment.

Description of the experiment:

The experiment investigates how a scribe writes the textual minutes of a facilitated workshop. The goal of this experiment is to investigate how different techniques affect the writing of the textual minutes. The duration of the experiment is limited to 60 minutes.

Risk and benefits:

Participation in the experiment is not associated with any risks or benefits.

Costs and rewards:

Apart from your investment of time, there are no other costs. Furthermore, no reward is paid for participation in the experiment.

Confidentiality:

All data collected during the experiment will be anonymous and only accessible for the software engineering group at Leibniz Universität Hannover. A random ID is assigned to each subject to ensure that the real person cannot be identified. The subject undertakes to keep the experiment contents confidential.

Cancellation of the experiment:

The subject can finish or cancel the experiment at any time. This decision does not result in any advantage or disadvantage for the subject.

Voluntary consent:

The above-listed points were explained to me and my questions were answered. Before, during, and after the experiment the experimenter answers my further questions. I confirm with my signature that I participate voluntarily in the described experiment.

_____

(First name, last name)

_____

(Place, date, and signature)

Questionnaire

ID: _____

Demographics of Students

Course of study: ( ) Undergraduate student   ( ) Graduate student

( ) _____

Semester: _____

I have visited the following lectures:

( ) Introduction to software engineering

( ) Software quality

( ) Software project

( ) _____

Demographics of Software Professionals

Occupation: _____

Years of Experience: _____

Demographics of Each Subject

How many workshops were you involved in?

Number of participated workshops in the role of a

Moderator: _____   Scribe: _____   Participant: _____

How many textual minutes have you written so far as a scribe of a workshop?

Number of textual minutes: _____

How long did the workshops last on average?

Hours: _____

Scenario of the Experiment

You are a scribe of a facilitated workshop. You have the task to take notes regarding requirements for a future software system that are stated by the participants during the workshop session. Based on your notes, you have to elicit and elaborate high-quality requirements that are included in the final textual minutes of the workshop.

Task 1 – Workshop Session

Watch the following ten-minute video clip of the workshop and take notes regarding requirements for the future system stated by the participants of the workshop.

In your opinion, what are the advantages and disadvantages of the used technique (ReqVidA) for taking notes in a workshop?

_____
_____
_____
_____
_____
_____

Indicate your degree of agreement with the following statements.

The effort of using ReqVidA for taking notes in a workshop is **lower** than the effort of using a text editor[1].

+2	+1	0	-1	-2		No
Agree		Neutral		Disagree		answer

The benefits of ReqVidA and its results for taking notes in a workshop is **higher** than the benefits of a text editor and its results.

+2	+1	0	-1	-2		No
Agree		Neutral		Disagree		answer

What is your preferred technique for taking notes in a workshop?

_____
_____
_____

---

[1] Before the subjects answer these statements, I briefly introduced them to a text editor.

Task 2 – Follow-up analysis

Based on your taken notes, elicit and elaborate high-quality requirements for the final textual minutes of the workshop. Please, state explicitly when you start the elicitation and elaboration of high-quality requirements and when you have finished the task.

Start time: _____   End time: _____

How many requirements have you elicited and elaborated?

Number of requirements: _____

In your opinion, what are the advantages and disadvantages of the used technique (ReqVidA) for taking notes in a workshop?

_____
_____
_____

Indicate your degree of agreement with the following statements.

The effort of using ReqVidA for eliciting and elaborating requirements is **lower** than the effort of using a text editor.

+2	+1	0	-1	-2		No
Agree		Neutral		Disagree		answer

The benefits of ReqVidA and its results for eliciting and elaborating requirements is **higher** than the benefits of a text editor and its results.

+2	+1	0	-1	-2		No
Agree		Neutral		Disagree		answer

The quality of elicited and elaborated requirements by using ReqVidA is **higher** than the quality of elicited and elaborated requirements by using a text editor.

+2	+1	0	-1	-2		No
Agree		Neutral		Disagree		answer

Experiment: Writing the Textual Minutes of a Facilitated Workshop

Consent Form

Please, read this consent form carefully before you decide whether you participate in this experiment.

Description of the experiment:

The experiment investigates how a scribe writes the textual minutes of a facilitated workshop. The goal of this experiment is to investigate how different techniques affect the writing of the textual minutes. The duration of the experiment is limited to 60 minutes.

Risk and benefits:

Participation in the experiment is not associated with any risks or benefits.

Costs and rewards:

Apart from your investment of time, there are no other costs. Furthermore, no reward is paid for participation in the experiment.

Confidentiality:

All data collected during the experiment will be anonymous and only accessible for the software engineering group at Leibniz Universität Hannover. A random ID is assigned to each subject to ensure that the real person cannot be identified. The subject undertakes to keep the experiment contents confidential.

Cancellation of the experiment:

The subject can finish or cancel the experiment at any time. This decision does not result in any advantage or disadvantage for the subject.

Voluntary consent:

The above-listed points were explained to me and my questions were answered. Before, during, and after the experiment the experimenter answers my further questions. I confirm with my signature that I participate voluntarily in the described experiment.

_____

(First name, last name)

_____

(Place, date, and signature)

Questionnaire

ID: _____

Demographics of Students

Course of study: ( ) Undergraduate student   ( ) Graduate student

( ) _____

Semester: _____

I have visited the following lectures:

( ) Introduction to software engineering

( ) Software quality

( ) Software project

( ) _____

Demographics of Software Professionals

Occupation: _____   _____

Years of Experience: _____

Demographics of Each Subject

How many workshops were you involved in?

Number of participated workshops in the role of a

Moderator: _____   Scribe: _____   Participant: _____

How many textual minutes have you written so far as a scribe of a workshop?

Number of textual minutes: _____

How long did the workshops last on average?

Hours: _____

Scenario of the Experiment

You are a scribe of a facilitated workshop. You have the task to take notes regarding requirements for a future software system that are stated by the participants during the workshop session. Based on your notes, you have to elicit and elaborate high-quality requirements that are included in the final textual minutes of the workshop.

Task 1 – Workshop Session

Watch the following ten-minute video clip of the workshop and take notes regarding requirements for the future system stated by the participants of the workshop.

In your opinion, what are the advantages and disadvantages of the used technique (text editor) for taking notes in a workshop?

_____
_____
_____
_____
_____
_____

Indicate your degree of agreement with the following statements.

The effort of using ReqVidA[1] for taking notes in a workshop is **lower** than the effort of using a text editor.

+2	+1	0	-1	-2		No
Agree		Neutral		Disagree		answer

The benefits of ReqVidA and its results for taking notes in a workshop is **higher** than the benefits of a text editor and its results.

+2	+1	0	-1	-2		No
Agree		Neutral		Disagree		answer

What is your preferred technique for taking notes in a workshop?

_____
_____
_____

---

[1] Before the subjects answer these statements, I briefly introduced them to ReqVidA.

Task 2 – Follow-up analysis

Based on your taken notes, elicit and elaborate high-quality requirements for the final textual minutes of the workshop. Please, state explicitly when you start the elicitation and elaboration of high-quality requirements and when you have finished the task.

Start time: _____   End time: _____

Would you have liked to watch the video of the workshop again when eliciting and elaborating the requirements?   ☐ Yes   ☐ No

Why would you (not) have liked to watch the video again?

_____
_____
_____

How many requirements have you elicited and elaborated?

Number of requirements: _____

In your opinion, what are the advantages and disadvantages of the used technique (ReqVidA) for taking notes in a workshop?

_____
_____
_____

Indicate your degree of agreement with the following statements.

The effort of using ReqVidA for eliciting and elaborating requirements is **lower** than the effort of using a text editor.

+2	+1	0	-1	-2		No
Agree		Neutral		Disagree		answer

The benefits of ReqVidA and its results for eliciting and elaborating requirements is **higher** than the benefits of a text editor and its results.

+2	+1	0	-1	-2		No
Agree		Neutral		Disagree		answer

The quality of elicited and elaborated requirements by using ReqVidA is **higher** than the quality of elicited and elaborated requirements by using a text editor.

+2	+1	0	-1	-2		No
Agree		Neutral		Disagree		answer

D.3 Data Set of the Experimental Results

Table D.1: Experimental results of the group $G_{ReqVidA}$

Subject	Writing time [s]	Quality ratio [%]	Standardized quality ratio [$\frac{\%}{min}$]
P2	981	100.0	6.12
P3	1750	100.0	3.43
P4	965	83.33	5.18
P9	1389	100.0	4.32
P11	1698	91.67	3.24
P12	840	83.33	5.95
Boxplot values			
Max	1750	100.0	6.12
Q3	1620.75	100.0	5.76
Mdn	1185	95.84	4.75
Q1	969	85.42	3.65
Min	840	83.33	3.24

Table D.2: Experimental results of the group $G_{Text\ editor}$

Subject	Writing time [s]	Quality ratio [%]	Standardized quality ratio [$\frac{\%}{min}$]
P1	531	16.67	1.88
P5	313	33.33	6.39
P6	344	16.67	2.90
P7	284	0.00	0.00
P8	489	16.67	2.05
P10	800	0.00	0.00
Boxplot values			
Max	800	33.33	2.90
Q3	520.5	16.67	2.69
Mdn	416.5	16.67	1.97
Q1	320.75	4.17	0.47
Min	284	0.00	0.00

Supplementary Materials of the Concept Awareness and Guidance

In the following, I present the supplementary materials for developing the concept *awareness and guidance*.

This appendix includes:

E.1 The manual coding results of the generic video production guidelines

E.2 The manual coding results of the literature on software project vision

E.3 The materials of the experiment for validating the quality model for vision videos

E.4 The condensed guideline for video production and use

E.5 The materials of the content validation study for validating the condensed guideline for video production and use

E.6 The condensed guideline for vision video production and use

E.1 Manual Coding Results of Video Production Guidelines

Table E.1: Dimension: Representation – Categories, sub-categories, and exemplary codes

			Representation	Coding frequency	Extracted from
Dimension	**Category**	**Sub-category**	*Video stimuli*	189	$[27, 57, 89, 105, 185, 242]$
			Image quality	105	$[27, 57, 89, 105, 185, 242]$
			Exemplary codes: Wide/tight shots, long/short shots, camera, auto focus, white balance, exposure, camcorder, shooting height, lighting, H.264, resolution, compression, aspect ratio format, mp4, Full HD, frame rate, zoom, equipment, framing, focus, stability, tripod, image		
			Sound quality	54	$[27, 57, 89, 105, 185, 242]$
			Exemplary codes: External microphone, sound level, stereo, shotgun microphone, audio, music, sound effects, ambient sound, check sound quality, microphone distance, omni-directional, ambient sound, background music/noise, clear audible sound, AAC-LC		
			Video length	30	$[57, 89, 105, 185]$
			Exemplary codes: Number of new scenes/minutes, length of final tape, longer than 5 minutes, record additionally 5-10 seconds, short-format projects, longer-format projects (over 30 minutes), not exceed five minutes length, hold shot for some time, how long?		

Table E.2: Dimension: Content – Categories, sub-categories, and exemplary codes

			Content	Coding frequency	Extracted from
Dimension	**Category**	**Sub-category**	*Accessibility*	79	$[27, 57, 89, 105, 185, 242]$
			Plot	59	$[27, 57, 89, 185, 242]$
			Exemplary codes: Tell a story, composition, scheduling, script or event, storyline, timing, tempo, vision and goal for the production, main action of each scene, storyboard, guide audience's thought process, shooting plan, outline, action, introduction & end, storytelling		
			Prior knowledge	20	$[57, 89, 105, 185]$
			Exemplary codes: Target audience, appropriate to audience, accuracy and grammar, who is the program being made for?, familiarity, how the audience react, what is the program about, puzzling, do not know, specific background, level: basic or intermediate or advanced		
			Relevance	145	$[27, 57, 89, 105, 185, 242]$
			Essence	91	$[27, 57, 89, 105, 185, 242]$
			Exemplary codes: Actions, location, background, people, places, relevant shots, message, rolls, natural opportunities, subjects, ideas, information, atmosphere, real subject, broad concepts, person, object, key shots, details, topics, arguments, explanation, foreground		
			Clutter	54	$[27, 57, 89, 105, 185, 242]$
			Exemplary codes: Limitations, masking sounds, mistakes, reflections, windows, posters, flashing signs, distraction, nearby noise, background noise, meaningless background, fading, dead air, no ambient noise, messy background, cluttered room, ill-placed items		

Table E.3: Dimension: Impact – Categories, sub-categories, and exemplary codes

Impact			Coding frequency	Extracted from
Dimension	Category	Sub-category		
		Attitude	173	$[27, 57, 89, 105, 185, 242]$
		Pleasure	69	$[27, 57, 89, 105, 185, 242]$
		Exemplary codes: Capture interest, special effects and mood, natural eye movement, hold viewer's interest, avoid motion sickness, impact, interesting, persuasive, convincing, attention, audience impact, pleasure, enjoy, appeal, emotion, drama, imagination, powerful		
		Intention	21	$[27, 57, 89, 105, 185, 242]$
		Exemplary codes: Introduce, demonstrate, fun, informational, documentation, training, entertainment, education, genre, promote, convey message, instructions, purpose of program, advertising, main purpose, production's impact, chief purpose, target audience		
		Sense of responsibility	83	$[27, 57, 89, 105, 185, 242]$
		Exemplary codes: Distribution, copyright, credits, fonts, health, safety, permissions, consent form, recording/publishing/performer rights, product names and labels, permissions, brand, approval process, privacy, legalities, private property, insurance, anonymity		

E.2 Manual Coding Results of Software Project Vision

Table E.4: Dimension: Representation – Categories and exemplary codes

Dimension	Category	Representation	Coding frequency	Extracted from
		Focus	10	[6, 149, 170, 195, 251]
		Exemplary codes: Described its essence in a compact way, few sentences or a relatively short text, no more than one page of paper, short and concise description of the essence, concise summary,high-level story, model-based view of new work practice [...] into one high-level picture, be compact, big picture story of the future, condensed form, conceptual image of what the future product will be, not sufficient to elicit and elaborate detailed requirements		

Table E.5: Dimension: Content – Categories and exemplary codes

Dimension	Category	Content	Coding frequency	Extracted from
		Completeness	17	[6, 37, 149, 170, 176, 195, 202, 240, 251]
		Exemplary codes: What the future product will be, why it is needed, and why it will be successful, problem, key idea, and improves state-of-art, aspired change, customer value proposition and business value, statement of need and key benefit unlike alternative, problem and solution, justifying the project based on seriousness of problem and reasons for solving the problem, description of the work the user wants to do		
		Clarity	11	[59, 67, 142, 149, 161, 162, 195, 202, 240]
		Exemplary codes: Firm's ability to define clear objectives, need for objective measures to determine whether the product is worthwhile and meets the goal, clearly define product and market objectives, ambiguous project concepts allow for greater speculation and conflict, unsuccessful projects lacked a clear vision, clarity, well-defined and verifiable goal, clearly signals [...] development goals, clear and easy-to-understand goal		

Table E.6: Dimension: Impact – Categories and exemplary codes

Dimension	Category	Impact	Coding frequency	Extracted from
		Support	10	[6, 149, 161, 162, 231, 240, 251]
		Exemplary codes: Balanced view that satisfy the needs of diverse stakeholders, to share these objectives and strategy with all those involved, motivating effect on stakeholders inside and outside of the company, support, guiding star, grounded in the realities of existing or anticipated markets, team tells story, desirable and ambitious but achievable future, share a common perception of objectives and strategy		
		Stability	7	[1, 51, 100, 161, 228]
		Exemplary codes: Stability, consistency of objectives over time, strategic intent is stable over time, consistency to short-term action while leaving room for reinterpretation, vision stability means that a company's vision remains consistent over time, having a stable vision reduces confusion, successful projects [...] had a stable vision, on the unsuccessful projects the visions were noticeably unstable, stable vision		

E.3 Materials of the Experiment

E.3.1 Specific Null Hypotheses of the Experiment

Table E.7: Specific null hypotheses of the 15 quality characteristics

ID	Specific null hypothesis
$H1_0$	The quality characteristic *image quality* does not relate to the overall quality of a vision video from a developer's point of view.
$H2_0$	The quality characteristic *sound quality* does not relate to the overall quality of a vision video from a developer's point of view.
$H3_0$	The quality characteristic *video length* does not relate to the overall quality of a vision video from a developer's point of view.
$H4_0$	The quality characteristic *focus* does not relate to the overall quality of a vision video from a developer's point of view.
$H5_0$	The quality characteristic *plot* does not relate to the overall quality of a vision video from a developer's point of view.
$H6_0$	The quality characteristic *prior knowledge* does not relate to the overall quality of a vision video from a developer's point of view.
$H7_0$	The quality characteristic *essence* does not relate to the overall quality of a vision video from a developer's point of view.
$H8_0$	The quality characteristic *clutter* does not relate to the overall quality of a vision video from a developer's point of view.
$H9_0$	The quality characteristic *completeness* does not relate to the overall quality of a vision video from a developer's point of view.
$H10_0$	The quality characteristic *clarity* does not relate to the overall quality of a vision video from a developer's point of view.
$H11_0$	The quality characteristic *pleasure* does not relate to the overall quality of a vision video from a developer's point of view.
$H12_0$	The quality characteristic *intention* does not relate to the overall quality of a vision video from a developer's point of view.
$H13_0$	The quality characteristic *sense of responsibility* does not relate to the overall quality of a vision video from a developer's point of view.
$H14_0$	The quality characteristic *support* does not relate to the overall quality of a vision video from a developer's point of view.
$H15_0$	The quality characteristic *stability* does not relate to the overall quality of a vision video from a developer's point of view.

Experiment: Assessment of Vision Videos

Consent Form

Please, read this consent form carefully before you decide whether you participate in this experiment.

Description of the experiment:

The experiment investigates the overall impression of vision videos from a developer's point of view. The goal of this experiment is to better understand how developers perceive and assess the quality of vision videos used for conveying the vision of a project. The duration of the experiment is limited to 60 minutes.

Risk and benefits:

Participation in the experiment is not associated with any risks or benefits.

Costs and rewards:

Apart from your investment of time, there are no other costs. Furthermore, no reward is paid for participation in the experiment. The participation in the experiment has no influence on passing the course.

Confidentiality:

All data collected during the experiment will be anonymous and only accessible for the software engineering group at Leibniz Universität Hannover. A random ID is assigned to each subject to ensure that the real person cannot be identified. The subject undertakes to keep the experiment contents confidential.

Cancellation of the experiment:

The subject can finish or cancel the experiment at any time. This decision does not result in any advantage or disadvantage for the subject.

Voluntary consent:

The above-listed points were explained to me and my questions were answered. Before, during, and after the experiment the experimenter answers my further questions. I confirm with my signature that I participate voluntarily in the described experiment.

_____

(First name, last name)

_____

(Place, date, and signature)

Assessment Form

ID: _____

Demographics

Semester: _____

How many years of experience do you have as a developer?

Years of experience: _____

Scenario of the Experiment

You are a developer who joins an ongoing project. You will receive a vision video which illustrates the vision of the system under development. This video conveys the vision of the project you will be working on in order to share this vision with you.

Please, assess the following statements from this perspective for every presented vision video.

Overall video quality
I perceive the overall video quality of the presented video as:

good   neutral   bad

Please, complete each of the following statements by selecting one of the items of the respective 5-point scale, taking into account the previously described scenario.

Image quality: considers the visual quality of the image of a video.	very good (2)	good (1)	neutral (0)	bad (-1)	very bad (-2)
The image of the vision video has a _____ visual quality.					
Sound quality: considers the auditory quality of the sound of a video.	very good (2)	good (1)	neutral (0)	bad (-1)	very bad (-2)
The sound of the vision video has a _____ auditory quality.					
Focus: considers the compact representation of a vision.	very compact (2)	compact (1)	neutral (0)	non-compact (-1)	very non-compact (-2)
The vision video represents the vision in a _____ way.					
Plot: considers the structured presentation of the content in a video.	very good (2)	good (1)	neutral (0)	bad (-1)	very bad (-2)
The vision video has a _____ plot.					
Prior knowledge: considers the presupposed prior knowledge to understand the content of a video.	very necessary (2)	necessary (1)	neutral (0)	unnecessary (-1)	very unnecessary (-2)
Prior knowledge is _____ to understand the vision video.					

Clarity: considers the intelligibility of the aspired goals of a vision by all parties involved.	very intelligible (2)	intelligible (1)	neutral (0)	unintelligible (-1)	very unintelligible (-2)
The vision video presents a vision with _____ aspired goals.					
Essence: considers the important core elements, e.g., persons, locations, and entities, which are to be presented in a video.	very much (2)	much (1)	neutral (0)	little (-1)	very little (-2)
The vision video contains _____ important core elements.					
Clutter: considers the disrupting and distracting elements, e.g., background actions and noises, that can be inadvertently recorded in a video.	very much (2)	much (1)	neutral (0)	little (-1)	very little (-2)
The vision video contains _____ disrupting and distracting elements.					
Completeness: considers the coverage of the three contents of a vison, i.e., problem, solution, and improvement.	very complete (2)	complete (1)	neutral (0)	incomplete (-1)	very incomplete (-2)
The vision video presents a _____ vision in terms of the considered problem, the proposed solution, and the improvement of the problem due to the solution.					
Pleasure: considers the enjoyment of watching a video.	very enjoyable (2)	enjoyable (1)	neutral (0)	unenjoyable (-1)	very unenjoyable (-2)
The vision video is _____ to watch.					

235

Intention: considers the intended purpose of a video.	very suitable (2)	suitable (1)	neutral (0)	unsuitable (-1)	very unsuitable (-2)
The vision video is _____ for the intended purpose of the scenario.					
Sense of responsibility: considers the compliance of a video with the legal regulations.	very compliant (2)	compliant (1)	neutral (0)	non-compliant (-1)	very non-compliant (-2)
The vision video is _____ with the legal regulations.					
Support: considers the level of acceptance of a vision, i.e., whether all parties involved share the vision.	totally agree (2)	agree (1)	neutral (0)	disagree (-1)	very disagree (-2)
I _____ that I accept and share the vision presented in the vision video.					
Stability: considers the consistency of a vision over time.	very stable (2)	stable (1)	neutral (0)	unstable (-1)	very unstable (-2)
The vision video presents a _____ vision.					

E.3.3 Data Set of the Experimental Results

Table E.8: Experimental results – Part 1

Assessments		Overall quality		In total
		Bad	**Good**	
Total sample (N)		281	671	952
Vision video characteristic		**Overall quality**		**In total**
		Bad	**Good**	
Image quality	Very bad	9	2	11
	Bad	38	18	56
	Neutral	68	73	141
	Good	95	229	324
	Very good	71	349	420
Sound quality	Very bad	21	25	46
	Bad	51	88	132
	Neutral	70	97	167
	Good	83	201	284
	Very good	56	260	316
Video length	Mean [s]	106.03	102.26	103.38
	Std. Deviation [s]	26.26	24.98	25.40
Focus	Very non-compact	19	6	25
	Non-compact	57	29	86
	Neutral	94	95	189
	Compact	85	281	366
	Very compact	26	260	286
Plot	Very bad	12	3	15
	Bad	37	26	63
	Neutral	79	74	153
	Good	119	299	418
	Very good	34	269	303
Prior knowledge	Very unnecessary	18	100	118
	Unnecessary	32	184	216
	Neutral	87	216	303
	Necessary	77	112	189
	Very necessary	67	59	126

Table E.9: Experimental results – Part 2

Vision video characteristic		Overall quality		In total
		Bad	Good	
Clarity	Very unintelligible	25	2	27
	Unintelligible	68	34	102
	Neutral	76	93	169
	Intelligible	78	244	322
	Very intelligible	34	298	332
Essence	Very little	23	12	35
	Little	58	41	99
	Neutral	100	170	270
	Much	76	263	339
	Very much	24	185	209
Clutter	Very little	69	140	209
	Little	92	136	228
	Neutral	89	233	322
	Much	27	109	136
	Very much	4	53	57
Completeness	Very incomplete	23	14	37
	Incomplete	53	73	126
	Neutral	80	96	176
	Complete	85	230	315
	Very complete	40	258	298
Pleasure	Very unenjoyable	15	3	18
	Unenjoyable	67	19	86
	Neutral	106	112	218
	Enjoyable	75	295	370
	Very enjoyable	18	242	260
Intention	Very unsuitable	10	4	14
	Unsuitable	38	11	49
	Neutral	107	89	196
	Suitable	95	326	421
	Very suitable	31	241	272
Sense of responsibility	Very non-compliant	77	150	227
	Non-compliant	102	170	272
	Neutral	85	252	337
	Compliant	11	67	78
	Very compliant	6	32	38

Table E.10: Experimental results – Part 3

Vision video characteristic		Overall quality		In total
		Bad	Good	
Support	Totally disagree	5	3	8
	Disagree	30	17	47
	Neutral	76	100	176
	Agree	121	263	384
	Totally agree	49	288	337
Stability	Very unstable	56	47	103
	Unstable	130	145	275
	Neutral	63	231	294
	Stable	27	155	182
	Very stable	5	93	98

E.4 The Condensed Guideline for Video Production and Use

01. Have preliminary meetings with your stakeholders to become sensitive to their concerns and different viewpoints.

    Rationale: These meetings help you to understand better your stakeholders by establishing trust between all parties involved.

    Steps: Preproduction

    Characteristics: Sense of responsibility

02. Define the intended purpose and target audience of your video to plan the content of your video.

    Rationale: You must know why you want to produce a video and for whom to better plan what content you must include in your video.

    Steps: Preproduction

    Characteristics: Intention, Prior knowledge

03. Create a list of topics that you want to address in your video to define the final number of topics addressed in your video.

    Rationale: If you have too many topics, the audience rarely remembers more than a fraction of them. If you have too few topics, the audience perceives the video as slow and labored.

    Steps: Preproduction, Viewing

    Characteristics: Essence, Pleasure

04. Keep your video simple by addressing only a few topics to reduce the amount of information in your video.

    Rationale: The audience can understand a video with fewer topics easier than a video with too many topics.

    Steps: Preproduction, Viewing

    Characteristics: Essence, Pleasure

05. Deal with one topic at a time to avoid cuts between different topics, flashbacks, and flashforwards.

    Rationale: Any cut, flashback, or flashforward can confuse the audience making it difficult to understand your video.

    Steps: Preproduction, Postproduction, Viewing

    Characteristics: Essence, Plot, Pleasure

06. Ensure that the image- and soundtrack deal with the same topic to present consistent visual and auditive information.

    Rationale: The audience can be easily distracted and confused if the visual and auditive information of the image- and soundtrack do not match.

    Steps: Preproduction, Shooting, Postproduction, Viewing

    Characteristics: Essence, Clutter, Pleasure

07. Tell the content of your video as a story that has a beginning, middle, and end to create a clear structure of the contents of your video.

> **Rationale:** This structure helps you to ensure that you introduce the prior knowledge (beginning) which the audience needs to know to understand the content (middle) which has a defined conclusion (end).
>
> **Steps:** Preproduction, Viewing
>
> **Characteristics:** Plot, Prior knowledge

08. Use a storyboard, script, or narration to create an outline of the story of your video.

> **Rationale:** It is essential to plan the entire plot and main action of each scene in advance to organize the entire video production.
>
> **Steps:** Preproduction
>
> **Characteristics:** Plot, Essence

09. Plan the plot of your video by designing the scenes in such a way that they can be trimmed or omitted as needed to shorten the final video if necessary.

> **Rationale:** It may be necessary to reduce the duration of the final video afterward.
>
> **Steps:** Preproduction, Postproduction
>
> **Characteristics:** Video length, Essence, Plot

10. Think about how long a shot should last to define the final duration of the shot.

> **Rationale:** The duration of a shot is crucial. If a shot is too long, the audience loses interest since they cannot capture, process, and understand the information. If a shot is too brief, the audience captures, but cannot process and understand, the information.
>
> **Steps:** Preproduction, Shooting, Postproduction, Viewing
>
> **Characteristics:** Video length, Pleasure

11. Hold a shot for at least 15 seconds to enable the audience to understand the information presented.

> **Rationale:** Fifteen seconds is the lower boundary of the average storage period of the human short-term memory for capturing, processing, and understanding information.
>
> **Steps:** Preproduction, Shooting, Postproduction, Viewing
>
> **Characteristics:** Video length, Pleasure

12. Hold a shot for a maximum of 30 seconds to avoid too long shots that the audience cannot understand.

> **Rationale:** Thirty seconds is the upper boundary of the average storage period of the human short-term memory for capturing, processing, and understanding information. If you exceed this duration, it is difficult for the audience to capture, process, understand, and remember the important details of a shot.
>
> **Steps:** Preproduction, Shooting, Postproduction, Viewing
>
> **Characteristics:** Video length, Pleasure

13. Plan to shoot shots of strategic moments of a long action to show the important moments of the long action in a condensed shot.

   Rationale: You must keep the duration of a shot short but at the same time show all important moments of a long action regardless of its length.

   Steps: Preproduction, Shooting, Viewing

   Characteristics: Plot, Video length

14. Compose a shot by keeping the important details of a scene within the safe area, which is the 70 percent area around the center of the screen, to ensure that the subject is properly framed and you do not accidentally cut off important details of the scene.

   Rationale: The audience might miss or not recognize the details that are outside of the safe area.

   Steps: Preproduction, Shooting, Viewing

   Characteristics: Image quality, Essence

15. Compose a shot by following the subsequent standards of the rule of thirds, which divides the screen into thirds horizontally and vertically, to create a shot that looks dynamic.

   The rule of thirds:
   1. The subject should not be exactly in the middle of the screen.
   2. The subject should be on one of those lines and, ideally, on the intersection of two lines.
   3. If the subject moves towards something, position the subject behind the center of the screen according to the direction of the camera motion.
   4. If the subject moves away from something, position the subject over the center of the screen according to the direction of the camera motion.
   5. The faster the movement of the subject, the greater the offset from the center of the screen.

   Rationale: The rule of thirds helps you produce a nicely balanced image that attracts the interest of the audience.

   Steps: Preproduction, Shooting, Viewing

   Characteristics: Image quality, Essence, Pleasure

16. Compose a shot by including a suitable back- and foreground for a scene to add additional information and a meaningful context to your video.

   Rationale: The back- and foreground must support the audience to understand the scene.

   Steps: Preproduction, Shooting

   Characteristics: Prior knowledge, Image quality, Essence

17. You have the subsequent options to obtain a suitable background for your scene.

   Options for the background of a scene:
   1. Use the real location.
   2. Use a substitute for the location you need.

3. Build a set that resembles the real location.

4. Combine photos from the real location and sound effects with your shots to make the audience think that you were shooting in the real location.

Rationale: It can be difficult or impossible to shoot in the real location. In this case, you need to think about alternatives to illustrate the scene of your video properly.

Steps: Preproduction, Shooting, Postproduction

Characteristics: Prior knowledge, Image quality, Essence

18. Ask the owner or responsible authority of private or public property to sign a consent form for shooting on the property to obtain the permission (signed consent form) to shoot on the property.

Rationale: You are responsible and legally liable to comply with the legal regulations in the context of a video production.

Steps: Preproduction, Shooting

Characteristics: Sense of responsibility

19. Ask each actor to sign a consent form covering the subsequent topics to obtain the permission (signed consent form of each actor) to use and distribute the individual shots and the final video.

Topics the consent form must cover:

1. A statement of how all shots and the final video will be used and distributed.

2. A statement that the actor has the right to withdraw at any time from the video production.

3. A statement of whether the actor may request the deletion of the recordings at any time.

4. A statement of how the actor can contact you (phone number or email).

Rationale: You are responsible and legally liable to comply with the legal regulation of the general data protection regulation (GDPR).

Steps: Preproduction, Shooting, Postproduction, Viewing

Characteristics: Sense of responsibility

20. Give each actor a suitable amount of time for reading the consent form as well as asking questions and clarifying issues and concerns to achieve that the actor is completely informed about the video production and use.

Rationale: You increase each actor's trust in you and your work by being transparent regarding the entire video production.

Steps: Preproduction

Characteristics: Sense of responsibility

21. Plan to shoot all of the action at one location before you go to the next location to simplify the shooting.

Rationale: Thus, ou save time by not following the running order of the scenes according to the plot.

Steps: Preproduction, Shooting

Characteristics: Plot, Sense of responsibility

22. Follow the subsequent steps to record a shot.

    Steps for recording:
    1. Review the details of the storyboard for the next scene.
    2. Call "Quiet, please!".
    3. Start recording.
    4. Call "Action!" to start the action.
    5. Call "Cut!" to announce the end of the action.
    6. Stop recording.
    7. Review the recording. If you are unsatisfied with the shot, repeat the recording.

    Rationale: These steps are an established process in video production for making a recording.

    Steps: Shooting

    Characteristics: Essence, Clutter, Video length, Image quality, Sound quality

23. Handle inexperienced actors by following the subsequent rules of conduct to calm the actors down.

    Rules of conduct for handling inexperienced actors:
    1. Making the actors feel welcome and that their contribution is important for the video.
    2. Give them instructions by telling them when, where, and how they should act in front of the camera.
    3. Make it clear to the actors that they do not have to worry that something goes wrong since the scene can be shot again.

    Rationale: Inexperienced actors are often nervous and afraid of doing something wrong that impedes shooting.

    Steps: Shooting

    Characteristics: Sense of responsibility

24. Use the best camera available (smartphone, tablet, consumer HD camera, etc.) which is small and light and has a display, mounting option for an external microphone, a large storage capacity, and sockets for a connection with a computer to obtain high image and sound quality.

    Rationale: Today's video cameras offer an image and sound quality that is sufficient for the most purposes.

    Steps: Shooting

    Characteristics: Image quality, Sound quality

25. Use an external microphone, i.e., a shotgun microphone, to achieve high sound quality.

    Rationale: The built-in microphones rarely provide sufficient sound quality. A shotgun microphone is ideal for isolating a subject and eliminating nearby noises.

    Steps: Shooting

Characteristics: Sound quality, Essence, Clutter

26. In general, let the camera control auto-focus, white balance, and exposure controls to obtain a high image quality.
Rationale:	These camera settings are complex and have a strong impact on the image. Therefore, you should only adjust them manually if you have the necessary knowledge and experience.
Steps:	Shooting
Characteristics:	Image quality

27. Use the 720p (1280 x 720) or better 1080p (1920 x 1080) HD format which utilizes a 16:9 aspect ratio to obtain a high-quality image.
Rationale:	These HD formats give your video a high-quality video look.
Steps:	Shooting
Characteristics:	Image quality

28. Use the standard recording speed to obtain high-quality image and sound.
Rationale:	The standard recording speed provides better image and sound quality.
Steps:	Shooting
Characteristics:	Image quality, Sound quality

29. Consider where you place the camera and microphone to create a video that enables the audience to experience the content of your video.
Rationale:	The more realistic the audience perceives the content of your video, the better they can understand the content of your video.
Steps:	Shooting, Viewing
Characteristics:	Image quality, Sound quality, Essence

30. When using the camera, keep in mind that you restrict the perspective of the image the audience can see in the video to avoid frustrating the audience.
Rationale:	The audience might get the impression that they are missing something.
Steps:	Shooting, Viewing
Characteristics:	Image quality, Essence, Pleasure

31. Have the light source, e.g., lamp or window, behind the camera to illuminate the subject.
Rationale:	The effect of light depends on the position of the camera. If you shoot against the light source, you leave the subject in deep shadow, making it difficult for the audience to recognize the subject.
Steps:	Shooting, Viewing
Characteristics:	Image quality, Essence

32. Place the microphone as close as possible to the subject by keeping the distance the same for all shots to get a higher sound quality.

Rationale:	The microphone is often too far away from the subject and strong reflections from nearby walls or loud background noises lower the quality of the sound.
Steps:	Shooting
Characteristics:	Sound quality, Clutter

33. For brief video production, shoot every action from start to finish to ensure that the audience misses none of the action.

Rationale:	The audience gets an accurate impression of the action of a scene and its duration.
Steps:	Shooting, Viewing
Characteristics:	Plot, Essence, Video length, Pleasure

34. Start the recording 5 – 10 seconds before the action starts and stop the recording 5 – 10 seconds after the action is completed to avoid too brief shots.

Rationale:	These additional buffers help you in the postproduction when you cut and combine the individual shots into the final video.
Steps:	Shooting, Postproduction
Characteristics:	Video length

35. Watch the elapsed time on the camera to know how much memory and battery are left.

Rationale:	A full memory and an empty battery delay the shooting, thus increase your costs, and waste the time of all parties involved.
Steps:	Shooting
Characteristics:	Sense of responsibility

36. Stabilize the camera by using your body or a camera mount (monopod or tripod) to create a steady and carefully controlled image of your video.

Rationale:	If the image of your video is blurred, bounce around, or lean over to one side, it is a pain to watch for the audience.
Steps:	Shooting, Viewing
Characteristics:	Image quality, Pleasure

37. When using a tripod, turn the auto-focus off. Instead, position the camera and manually focus the image on a fixed point of interest.

Rationale:	If you use the auto-focus, any movement in the scene may cause the camera to adjust and re-adjust which in turn blurs the image for a moment.
Steps:	Shooting
Characteristics:	Image quality

38. Use only as much camera motions, pans, zooms, and tilts as necessary by always ensuring that the motions are slow and smooth to create a shot with a low compression.

| **Rationale:** | Any camera motion results in more compression of the image of a video and can cause motion sickness by the audience. |
| **Steps:** | Shooting, Viewing |

Characteristics: Image quality, Pleasure

39. If possible, do not zoom in or out to obtain a high image quality of your video.
    Rationale: Zooming is an unnatural eye movement that can confuse the
                         audience.
    Steps: Shooting, Viewing
    Characteristics: Image quality, Pleasure

40. Sharpen the focus on the most important part of the scene and leave the rest defocused
    to highlight the important content of a scene.
    Rationale: Although this presentation style is not ideal, it enables you to show
                         the audience exactly what you want them to see.
    Steps: Shooting, Viewing
    Characteristics: Image quality, Essence

41. Light the subject well by switching on the room lights or open the curtain to obtain a
    high image quality.
    Rationale: There is usually not enough light in a building to present a subject
                         in such a way that the audience can recognize all details of the
                         subject.
    Steps: Shooting, Viewing
    Characteristics: Image quality, Essence

42. Use a close shot to show the audience the action of a scene.
    Rationale: A close shot enables you to show the details of the scene by
                         showing the audience the concrete action more closely.
    Steps: Shooting, Viewing
    Characteristics: Image quality, Essence

43. Use a wide shot to show the audience a wide view of the scene.
    Rationale: A wide shot enables you to establish the scene by showing the
                         audience where the action is located.
    Steps: Shooting, Viewing
    Characteristics: Image quality, Essence

44. Prefer close to wide shots to create a video with more impact on the audience.
    Rationale: In contrast to wide shots, close shots add more emotion and drama
                         to a video.
    Steps: Shooting, Viewing
    Characteristics: Image quality, Pleasure

45. Shoot scenes from different angles and heights to obtain a pleasant and interesting
    image.
    Rationale: Different angles and heights arouse the interest of the audience.
    Steps: Shooting, Viewing
    Characteristics: Image quality, Pleasure

46. Avoid extreme angles to obtain a high-quality image.

Rationale:	Extreme angles distort the image of your video.
Steps:	Shooting
Characteristics:	Image quality

47. Do not shoot a subject in front of a black or strong colored (red, yellow, or bright-green) background to avoid a lower image quality.

Rationale:	A black or strong colored background does not only distract the audience but such a background also modifies the apparent colors of the subject.
Steps:	Shooting, Viewing
Characteristics:	Image quality, Clutter, Pleasure

48. When you record a group of persons with one camera, zoom out to include a new person in a wide shot and then zoom in on this person in a close shot to avoid continually panning across the group from one person to another.

Rationale:	Any camera motion results in more compression of your video and can cause motion sickness by the audience.
Steps:	Shooting, Viewing
Characteristics:	Image quality, Pleasure

49. Present a small object by placing it on a turntable (manual- or motor-driven) to avoid having to move the camera in an arc around the object.

Rationale:	This motion is complex and therefore difficult to carry out smoothly.
Steps:	Shooting
Characteristics:	Image quality

50. Carefully review the back- and foreground of a scene to ensure that there are no unplanned actions and objects included in a shot.

Rationale:	Any unplanned action and object may distract the audience from the actual content that you want to convey.
Steps:	Shooting, Viewing
Characteristics:	Clutter, Pleasure

51. Review the background of your scene for the subsequent factors to avoid inadvertently recording these factors.

Factors to avoid in a shot:

1. Reflections and contents of windows.
2. Reflecting surfaces which may show the camera.
3. Flashing signs, posters, directions signs, billboards, persons, etc. which may distract the audience.

Rationale:	These factors can disrupt and distract the audience from the actual content of your video and thus must be excluded.
Steps:	Shooting, Postproduction, Viewing
Characteristics:	Clutter, Pleasure

52. During the shooting, you have the subsequent options to achieve a suitable background for your scene.

Options for the background:
1. Rearrange the furniture.
2. Replace the furniture with pieces from nearby rooms.
3. Attach posters, notices, and signs to walls.

Rationale: These are quick, inexpensive, and simple options to customize the background of your scene to better suit your needs.

Steps: Shooting

Characteristics: Essence, Clutter

53. After a shot, check the sound quality and balance by listening to the recording with high-grade earphones or a loudspeaker to detect any unwanted background noises.

Rationale: Any unwanted background noise may disrupt and distract the audience from the actual content of your video.

Steps: Shooting, Viewing

Characteristics: Sound quality, Clutter, Pleasure

54. If something goes wrong during the recording of a scene, record the whole scene again to create one individual shot for one scene.

Rationale: Otherwise, the scene may not seem to be smooth and combining several shots for one scene increases your effort in the postproduction.

Steps: Shooting, Postproduction, Viewing

Characteristics: Image quality, Plot, Pleasure

55. Keep all shots, even the unsuccessful ones, to have a large collection of shots.

Rationale: Parts of, even the unsuccessful ones, may be used in the postproduction.

Steps: Shooting, Postproduction

Characteristics: Essence

56. Follow the subsequent steps of the non-linear editing process to create the final video.

Steps of the non-linear editing process:
1. Phase: Rough edit
   (a) Digitize footage on your computer to choose the best shots.
   (b) Trim and clean up each shot by deleting unwanted frames.
   (c) Place the shots on the timeline to assemble simply the structure of your video according to your planned story.
2. Phase: Tight edit
   (a) Add effects and transitions to and between the shots.
   (b) Clean up and insert the necessary sound.
   (c) Before you create the final video, add titles to identify persons, places, and things supporting to the tell story and to give credits.

Rationale:	This process is established in video production for highly structured, short-format videos due to its simplicity in making changes to the video by simply moving the shots around.
Steps:	Postproduction
Characteristics:	Plot, Clutter, Image quality, Sound quality

57. Keep the final video short (up to 5 minutes) to ensure that you only show the important details to the audience.

Rationale:	You must focus the audience's attention on the important details which they need to understand.
Steps:	Postproduction, Viewing
Characteristics:	Video length, Essence, Pleasure

58. Do not create a rapid succession of unrelated shots or quick cuts between different viewpoints in the postproduction to avoid annoying, confusing, or boring your audience.

Rationale:	The audience can hardly follow these presentation styles which in turn impede their understanding of the video.
Steps:	Postproduction, Viewing
Characteristics:	Plot, Pleasure

59. Follow the subsequent rules for cutting in the postproduction to avoid irritating transitions in your final video.

Rules for cutting:
1. Plan to cut between shots as eye blinks when looking around.
2. Do not cut between shots of extremely different sizes of the same subject, e.g., a close to a wide shot.
3. Do not cut between shots that are similar or even match, e.g., two close shots of two different persons.
4. Do not cut between two shots of the same size of the same subject, e.g., a close to a close shot.

Rationale:	These rules are based on experience and help you to ensure that your final video is pleasant to watch for your audience.
Steps:	Postproduction, Viewing
Characteristics:	Image quality, Pleasure

60. Include the subsequent graphical elements in your video to obtain a well structure.

Graphical elements to structure your video:
1. Opening title to announce the video.
2. Subtitles to identify persons and locations.
3. Credits to recognize the persons appearing in and contributing to the video.
4. Ending titles to draw the video to its conclusion.

Rationale:	These graphical elements add clarity to your video and thus help the audience to follow the video and its content.

Steps: Postproduction, Viewing
Characteristics: Plot, Essence, Sense of responsibility, Pleasure

61. Consider the subsequent standards to design well-legible graphics.

    Standards for well-legible graphics:
    1. Place the graphic within the safe area, which is the 70 percent area around the center of the screen.
    2. Limit the number of fonts.
    3. Sans-serif bold fonts, e.g., Arial or Trade Gothic Bold, are best readable, especially on smaller displays.
    4. Avoid serif fonts since they create a flicker effect, especially on smaller displays.
    5. Letters smaller than one-tenth of the screen height are difficult to read.
    6. Black-edged letters are difficult to read.
    7. Do not use abbreviations to be unambiguous.
    8. Letters are usually much lighter than the background.
    9. Warm bright colors attract the most attention.

    Rationale: Well-legible graphics add clarity to the presentation of your video and thus help the audience to follow the video and its content.
    Steps: Postproduction, Viewing
    Characteristics: Image quality, Pleasure

62. When using materials (music, videos, images, texts, etc.) of third parties, verify that you comply with the respective regulations of copyright law to obtain a copy clearance for using the materials of third parties.
    Rationale: You are responsible and legally liable to comply with the legal regulations for copyright.
    Steps: Postproduction
    Characteristics: Sense of responsibility

63. Label the final video by adding the subsequent metadata to have a fully labeled video.

    Metadata:
    1. Title.
    2. Subtitle.
    3. Department.
    4. Producer/client.
    5. Editor.
    6. Video length.

    Rationale: This information is important for future informational purposes, e.g., for distributing the video.
    Steps: Postproduction
    Characteristics: Sense of responsibility

E.5 Materials of the Content Validation Study

E.5.1 Content Validation Form

Content Validation Study

Consent Form

Please, read this consent form carefully before you decide whether you participate in this study. I invite you to participate in this study as an expert since you have already produced and used videos in requirements engineering in your previous work.

Description of the study:

The content validation study investigates the content validity of structured recommendations for video production and use by inexperienced software professionals who want to produce and use videos in requirements engineering. The goal of this study is to evaluate how valid the individual recommendations are in terms of content with respect to providing essential knowledge (RELEVANCE) on how something in video production and use should be done (HOW) to achieve a particular result (WHAT) by emphasizing the motivation, reason, or purpose for following the given advice (WHY). Each recommendation is structured according to the following pattern:

> **ID.** <HOW> to <WHAT>.
> **Rationale:** <WHY>.

Task:

Your task is to rate your agreement with four defined statements regarding the four aspects RELEVANCE, HOW, WHAT, and WHY for each structured recommendation based on a 4-point Likert scale ranging from 1 (strongly disagree) to 4 (strongly agree).

Confidentiality:

All data collected during the study will be anonymous and only accessible for the software engineering group at Leibniz Universität Hannover. A random ID is assigned to each participant to ensure that the real person cannot be identified. The participant undertakes to keep the study contents confidential.

Voluntary consent:

The above-listed points were explained to me and my questions were answered. I confirm with my signature that I participate voluntarily in the described study.

_____

(First name, last name)

_____

(Place, date, and signature)

Content Validation Form

Below, the table provides a column for your assessment of your agreement with each of the four following four statements. The ID of each row corresponds to the ID of the respective structured recommendation. The structured recommendations are provided in a separate PDF file, called "Guideline".

Statements:

HOW: The structured recommendation explains how something in video production and use should be done by describing a process or method.

WHAT: The structured recommendation explains what result is achieved by the process or method described.

WHY: The structured recommendation explains the motivation, reason, or purpose for following the given advice.

RELEVANCE: The structured recommendation provides essential knowledge that is relevant for an inexperienced software professional who wants to produce and use a video in requirements engineering.

ID	HOW	WHAT	WHY	RELEVANCE
	Scale: 4 := strongly agree, 3 := agree, 2 := disagree, 1 := strongly disagree			
01				
02				
03				
04				
05				
06				
07				
08				
09				
10				
11				
12				
13				
14				
15				
16				

ID	HOW	WHAT	WHY	RELEVANCE
	Scale: 4 := strongly agree, 3 := agree, 2 := disagree, 1 := strongly disagree			
17				
18				
19				
20				
21				
22				
23				
24				
25				
26				
27				
28				
29				
30				
31				
32				
33				
34				
35				
36				
37				
38				
39				
40				
41				
42				
43				
44				
45				
46				
47				

ID	HOW	WHAT	WHY	RELEVANCE
	Scale: 4 := strongly agree, 3 := agree, 2 := disagree, 1 := strongly disagree			
48				
49				
50				
51				
52				
53				
54				
55				
56				
57				
58				
59				
60				
61				
62				
63				

E.5.2 Detailed Analysis Results using the Content Validity Index

Table E.12: Results of the content validity study – Part 1. Remark: Int. := Interpretation, AP := Almost perfect agreement, S := Substantial agreement, and M := Moderate agreement.

Item	HOW			WHAT			WHY			RELEVANCE		
	I-CVI	κ^*	Int.	I-CVI	κ^*	Int.	I-CVI	κ^*	Int.	I-CVI	κ^*	Int.
01	1.0	1.0	AP	0.8	0.76	S	0.8	0.76	S	0.6	0.42	M
02	1.0	1.0	AP	0.8	0.76	S	0.8	0.76	S	0.8	0.76	S
03	0.8	0.76	S	1.0	1.0	AP	1.0	1.0	AP	1.0	1.0	AP
04	0.8	0.76	S	0.8	0.76	S	1.0	1.0	AP	1.0	1.0	AP
05	1.0	1.0	AP	1.0	1.0	AP	1.0	1.0	AP	1.0	1.0	AP
06	0.8	0.76	S	1.0	1.0	AP	1.0	1.0	AP	1.0	1.0	AP
07	1.0	1.0	AP	1.0	1.0	AP	1.0	1.0	AP	1.0	1.0	AP
08	1.0	1.0	AP	1.0	1.0	AP	1.0	1.0	AP	1.0	1.0	AP
09	0.8	0.76	S	1.0	1.0	AP	1.0	1.0	AP	0.6	0.42	M
10	0.8	0.76	S	1.0	1.0	AP	1.0	1.0	AP	1.0	1.0	AP
11	1.0	1.0	AP	1.0	1.0	AP	1.0	1.0	AP	1.0	1.0	AP
12	1.0	1.0	AP	1.0	1.0	AP	1.0	1.0	AP	1.0	1.0	AP
13	0.8	0.76	S	1.0	1.0	AP	1.0	1.0	AP	1.0	1.0	AP
14	1.0	1.0	AP	1.0	1.0	AP	1.0	1.0	AP	1.0	1.0	AP
15	1.0	1.0	AP	1.0	1.0	AP	1.0	1.0	AP	1.0	1.0	AP
16	0.8	0.76	S	1.0	1.0	AP	1.0	1.0	AP	1.0	1.0	AP
17	1.0	1.0	AP	1.0	1.0	AP	1.0	1.0	AP	1.0	1.0	AP
18	0.8	0.76	S	1.0	1.0	AP	1.0	1.0	AP	1.0	1.0	AP
19	1.0	1.0	AP	1.0	1.0	AP	1.0	1.0	AP	1.0	1.0	AP
20	1.0	1.0	AP	1.0	1.0	AP	1.0	1.0	AP	1.0	1.0	AP
21	1.0	1.0	AP	1.0	1.0	AP	1.0	1.0	AP	1.0	1.0	AP
22	1.0	1.0	AP	0.8	0.76	S	0.8	0.76	S	1.0	1.0	AP
23	1.0	1.0	AP	1.0	1.0	AP	1.0	1.0	AP	1.0	1.0	AP
24	1.0	1.0	AP	1.0	1.0	AP	0.8	0.76	S	1.0	1.0	AP
25	1.0	1.0	AP	1.0	1.0	AP	1.0	1.0	AP	1.0	1.0	AP
26	1.0	1.0	AP	1.0	1.0	AP	1.0	1.0	AP	1.0	1.0	AP
27	1.0	1.0	AP	1.0	1.0	AP	0.8	0.76	S	0.8	0.76	S
28	1.0	1.0	AP	0.8	0.76	S	0.8	0.76	S	0.8	0.76	S
29	0.8	0.76	S	1.0	1.0	AP	1.0	1.0	AP	1.0	1.0	AP
30	0.8	0.76	S	0.8	0.76	S	1.0	1.0	AP	0.8	0.76	S
31	1.0	1.0	AP	1.0	1.0	AP	1.0	1.0	AP	1.0	1.0	AP
32	1.0	1.0	AP	1.0	1.0	AP	1.0	1.0	AP	1.0	1.0	AP

Table E.13: Results of the content validity study – Part 2. Remark: Int. := Interpretation, AP := Almost perfect agreement, S := Substantial agreement, and M := Moderate agreement.

Item	HOW			WHAT			WHY			RELEVANCE		
	I-CVI	κ^*	Int.	I-CVI	κ^*	Int.	I-CVI	κ^*	Int.	I-CVI	κ^*	Int.
33	1.0	1.0	AP	1.0	1.0	AP	1.0	1.0	AP	1.0	1.0	AP
34	1.0	1.0	AP	1.0	1.0	AP	1.0	1.0	AP	1.0	1.0	AP
35	1.0	1.0	AP	0.8	0.76	S	1.0	1.0	AP	0.8	0.76	S
36	1.0	1.0	AP	0.8	0.76	S	0.8	0.76	S	1.0	1.0	AP
37	1.0	1.0	AP	1.0	1.0	AP	1.0	1.0	AP	1.0	1.0	AP
38	1.0	1.0	AP	1.0	1.0	AP	1.0	1.0	AP	1.0	1.0	AP
39	1.0	1.0	AP	1.0	1.0	AP	1.0	1.0	AP	1.0	1.0	AP
40	1.0	1.0	AP	1.0	1.0	AP	1.0	1.0	AP	1.0	1.0	AP
41	1.0	1.0	AP	1.0	1.0	AP	1.0	1.0	AP	1.0	1.0	AP
42	1.0	1.0	AP	1.0	1.0	AP	0.8	0.76	S	1.0	1.0	AP
43	1.0	1.0	AP	1.0	1.0	AP	0.8	0.76	S	1.0	1.0	AP
44	0.8	0.76	S	0.8	0.76	S	1.0	1.0	AP	1.0	1.0	AP
45	1.0	1.0	AP	1.0	1.0	AP	1.0	1.0	AP	0.8	0.76	S
46	0.8	0.76	S	1.0	1.0	AP	1.0	1.0	AP	0.8	0.76	S
47	1.0	1.0	AP	1.0	1.0	AP	1.0	1.0	AP	0.8	0.76	S
48	1.0	1.0	AP	1.0	1.0	AP	1.0	1.0	AP	0.8	0.76	S
49	1.0	1.0	AP	1.0	1.0	AP	1.0	1.0	AP	0.6	0.42	M
50	0.8	0.76	S	1.0	1.0	AP	1.0	1.0	AP	1.0	1.0	AP
51	1.0	1.0	AP	1.0	1.0	AP	1.0	1.0	AP	1.0	1.0	AP
52	1.0	1.0	AP	1.0	1.0	AP	1.0	1.0	AP	1.0	1.0	AP
53	1.0	1.0	AP	1.0	1.0	AP	1.0	1.0	AP	1.0	1.0	AP
54	1.0	1.0	AP	1.0	1.0	AP	1.0	1.0	AP	1.0	1.0	AP
55	1.0	1.0	AP	1.0	1.0	AP	0.8	0.76	S	0.6	0.42	M
56	1.0	1.0	AP	1.0	1.0	AP	1.0	1.0	AP	1.0	1.0	AP
57	0.8	0.76	S	0.8	0.76	S	1.0	1.0	AP	0.8	0.76	S
58	1.0	1.0	AP	1.0	1.0	AP	1.0	1.0	AP	1.0	1.0	AP
59	1.0	1.0	AP	1.0	1.0	AP	1.0	1.0	AP	0.6	0.42	M
60	1.0	1.0	AP	1.0	1.0	AP	1.0	1.0	AP	1.0	1.0	AP
61	1.0	1.0	AP	1.0	1.0	AP	0.8	0.76	S	1.0	1.0	AP
62	1.0	1.0	AP	0.8	0.76	S	1.0	1.0	AP	1.0	1.0	AP
63	1.0	1.0	AP	1.0	1.0	AP	1.0	1.0	AP	1.0	1.0	AP

E.6 The Condensed Guideline for Vision Video Production and Use

01. Have preliminary meetings with your stakeholders to become sensitive to their concerns and different viewpoints.

Rationale:	These meetings help you to understand better your stakeholders by establishing trust between all parties involved.
Steps:	*Preproduction*
Characteristics:	Sense of responsibility, Clarity, Support
Based on:	Recommendation 01

02. Define the intended purpose and target audience of your vision video to clearly indicate your intention for what the vision video should be used for.

Intended purposes of vision videos:

1. Convey or obtain knowledge and/or new information (declarative knowledge) to share an integrated view of a future system and its use within a heterogeneous group of stakeholders for aligning their actions and views.
2. Convey or obtain knowledge and/or new information (declarative knowledge) to share an integrated view of the future system and its use with the development team that will implement the vision.
3. Convey or obtain particular experiences to share an integrated view of a future system and its use for validating this view and for eliciting new or diverging aspects. The vision video serves as a replacement of the future system and its use so that the viewers can experience the envisioned product.

Rationale:	You must know the purpose and target audience for whom you want to produce a vision video to clearly indicate your intended use of the vision video for later viewing.
Steps:	*Preproduction*, Viewing
Characteristics:	Intention, Prior knowledge, Clarity, Support, Stability
Based on:	Recommendation 02

03. Define the topics of a vision (addressed problem, key idea of the solution, and improvement of the problem by the solution) that you want to address in your vision video to clarify the content addressed in your vision video.

Rationale:	These topics are crucial for a vision video since a vision video is a video that presents a vision or parts of it.
Steps:	*Preproduction*, Viewing
Characteristics:	Essence, Pleasure, Completeness
Based on:	Recommendation 03

04. Keep your vision video simple by addressing a maximum of the three topics of a vision to reduce the amount of information in your vision video.

Rationale:	The audience can understand a vision video with fewer topics easier than a vision video with too many topics.
Steps:	*Preproduction*, Viewing
Characteristics:	Essence, Pleasure, Focus, Completeness

Based on: Recommendation 04

05. Tell the content of your vision video by inventing a story with a beginning, middle, and end to create a clear structure of the contents of your vision video.

    Rationale: This structure helps you to ensure that you introduce the prior knowledge (beginning) which the audience needs to know to understand the main content (middle) which has a defined conclusion (end).

    Steps: *Preproduction*, Viewing

    Characteristics: Plot, Prior knowledge, Completeness

    Based on: Recommendation 07

06. If you are not sure how to invent the story of your vision video, you can use one of the subsequent storylines to tell the content of your vision video.

    1. Storyline:

      (a) Beginning: Address the audience emotionally by introducing the problem of your vision with its negative consequences.

      (b) Middle: Address the audience emotionally by introducing the key idea of the solution of your vision with its positive consequences.

      (c) End: Emphasize the envisioned improvement of the problem by the solution by concluding with its benefits.

    2. Storyline: (Requires that the audience knows the problem of the vision.)

      (a) Beginning: Introduce the key idea of the solution of your vision.

      (b) Middle: Emphasize the envisioned improvements of the solution.

      (c) End: Conclude with the benefits of your vision.

    Rationale: Both storylines have been applied in the production of vision videos. Based on experience, it can be confirmed that these two storylines work for vision videos.

    Steps: *Preproduction*, Viewing

    Characteristics: Plot, Prior knowledge, Pleasure, Focus, Completeness

    Based on: Experience

07. Use a storyboard, script, or narration to create an outline of the story of your vision video.

A storyboard is a series of drawings that visualize the content of each scene used to plan the order of actions and events in the particular scene.

Each element in the series consists of:

    1. An ID for each drawing.

    2. A hand-drawn sketch of a key image of the scene.

    3. A short textual description what happens in this part of the scene.

    4. If necessary, a textual description of the content of the audio track.

    Rationale: It is essential to plan the entire plot and main action of each scene in advance to organize the entire video production.

Steps:	*Preproduction*
Characteristics:	Plot, Essence
Based on:	Recommendation 08

08. In the case of recording a long action, plan to shoot or cut out only shots of strategic moments of the action to show its important moments in a condensed shot.

Rationale:	You must keep the duration of a shot short but at the same time show all important moments of a long action regardless of its length.
Steps:	*Preproduction*, Shooting, Viewing
Characteristics:	Plot, Video length
Based on:	Recommendation 13

09. Compose a shot by including a suitable back- and foreground for a scene to add additional information and a meaningful context to your vision video.

Options for the back- and foreground of a scene:
1. Use the real location.
2. Use a substitute for the location you need.
3. Build a set that resembles the real location.
4. Combine photos from the real location and sound effects with your shots to make the audience think that you were shooting in the real location.

Rationale:	It can be difficult or impossible to shoot in the real location. In this case, you need to think about alternatives to illustrate the scene of your vision video properly. The back- and foreground must support the audience to understand the scene.
Steps:	*Preproduction*, Shooting, Postproduction
Characteristics:	Prior knowledge, Image quality, Essence
Based on:	Recommendation 16, Recommendation 17

10. Create a list of all shots based on the storyboard by following the subsequent rules to plan the shooting order.

Rules for planning the shooting:
1. Create a list of one-liners that consist of the ID of the drawing of the storyboard and a short title of the respective shot.
2. Sort the list by location.
3. For each location, sort the shots again starting with shots that are easy to shoot and to understand for the actors.

Rationale:	You save time by shooting all shots of one location at once instead of shooting shots according to the running order of the plot.
Steps:	*Preproduction*, Shooting
Characteristics:	Plot, Sense of responsibility
Based on:	Recommendation 21

11. Ask the responsible authority of property you will use for your vision video to sign a consent form for shooting on the property to obtain the permission (signed consent form) to shoot on the property.

   Rationale: You are responsible and legally liable to comply with the legal regulations in the context of a video production.

   Steps: *Preproduction*, Shooting

   Characteristics: Sense of responsibility

   Based on: Recommendation 18

12. Ask each actor, even ad-hoc ones, to sign a consent form covering the subsequent topics to obtain the permission (signed consent form of each actor) to use and distribute the individual shots and the final vision video.

   Topics the consent form must cover:

   1. A statement of how all shots and the final vision video will be used and distributed.
   2. A statement that the actor has the right to withdraw at any time from the video production.
   3. A statement of whether the actor may request the deletion of the recordings at any time.
   4. A statement of how the actor can contact you (phone number or email).

   Rationale: You are responsible and legally liable to comply with the legal regulation of the general data protection regulation (GDPR).

   Steps: *Preproduction*, Shooting, Postproduction, Viewing

   Characteristics: Sense of responsibility

   Based on: Recommendation 19

13. Follow the subsequent steps to record a shot.

   Steps for recording:

   1. Review the details of the storyboard for the next scene.
   2. Call "Quiet, please!".
   3. Start recording.
   4. Call "Action!" to start the action.
   5. Call "Cut!" to announce the end of the action.
   6. Stop recording.
   7. Review the recording. If you are unsatisfied with the shot, repeat the recording of the entire shot.

   Rationale: These steps are an established process in video production for making a recording. It is important to record the entire shot again, otherwise, the scene may not appear smooth, and combining several shots for one scene increases your effort in the post production.

   Steps: *Shooting*, Postproduction, Viewing

   Characteristics: Essence, Clutter, Video length, Image quality, Sound quality, Plot, Pleasure

Based on: Recommendation 22, Recommendation 54

14. Handle inexperienced actors by following the subsequent rules of conduct to calm the actors down.

    Rules of conduct for handling inexperienced actors:
    1. Making the actors feel welcome and that their contribution is important for the vision video.
    2. Give them instructions by telling them when, where, and how they should act in front of the camera.
    3. Make it clear to the actors that they do not have to worry that something goes wrong since the scene can be shot again.

    Rationale: Inexperienced actors are often nervous and afraid of doing something wrong that impedes shooting.

    Steps: *Shooting*

    Characteristics: Sense of responsibility

    Based on: Recommendation 23

15. Take the storyboard and sorted list of all shots with you to each scene during the shooting to know how to proceed.

    Rationale: The storyboard and sorted list of shots are your orientation for the shooting. Based on these two artifacts, you can plan your next shooting steps and check that each recorded shot corresponds to your expectations.

    Steps: *Shooting*

    Characteristics: Plot, Sense of responsibility, Completeness

    Based on: Experience

16. Before recording a shot, check the details of the storyboard and sorted list of all shots to ensure that you prepared everything.

    Rationale: There are often similar scenes. Therefore, you must check whether everything is prepared for a shot by having an explicit checklist. Otherwise, you can get easily confused.

    Steps: *Shooting*

    Characteristics: Plot, Sense of responsibility, Completeness

    Based on: Experience

17. Use the best camera available (smartphone, tablet, consumer HD camera, etc.) which is small and light and has a display, mounting option for an external microphone, a large storage capacity, and sockets for a connection with a computer to obtain high image quality and sound quality.

    Rationale: Today's video cameras offer an image quality and sound quality that is sufficient for the most purposes.

    Steps: *Shooting*

    Characteristics: Image quality, Sound quality

    Based on: Recommendation 24

18. Ensure that you have sufficient free memory capacity (SD cards) and at least two fully loaded batteries to avoid unnecessary interruptions during the shooting.

    Rationale: A full memory and an empty battery delay the shooting, thus increase your costs, and waste the time of all parties involved.

    Steps: *Shooting*

    Characteristics: Sense of responsibility

    Based on: Recommendation 35

19. In general, let the camera control auto-focus, white balance, and exposure controls to obtain a high image quality.

    Rationale: These camera settings are complex and have a strong impact on the image. Therefore, you should only adjust them manually if you have the necessary knowledge and experience.

    Steps: *Shooting*

    Characteristics: Image quality

    Based on: Recommendation 26

20. Use the standard recording speed to obtain a high image quality and sound quality.

    Rationale: The standard recording speed provides better image quality and sound quality.

    Steps: *Shooting*

    Characteristics: Image quality, Sound quality

    Based on: Recommendation 28

21. Use an external microphone, i.e., a shotgun microphone, to achieve high sound quality.

    Rationale: The built-in microphones rarely provide sufficient sound quality. A shotgun microphone is ideal for isolating a subject and eliminating nearby noises.

    Steps: *Shooting*

    Characteristics: Sound quality, Essence, Clutter

    Based on: Recommendation 25

22. For each shot, think about where you place the camera and microphone to create a vision video that enables the audience to experience the content of your vision video.

    Rationale: The more realistic the audience perceives the content of your vision video, the better they can understand the content of your vision video.

    Steps: *Shooting*, Viewing

    Characteristics: Image quality, Sound quality, Essence

    Based on: Recommendation 29

23. Have the light source, e.g., lamp or window, behind the camera to illuminate the subject.

    Rationale: The effect of light depends on the position of the camera. If you shoot against the light source, you leave the subject in deep shadow, making it difficult for the audience to recognize the subject.

Steps: *Shooting*, Viewing
Characteristics: Image quality, Essence
Based on: Recommendation 31

24. Light the subject well by switching on the room lights or open the curtain to obtain a high image quality.

Rationale: There is usually not enough light in a building to present a subject in such a way that the audience can recognize all details of the subject.

Steps: *Shooting*, Viewing
Characteristics: Image quality, Essence
Based on: Recommendation 41

25. Place the microphone as close as possible to the subject by keeping the distance the same for all shots to get a higher sound quality.

Rationale: The microphone is often too far away from the subject and strong reflections from nearby walls or loud background noises lower the quality of the sound.

Steps: *Shooting*
Characteristics: Sound quality, Clutter
Based on: Recommendation 32

26. Compose a shot by keeping the important details of a scene within the safe area, which is the 70 percent area around the center of the screen, to ensure that the subject is properly framed and you do not accidentally cut off important details of the scene.

Rationale: The audience might miss or not recognize the details that are outside of the safe area.

Steps: Preproduction, *Shooting*, Viewing
Characteristics: Image quality, Essence
Based on: Recommendation 14

27. Compose a shot by following the subsequent standards of the rule of thirds, which divides the screen into thirds horizontally and vertically, to create a shot that looks dynamic.

The rule of thirds:

1. The subject should not be exactly in the middle of the screen.
2. The subject should be on one of those lines and, ideally, on the intersection of two lines.
3. If the subject moves towards something, position the subject behind the center of the screen according to the direction of the camera motion.
4. If the subject moves away from something, position the subject over the center of the screen according to the direction of the camera motion.
5. The faster the movement of the subject, the greater the offset from the center of the screen.

Rationale: The rule of thirds helps you produce a nicely balanced image that attracts the interest of the audience.

Steps: Preproduction, *Shooting*, Viewing

Characteristics: Image quality, Essence, Pleasure

Based on: Recommendation 15

28. Shoot scenes from different angles and heights to obtain a pleasant and interesting image.

Rationale: Different angles and heights arouse the interest of the audience.

Steps: *Shooting*, Viewing

Characteristics: Image quality, Pleasure

Based on: Recommendation 45

29. Avoid extreme angles to obtain a high-quality image.

Rationale: Extreme angles distort the image of your vision video.

Steps: *Shooting*

Characteristics: Image quality

Based on: Recommendation 46

30. Do not shoot a subject in front of a black or strong colored (red, yellow, or bright green) background to avoid a lower image quality.

Rationale: A black or strong colored background does not only distract the audience but such a background also modifies the apparent colors of the subject.

Steps: *Shooting*, Viewing

Characteristics: Image quality, Clutter, Pleasure

Based on: Recommendation 47

31. Review the back- and foreground of your scene for the subsequent factors to avoid inadvertently recording these factors.

Factors to avoid in a shot:

1. Reflections and contents of windows.
2. Reflecting surfaces which may show the camera.
3. Flashing signs, posters, directions signs, billboards, persons etc. which may distract the audience.

Rationale: These factors can disrupt and distract the audience from the actual content of your vision video and thus must be excluded.

Steps: *Shooting*, Postproduction, Viewing

Characteristics: Clutter, Pleasure

Based on: Recommendation 50, Recommendation 51

32. During the shooting, you have the subsequent options to achieve a suitable background for your scene.

Options for the background:

1. Rearrange the furniture.

2. Replace the furniture with pieces from nearby rooms.
3. Attach posters, notices, and signs to walls.

Rationale:	These are quick, inexpensive, and simple options to customize the background of your scene to better suit your needs.
Steps:	*Shooting*
Characteristics:	Essence, Clutter
Based on:	Recommendation 52

33. Stabilize the camera by using your body or a camera mount (monopod or tripod) to create a steady and carefully controlled image of your vision video.

Rationale:	If the image of your vision video is blurred, bounce around, or lean over to one side, it is a pain to watch for the audience.
Steps:	*Shooting*, Viewing
Characteristics:	Image quality, Pleasure
Based on:	Recommendation 36

34. When using a tripod, turn the auto-focus off. Instead, position the camera and manually focus the image on a fixed point of interest.

Rationale:	If you use the auto-focus, any movement in the scene may cause the camera to adjust and re-adjust which in turn blurs the image for a moment.
Steps:	*Shooting*
Characteristics:	Image quality
Based on:	Recommendation 37

35. Sharpen the focus on the most important part of the scene and leave the rest defocused to highlight the important content of a scene.

Rationale:	Although this presentation style is not ideal, it enables you to show the audience exactly what you want them to see.
Steps:	*Shooting*, Viewing
Characteristics:	Image quality, Essence
Based on:	Recommendation 40

36. Use only as much camera motions, pans, zooms, and tilts as necessary by always ensuring that the motions are slow and smooth to create a shot with a low compression.

Rationale:	Any camera motion results in more compression of the image of a vision video and can cause motion sickness by the audience. Especially, zooming is an unnatural eye movement that can confuse the audience.
Steps:	*Shooting*, Viewing
Characteristics:	Image quality, Pleasure
Based on:	Recommendation 38, Recommendation 39

37. When you record a group of persons with one camera, zoom out to include a new person in a wide shot and then zoom in on this person in a close shot to avoid continually panning across the group from one person to another.

Rationale:	Any camera motion results in more compression of your video and can cause motion sickness by the audience.
Steps:	*Shooting*, Viewing
Characteristics:	Image quality, Pleasure
Based on:	Recommendation 48

38. Shoot every action from start to finish to ensure that the audience misses none of the action.

Rationale:	The audience gets an accurate impression of the action of a scene and its duration.
Steps:	*Shooting*, Viewing
Characteristics:	Plot, Essence, Video length, Pleasure
Based on:	Recommendation 33

39. Start the recording 5 seconds before the action starts and stop the recording 5 seconds after the action is completed to avoid too brief shots.

Rationale:	These additional buffers help you in the postproduction when you cut and combine the individual shots into the final vision video.
Steps:	*Shooting*, Postproduction
Characteristics:	Video length
Based on:	Recommendation 34

40. Hold each shot for at least 15 seconds and a maximum of 30 seconds to avoid to brief and too long shots.

Rationale:	These two times are the lower and upper boundary of the average storage period of the human short-term memory for capturing, processing, and understanding information. If you undercut respective exceed this duration, it is difficult for the audience to capture, process, understand, and remember the details of the shot.
Steps:	Preproduction, *Shooting*, Postproduction, Viewing
Characteristics:	Video length, Pleasure
Based on:	Recommendation 11, Recommendation 12

41. After recording a shot, check the image quality and sound quality by viewing the recording with high-grade earphones or a loudspeaker to detect any unwanted background or foreground actions and noises.

Rationale:	Any unwanted actions and noises may disrupt and distract the audience from the actual content of your vision video.
Steps:	*Shooting*, Viewing
Characteristics:	Image quality, Sound quality, Clutter, Pleasure
Based on:	Recommendation 50, Recommendation 53

42. Keep all shots, even the unsuccessful ones, to have a large collection of shots.

Rationale:	Parts of, even the unsuccessful shots, may be used in the postproduction.
Steps:	*Shooting*, Postproduction
Characteristics:	Essence
Based on:	Recommendation 55

43. Follow the subsequent steps of the non-linear editing process to create the final vision video.

Steps of the non-linear editing process:

1. Phase: Rough edit

   (a) Digitize footage on your computer to choose the best shots.
   (b) Trim and clean up each shot by deleting unwanted frames.
   (c) Place the shots on the timeline to assemble simply the structure of your vision video according to your planned story.

2. Phase: Tight edit

   (a) Add effects and transitions to and between the shots.
   (b) Clean up and insert the necessary sound.
   (c) Before you create the final vision video, add titles to identify persons, places, and things supporting to the tell story and to give credits.

Rationale:	This process worked well for highly structured, short-format vision videos due to its simplicity in making changes to the vision video by simply moving the shots around.
Steps:	*Postproduction*
Characteristics:	Plot, Clutter, Image quality, Sound quality
Based on:	Recommendation 56

44. Ensure that the image- and soundtrack deal with the same topic to present consistent visual and auditive information.

Rationale:	The audience can be easily distracted and confused if the visual and auditive information of the image- and soundtrack do not match.
Steps:	Preproduction, Shooting, *Postproduction*, Viewing
Characteristics:	Essence, Clutter, Pleasure
Based on:	Recommendation 05, Recommendation 06

45. If the image- and soundtrack do not deal with the same topic, delete the soundtrack and maybe replace it to ensure that both tracks deal with the same topic.

Rationale:	It is easier to replace the soundtrack instead of the imagetrack. Therefore, you should always try to keep the image of a shot and replace the sound.
Steps:	*Postproduction*
Characteristics:	Essence, Clutter
Based on:	Experience

46. Do not create a rapid succession of unrelated shots or quick cuts between different viewpoints to avoid annoying, confusing, or boring your audience.

Rationale: The audience can hardly follow these presentation styles which in turn impede their understanding of the vision video.

Steps: *Postproduction*, Viewing

Characteristics: Plot, Pleasure

Based on: Recommendation 58

47. Follow the subsequent rules for cutting in the postproduction to avoid irritating transitions in your final vision video.

Rules for cutting:

1. Plan to cut between shots as eye blinks when looking around.
2. Do not cut between shots of extremely different sizes of the same subject, e.g., a close to a wide shot.
3. Do not cut between shots that are similar or even match, e.g., two close shots of two different persons.
4. Do not cut between two shots of the same size of the same subject, e.g., a close to a close shot.

Rationale: These rules are based on experience and help you to ensure that your final vision video is pleasant to watch for your audience.

Steps: *Postproduction*, Viewing

Characteristics: Image quality, Pleasure

Based on: Recommendation 59

48. Include the subsequent graphical elements in your vision video to obtain a well structure.

Graphical elements to structure your vision video:

1. Opening title to announce the vision video.
2. Subtitles to identify persons and locations.
3. Credits to recognize the persons appearing in and contributing to the vision video.
4. Ending titles to draw the vision video to its conclusion.

Rationale: These graphical elements add clarity to your vision video and thus help the audience to follow the vision video and its content.

Steps: *Postproduction*, Viewing

Characteristics: Plot, Essence, Sense of responsibility, Pleasure

Based on: Recommendation 60

49. When using materials (music, videos, images, texts, etc.) of third parties, verify that you comply with the respective regulations of copyright law to obtain a copy clearance for using the materials of third parties.

Rationale: You are responsible and legally liable to comply with the legal regulations for copyright.

Steps: *Postproduction*

Characteristics: Sense of responsibility

Based on: Recommendation 62

50. Consider the subsequent standards to design well-legible graphics.

    Standards for well-legible graphics:
    1. Place the graphic within the safe area, which is the 70 percent area around the center of the screen.
    2. Limit the number of fonts.
    3. Sans-serif bold fonts, e.g., Arial or Trade Gothic Bold, are best readable, especially on smaller displays.
    4. Avoid serif fonts since they create a flicker effect, especially on smaller displays.
    5. Letters smaller than one-tenth of the screen height are difficult to read.
    6. Black-edged letters are difficult to read.
    7. Do not use abbreviations to be unambiguous.
    8. Letters are usually much lighter than the background.
    9. Warm bright colors attract the most attention.

    Rationale: Well-legible graphics add clarity to the presentation of your vision video and thus help the audience to follow the vision video and its content.

    Steps: *Postproduction*, Viewing

    Characteristics: Image quality, Pleasure

    Based on: Recommendation 61

51. Keep the final vision video short (up to 5 minutes) to ensure that you only show the important details to the audience.

    Rationale: You must focus the audience's attention on the important details which they need to understand. The duration of a shot is crucial. If a shot is too long, the audience loses interest since they cannot capture, process, and understand the information presented. If a shot is too brief, the audience captures, but cannot process and understand, the information presented.

    Steps: Preproduction, Shooting, *Postproduction*, Viewing

    Characteristics: Video length, Essence, Pleasure, Focus

    Based on: Recommendation 10, Recommendation 57

52. Before you produce the final vision video, ask a second person to review your vision video for comprehensibility as well as visual and auditory problems.

    Rationale: You must exclude blurred images, poor sound, and tacit assumptions which often tend to be unnoticed by you as the video producer. Ask someone to review the vision video to see if this person can follow the logic and speed of the story of your vision video.

    Steps: *Postproduction*, Viewing

    Characteristics: Image quality, Sound quality, Plot, Essence, Pleasure, Clarity, Completeness

    Based on: Experience

Supplementary Materials of the Case Study

In the following, I present the supplementary materials for validating the candidate solution in the industry.

This appendix includes:

Questionnaire 1 – Initial Assessment

1   Demographics

a) What is your primary business role?

( ) Project manager   ( ) Requirements Engineer   ( ) Software architect

( ) Developer   ( ) Tester   ( ) Administrator

( ) IT-Operator   ( ) Quality manager

( ) Other:

b) How many years of experience do you have in your business role?

< 1 year: ☐   1-2 years: ☐   3-4 years: ☐   5-10 years: ☐   > 10 years: ☐

c) How many years of experience do you have overall in the industry?

< 1 year: ☐   1-2 years: ☐   3-4 years: ☐   5-10 years: ☐   > 10 years: ☐

2   Pre-Assessment of Awareness and Knowledge

Before working with the quality model for vision videos and the guideline for video production and use, please, assess your level of agreement with the following statements.

a) I am aware of what constitutes the quality of a video.

Totally disagree   Neutral   Totally agree

b) I have the knowledge to produce a good video.

Totally disagree   Neutral   Totally agree

c) I have the knowledge to use a video for effective communication with the parties involved.

Totally disagree   Neutral   Totally agree

Questionnaire 2 –
After Preproduction

1   Post-Assessment of Awareness and Knowledge

After working with the quality model for vision videos and the guideline for video production and use, please, assess your level of agreement with the following statements.

a) I am aware of what constitutes the quality of a video.

Totally disagree			Neutral			Totally agree

b) I have the knowledge to produce a good video.

Totally disagree			Neutral			Totally agree

c) I have the knowledge to use a video for effective communication with the parties involved.

Totally disagree			Neutral			Totally agree

Questionnaire 3 – After Production

1   Values of the Video as a By-Product Approach

As a reminder, the three concepts of the Mockup Recorder and its key features are summarized below.

Concept 1: Support of arbitrarily created mockups

- Mockups can be hand-drawn and digitally created (import and creation of mockups)
- Support of different levels of detail (use of graphical user interface elements)
- Support of visual refinement (use of CSS and rearrangement of graphical user interface elements with reuse of defined interaction sequences)

Concept 2: Evolutionary specification of scenarios

- Fast and easy definition and modification of a scenario (drag and drop of mockups)
- Manage the scenario sequence by adding, rearranging, and deleting mockups (in the film strip)
- Manage the interaction event sequence for each mockup individually (for each mockup in the film strip)

Concept 3: Independence from videos

- Playback of interactions at any time without a created video (in the Mockup Recorder)
- A video is only an exportable documentation option (export function)

In consideration of these concepts and after working with the Mockup Recorder, please, assess your level of agreement with the following statements.

a) Integration: The production and use of a video with the Mockup Recorder are integrated into the practice "prototyping of scenarios" that belongs to an activity within the software development process.

Totally disagree   Neutral   Totally agree

b) Involvement: The production and use of a video with the Mockup Recorder concern only the parties who are already involved in the practice "prototyping of scenarios".

Totally disagree   Neutral   Totally agree

c) Involvement: The production and use of a video with the Mockup Recorder are as little intrusive as possible to the parties who are already involved in the practice "prototyping of scenarios".

Totally disagree   Neutral   Totally agree

d) Simplicity: The production and use of a video with the Mockup Recorder is easy for the parties involved in the practice "prototyping of scenarios" regarding …

… the knowledge required.

Totally disagree   Neutral   Totally agree

… the skills required.

Totally disagree   Neutral   Totally agree

… the process used.

Totally disagree   Neutral   Totally agree

… the technology used.

Totally disagree   Neutral   Totally agree

e) Supplementation: A video produced with the Mockup Recorder is only a supplementary material in addition to the actual results of the practice "prototyping of scenarios".

Remark: The typical use case of the Mockup Recorder is to create the mockups with the tool. For this reason, you can export all mockups in the Mockup Recorder, even the mockups based on imported images, as images. Thus, a video is actually an additional exportable result.

Totally disagree   Neutral   Totally agree

2 Perceived Usability of the Mockup Recorder

After using the Mockup Recorder, please, assess your level of agreement with the following statements.

a) I think that I would like to use the Mockup Recorder frequently.

Totally disagree   Neutral   Totally agree

b) I found the Mockup Recorder unnecessarily complex.

Totally disagree   Neutral   Totally agree

c) I thought the Mockup Recorder was easy to use.

Totally disagree   Neutral   Totally agree

d) I think that I would need the support of a technical person to be able to use the Mockup Recorder.

Totally disagree   Neutral   Totally agree

e) I found the various functions in the Mockup Recorder were well integrated.

Totally disagree   Neutral   Totally agree

f) I thought there was too much inconsistency in the Mockup Recorder.

Totally disagree   Neutral   Totally agree

g) I would imagine that most people would learn to use the Mockup Recorder very quickly.

Totally disagree   Neutral   Totally agree

h) I found the Mockup Recorder very cumbersome (awkward) to use.

Totally disagree   Neutral   Totally agree

i) I felt very confident using the Mockup Recorder.

Totally disagree   Neutral   Totally agree

j) I needed to learn a lot of things before I could get going with the Mockup Recorder.

Totally disagree Neutral Totally agree

3 Time Needed for Video Production

a) For the video that you have created with the Mockup Recorder, please, indicate how long it took you to produce the video.

Duration (in minutes): _____

4 Post-Assessment of Awareness and Knowledge

After working with the Mockup Recorder, please, assess your level of agreement with the following statements.

a) I am aware of what constitutes the quality of a video.

Totally disagree Neutral Totally agree

b) I have the knowledge to produce a good video.

Totally disagree Neutral Totally agree

c) I have the knowledge to use a video for effective communication with the parties involved.

Totally disagree Neutral Totally agree

Questionnaire 4 – After Viewing

Consent Form

Please, read this consent form carefully.

Description of the study:

This case study investigates the overall impression of vision videos from your point of view. The goal of this study is to understand better how video producers and their target audience perceive and assess the quality of videos used for illustrating scenarios of interaction processes between a user and a future system.

Task:

Your task is to view a video and then assess 14 quality characteristics for the video. In addition, we ask you to assess your level of agreement with four statements regarding the video presentation.

Confidentiality:

All data collected during the study will be anonymous and only accessible for the software engineering group at Leibniz Universität Hannover. A random ID is assigned to each participant to ensure that the real person cannot be identified. The participant undertakes to keep the content of the study confidential.

Voluntary consent:

The above-listed points were explained to me and my questions were answered. I confirm with my signature that I participate voluntarily in the described study.

_____

(First name, last name)

_____

(Place, date, and signature)

1 Demographics

a) What is your primary business role?

Administration staff: ☐ Others: ☐ _____

b) How many years of experience do you have in your business role?

< 1 year: ☐ 1-2 years: ☐ 3-4 years: ☐ 5-10 years: ☐ > 10 years: ☐

c) How many years of experience do you have overall in the industry?

< 1 year: ☐ 1-2 years: ☐ 3-4 years: ☐ 5-10 years: ☐ > 10 years: ☐

2 Video Quality Assessment

Please, assess your level of agreement with the following statements for the video shown.

Video:

The presented vision video has a good overall quality.

Totally disagree	Neutral	Totally agree

Please, assess your level of agreement with the following statements by selecting one of the items of the respective 5-point scale.

Image quality: considers the visual quality of the image of a video.	Totally disagree (2)	Disagree (1)	Neutral (0)	Agree (-1)	Totally agree (-2)
The image of the produced vision video has a good visual quality.					
Focus: considers the compact representation of a vision.	Totally disagree (2)	Disagree (1)	Neutral (0)	Agree (-1)	Totally agree (-2)
The vision video presents the visionary scenario of the prototype and its use in a compact way.					
Pleasure: considers the enjoyment of watching a video.	Totally disagree (2)	Disagree (1)	Neutral (0)	Agree (-1)	Totally agree (-2)
The vision video is enjoyable to watch.					

Intention: considers the intended purpose of a video.	Totally disagree (2)	Disagree (1)	Neutral (0)	Agree (-1)	Totally agree (-2)
The vision video is suitable for presenting scenarios of an interaction process between a user and the prototype to validate the scenario and collect feedback.					

Questionnaire 4 –
After Viewing

Consent Form

Please, read this consent form carefully.

Description of the study:

This case study investigates the overall impression of vision videos from your point of view. The goal of this study is to understand better how video producers and their target audience perceive and assess the quality of videos used for illustrating scenarios of interaction processes between a user and a future system.

Task:

Your task is to view your produced video and then assess 14 quality characteristics for the video. In addition, I ask you to assess your level of agreement with four statements regarding the video presentation.

Confidentiality:

All data collected during the study will be anonymous and only accessible for the software engineering group at Leibniz Universität Hannover. A random ID is assigned to each participant to ensure that the real person cannot be identified. The participant undertakes to keep the content of the study confidential.

Voluntary consent:

The above-listed points were explained to me and my questions were answered. I confirm with my signature that I participate voluntarily in the described study.

(First name, last name)

(Place, date, and signature)

1 Video Quality Assessment

Please, assess your level of agreement with the following statements for the video shown.

Video:
The presented vision video has a good overall quality.

| Totally disagree | Neutral | Totally agree |

Please, assess your level of agreement with the following statements by selecting one of the items of the respective 5-point scale.

Image quality: considers the visual quality of the image of a video.	Totally disagree (2)	Disagree (1)	Neutral (0)	Agree (-1)	Totally agree (-2)
The image of the produced vision video has a good visual quality.					
Focus: considers the compact representation of a vision.	Totally disagree (2)	Disagree (1)	Neutral (0)	Agree (-1)	Totally agree (-2)
The vision video presents the visionary scenario of the prototype and its use in a compact way.					
Pleasure: considers the enjoyment of watching a video.	Totally disagree (2)	Disagree (1)	Neutral (0)	Agree (-1)	Totally agree (-2)
The vision video is enjoyable to watch.					
Intention: considers the intended purpose of a video.	Totally disagree (2)	Disagree (1)	Neutral (0)	Agree (-1)	Totally agree (-2)
The vision video is suitable for presenting scenarios of an interaction process between a user and the prototype to validate the scenario and collect feedback.					

2 Post-Assessment of Awareness and Knowledge

After presenting the produced videos to your target audience, please, assess your level of agreement with the following statements.

a) I am aware of what constitutes the quality of a video.

Totally disagree   Neutral   Totally agree

b) I have the knowledge to produce a good video.

Totally disagree   Neutral   Totally agree

c) I have the knowledge to use a video for effective communication with the parties involved.

Totally disagree   Neutral   Totally agree

Bibliography

[1]   AAKER, D. A.; MCLOUGHLIN, D.: *Strategic Market Management: Global Perspectives*. John Wiley & Sons, 2009

[2]   ABAD, Z. S. H.; NOAEEN, M.; RUHE, G.:   Requirements Engineering Visualization: A Systematic Literature Review. In: *2016 IEEE 24th International Requirements Engineering Conference (RE)*, 2016, pp. 6–15

[3]   ABELEIN, U.; PAECH, B.: State of Practice of User-Developer Communication in Large-Scale IT Projects. In: *International Working Conference on Requirements Engineering: Foundation for Software Quality* Springer, 2014, pp. 95–111

[4]   AKRAMULLAH, S.:   *Digital Video Concepts, Methods, and Metrics: Quality, Compression, Performance, and Power Trade-off Analysis*. Apress, 2014

[5]   AL-RAWAS, A.; EASTERBROOK, S.:   Communication Problems in Requirements Engineering: A Field Study. In: *Proceedings of the 1st Westminster Conference on Professional Awareness in Software Engineering*, Royal Society, 1996

[6]   ALEXANDER, I. F.; MAIDEN, N.: *Scenarios, Stories, Use Cases: Through the Systems Development Life-Cycle*. John Wiley & Sons, 2005

[7]   ALEXANDER, I. F.; STEVENS, R.: *Writing Better Requirements*. Pearson Education, 2002

[8]   AMBLER, S. W.: *Agile Modeling: Effective Practices for eXtreme Programming and the Unified Process*. John Wiley & Sons, 2002

[9]   ANTON, A. I.; POTTS, C.: The Use of Goals to Surface Requirements for Evolving Systems. In: *Proceedings of the 20th International Conference on Software Engineering* IEEE, 1998, pp. 157–166

[10]   ANTONY, M. M.; SWINSON, R. P.: *When Perfect isn't Good Enough: Strategies for Coping with Perfectionism*. New Harbinger Publications, 2009

[11]   ARANDA, J.: *A Theory of Shared Understanding for Software Organizations*. University of Toronto, 2010

[12]   ARULMANI SANKARANARAYANAN, V.: *Tool-Supported Data Collection for Experiments to Subjectively Assess Vision Videos*, Leibniz Universität Hannover, Bachelor thesis, 2019

[13]   AURUM, A.; WOHLIN, C.: *Engineering and Managing Software Requirements*. Springer-Verlag, 2005

[14]   AVERBAKH, A.: *Light-Weight Experience Collection in Distributed Software Engineering*. Logos Verlag Berlin GmbH, 2015

[15] BACKHAUS, K.; ERICHSON, B.; PLINKE, W.; WEIBER, R.: *Multivariate Analysemethoden: Eine anwendungsorientierte Einführung.* Springer, 2016

[16] BANGOR, A.; KORTUM, P.; MILLER, J.: Determining What Individual SUS Scores Mean: Adding an Adjective Rating Scale. In: *Journal of Usability Studies* 4 (2009), No. 3, pp. 114–123

[17] BARTHOLOMEW, D. J.; STEELE, F.; MOUSTAKI, I.; GALBRAITH, J. I.: *Analysis of Multivariate Social Science Data.* Chapman and Hall/CRC, 2008

[18] BASILI, V. R.; CALDIERA, C.; ROMBACH, H. D.: Goal Question Metric Paradigm. In: *Encyclopedia of Software Engineering* 1 (1994), pp. 528–532

[19] BECK, K.; ANDRES, C.: *Extreme Programming Explained: Embrace Change (2nd Edition).* Addison-Wesley Professional, 2004

[20] BEIMEL, D.; KEDMI-SHAHAR, E.: Improving the Identification of Functional System Requirements When Novice Analysts Create Use Case Diagrams: The Benefits of Applying Conceptual Mental Models. In: *Requirements Engineering* 24 (2019), No. 4, pp. 483–502

[21] BENNACEUR, A.; MCCORMICK, C.; GARCÍA-GALÁN, J.; PERERA, C.; SMITH, A.; ZISMAN, A.; NUSEIBEH, B.: Feed me, Feed me: An Exemplar for Engineering Adaptive Software. In: *2016 IEEE/ACM 11th International Symposium on Software Engineering for Adaptive and Self-Managing Systems (SEAMS)* IEEE, 2016, pp. 89–95

[22] BITTNER, E. A. C.; LEIMEISTER, J. M.: Creating Shared Understanding in Heterogeneous Work Groups: Why it Matters and How to Achieve it. In: *Journal of Management Information Systems* 31 (2014), No. 1, pp. 111–144

[23] BJARNASON, E.; SHARP, H.: The Role of Distances in Requirements Communication: A Case Study. In: *Requirements Engineering* 22 (2017), No. 1, pp. 1–26

[24] BJARNASON, E.; SHARP, H.; REGNELL, B.: Improving Requirements-Test Alignment by Prescribing Practices that Mitigate Communication Gaps. In: *Empirical Software Engineering* 24 (2019), No. 4, pp. 2364–2409

[25] BJARNASON, E.; WNUK, K.; REGNELL, B.: Requirements are Slipping Through the Gaps – A Case Study on Causes & Effects of Communication Gaps in Large-Scale Software Development. In: *2011 IEEE 19th International Requirements Engineering Conference (RE)* IEEE, 2011, pp. 37–46

[26] BOEHM, B. W.; BROWN, J. R.; LIPOW, M.: Quantitative Evaluation of Software Quality. In: *Proceedings of the 2nd International Conference on Software Engineering* IEEE Computer Society Press, 1976, pp. 592–605

[27] BOISE STATE UNIVERSITY: *Video Production Standards.* https://brandstandards .boisestate.edu/wp-content/uploads/2014/10/VideoGuidelinesB oiseState.2014-10-14.pdf

[28] BOJIC, M.; GOULATI, A.; SZOSTAK, D.; MARKOPOULOS, P.: On the Effect of Visual Refinement upon User Feedback in the Context of Video Prototyping. In: *Proceedings of the 29th ACM International Conference on Design of Communication*, 2011, pp. 115–118

[29] BOOK, M.; GRAPENTHIN, S.; GRUHN, V.: Seeing the Forest and the Trees: Focusing Team Interaction on Value and Effort Drivers. In: *Proceedings of the ACM SIGSOFT 20th International Symposium on the Foundations of Software Engineering* ACM, 2012, pp. 1–4

[30] BÖRGER, E.; HÖRGER, B.; PARNAS, D.; ROMBACH, H.: Requirements Capture, Documentation, and Validation. In: *Dagstuhl Seminar*, 1999

[31] BORUSZEWSKI, O.: *Unterstützung der Koexistenz von agilen und traditionellen Anforderungsartefakten*, Gottfried Wilhelm Leibniz Universität Hannover, PhD thesis, 2017

[32] BRILL, O.; SCHNEIDER, K.; KNAUSS, E.: Videos vs. Use Cases: Can Videos Capture More Requirements under Time Pressure? In: *International Working Conference on Requirements Engineering: Foundation for Software Quality* Springer, 2010, pp. 30–44

[33] BRINGS, J.; DAUN, M.; KEMPE, M.; WEYER, T.: On Different Search Methods for Systematic Literature Reviews and Maps: Experiences from a Literature Search on Validation and Verification of Emergent Behavior. In: *Proceedings of the 22nd International Conference on Evaluation and Assessment in Software Engineering 2018* ACM, 2018, pp. 35–45

[34] BROLL, G.; HUSSMANN, H.; RUKZIO, E.; WIMMER, R.: Using Video Clips to Support Requirements Elicitation in Focus Groups – An Experience Report. In: *SE 2007 Workshop on Multimedia Requirements Engineering*, 2007

[35] BROOKE, J.: SUS: A "Quick and Dirty" Usability Scale. In: *Usability Evaluation in Industry* (1996), pp. 189–194

[36] BROUSE, P. L.; FIELDS, N. A.; PALMER, J. D.: A Multimedia Computer Supported Cooperative Work Environment for Requirements Engineering. In: *1992 IEEE International Conference on Systems, Man, and Cybernetics* IEEE, 1992, pp. 954–959

[37] BROWN, S. L.; EISENHARDT, K. M.: Product Development: Past Research, Present Findings, and Future Directions. In: *Academy of Management Review* 20 (1995), No. 2, pp. 343–378

[38]   BRUEGGE, B.; CREIGHTON, O.; REISS, M.; STANGL, H.:   Applying a Video-Based Requirements Engineering Technique to an Airport Scenario. In: *3rd International Workshop
on Multimedia and Enjoyable Requirements Engineering – Beyond Mere Descriptions and with
More Fun and Games* IEEE, 2008, pp. 9–11

[39]   BRUEGGE, B.; STANGL, H.; REISS, M.: An Experiment in Teaching Innovation in Software
Engineering: Video Presentation. In: *Companion to the 23rd ACM SIGPLAN Conference on
Object-Oriented Programming Systems Languages and Applications* ACM, 2008, pp. 807–810

[40]   BRUN-COTTAN, F.; WALL, P.: Using Video to Re-Present the User. In: *Communications of
the ACM* 38 (1995), No. 5, pp. 61–71

[41]   BUBENKO, J. A.: Challenges in Requirements Engineering. In: *Proceedings of 1995 IEEE
International Symposium on Requirements Engineering*, 1995, pp. 160–162

[42]   BUCHAN, J.: An Empirical Cognitive Model of the Development of Shared Understanding of Requirements. In: *Requirements Engineering. Communications in Computer and Information Science*. Springer, 2014, pp. 165–179

[43]   BUCHHOLZ, A.; SCHULT, G.:   *Fernseh-Journalismus: Ein Handbuch für Ausbildung und
Praxis*. Springer-Verlag, 2016

[44]   BURGE, J. E.; KIPER, J. D.: Capturing Decisions and Rationale from Collaborative Design.
In: *Design Computing and Cognition'08*. Springer, 2008, pp. 221–239

[45]   BUSCH, M.; KARRAS, O.; SCHNEIDER, K.; AHRENS, M.: Vision Meets Visualization: Are
Animated Videos an Alternative? In: *International Working Conference on Requirements
Engineering: Foundation for Software Quality* Springer, 2020, pp. 277–292

[46]   CALLELE, D.; NEUFELD, E.; SCHNEIDER, K.: Requirements Engineering and the Creative
Process in the Video Game Industry. In: *13th IEEE International Conference on Requirements
Engineering (RE)* IEEE, 2005, pp. 240–250

[47]   CARROLL, J. M.: *Scenario-Based Design: Envisioning Work and Technology in System Development*. John Wiley & Sons, Inc., 1995

[48]   CARTER, L. R.; KARATSOLIS, A.: Lessons from Trying to Develop a Robust Documentation Exemplar. In: *Proceedings of the 27th ACM International Conference on Design of
Communication* ACM, 2009, pp. 199–204

[49]   CHAPPELL, G.; POTTS, J.; HILDEBRANDT, N.: *JavaFX – Getting Started with JavaFX*. Release 2.2.40, 2013

[50] CHIKKERUR, S.; SUNDARAM, V.; REISSLEIN, M.; KARAM, L. J.: Objective Video Quality Assessment Methods: A Classification, Review, and Performance Comparison. In: *IEEE Transactions on Broadcasting* 57 (2011), No. 2, pp. 165–182

[51] CLARK, K. B.; WHEELWRIGHT, S. C.: *Managing New Product and Process Development: Text Cases.* Simon and Schuster, 2010

[52] CLAYTON, M. J.: Delphi: A Technique to Harness Expert Opinion for Critical Decision-Making Tasks in Education. In: *Educational Psychology* 17 (1997), No. 4, pp. 373–386

[53] COCKBURN, A.: *Writing Effective Use Cases.* Addison-Wesley Professional, 2000

[54] COCKBURN, A.: *Agile Software Development: The Cooperative Game.* Pearson Education, 2006

[55] COHEN, J.: A Coefficient of Agreement for Nominal Scales. In: *Educational and Psychological Measurement* 20 (1960), No. 1, pp. 37–46

[56] COHEN, J.: *Statistical Power Analysis for the Behavioral Sciences.* Routledge, 2013

[57] COLLIER, J.; BREWER, K.: *Video Production Guide.* http://web.mit.edu/techtv/videoprodguide/videoprodguide.pdf

[58] COUGHLAN, J.; MACREDIE, R. D.: Effective Communication in Requirements Elicitation: A Comparison of Methodologies. In: *Requirements Engineering* 7 (2002), No. 2, pp. 47–60

[59] CRAWFORD, C. M.; DI BENEDETTO, A.: *New Products Management.* Tata McGraw-Hill Education, 2008

[60] CREIGHTON, O.; OTT, M.; BRUEGGE, B.: Software Cinema – Video-Based Requirements Engineering. In: *2006 IEEE 14th International Requirements Engineering Conference (RE)* IEEE, 2006, pp. 109–118

[61] CREIGHTON, O.: *Software Cinema: Employing Digital Video in Requirements Engineering.* Verlag Dr. Hut, 2006

[62] CRESWELL, J. W.; CRESWELL, J. D.: *Research Design: Qualitative, Quantitative, and Mixed Methods Approaches.* Sage publications, 2017

[63] DALY, S. J.: Visible Differences Predictor: An Algorithm for the Assessment of Image Fidelity. In: *Human Vision, Visual Processing, and Digital Display III* Vol. 1666 International Society for Optics and Photonics, 1992, pp. 2–16

[64]   DARBY, A.; TSEKLEVES, E.; SAWYER, P.: Speculative Requirements: Design Fiction and RE. In: *2018 IEEE 26th International Requirements Engineering Conference (RE)* IEEE, 2018, pp. 388–393

[65]   DODGE, Y.: *The Concise Encyclopedia of Statistics*. Springer Science & Business Media, 2008

[66]   DOERR, J.; KOENIG, T.; OLSSON, T.; ADAM, S.: Das ReqMan Prozessrahmenwerk. In: *IESE-Report Nr. 141* (2006)

[67]   DYER, B.; GUPTA, A. K.; WILEMON, D.: What First-to-Market Companies Do Differently. In: *Research-Technology Management* 42 (1999), No. 2, pp. 15–21

[68]   EASTERBROOK, S.: Coordination Breakdowns: Why Groupware is So Difficult to Design. In: *Proceedings of the 28th Hawaii International Conference on System Sciences (HICSS '95)*, IEEE Computer Society, 1995, pp. 191–199

[69]   EASTERBROOK, S.; SINGER, J.; STOREY, M.-A.; DAMIAN, D.: Selecting Empirical Methods for Software Engineering Research. In: *Guide to Advanced Empirical Software Engineering*. Springer, 2008, pp. 285–311

[70]   EDITORS OF VIDEOMAKER MAGAZINE; YORK, M.; BURKHART, J.: *The Videomaker Guide to Video Production*. Focal Press, 2008

[71]   ELIASSON, U.; HELDAL, R.; KNAUSS, E.; PELLICCIONE, P.: The Need of Complementing Plan-Driven Requirements Engineering with Emerging Communication: Experiences from Volvo Car Group. In: *2015 IEEE 23rd International Requirements Engineering Conference (RE)* IEEE, 2015, pp. 372–381

[72]   EU GENERAL DATA PROTECTION REGULATION (GDPR): Regulation (EU) 2016/679 of the European Parliament and of the Council of 27 April 2016 on the Protection of Natural Persons with Regard to the Processing of Personal Data and on the Free Movement of such Data, and Repealing Directive 95/46/EC (General Data Protection Regulation). In: *Official Journal of the European Union* L 119/1 (2016)

[73]   FEENEY, W.: Documenting Software Using Video. In: *IEEE Computer Society Workshop on Software Engineering Technology Transfer*, 1983

[74]   FEMMER, H.; VOGELSANG, A.: Requirements Quality is Quality in Use. In: *IEEE Software* 36 (2018), No. 3, pp. 83–91

[75]   FERNÁNDEZ, D. M.; WAGNER, S.; KALINOWSKI, M.; FELDERER, M.; MAFRA, P.; VETRÒ, A.; CONTE, T.; CHRISTIANSSON, M.-T.; GREER, D.; LASSENIUS, C. et al.: Naming the Pain in Requirements Engineering. In: *Empirical Software Engineering* 22 (2017), No. 5, pp. 2298–2338

[76] FERRARI, A.; SPOLETINI, P.; GNESI, S.: Ambiguity as a Resource to Disclose Tacit Knowledge. In: *2015 IEEE 23rd International Requirements Engineering Conference (RE)* IEEE, 2015, pp. 26–35

[77] FICKERT, S.; GÜNTHER, A.: *Rückblick auf unsere Innovations-Themen 2019.* https://blog.sophist.de/2020/05/12/rueckblick-auf-unsere-innovations-themen-2019/. 2020

[78] FINK, A.: *The Survey Handbook.* Sage, 2003

[79] FORWARD, A.; LETHBRIDGE, T. C.: The Relevance of Software Documentation, Tools and Technologies: A Survey. In: *Proceedings of the 2002 ACM Symposium on Document Engineering* ACM, 2002, pp. 26–33

[80] FRICKER, S. A.: *Pragmatic Requirements Communication: The Handshaking Approach.* Shaker Verlag GmbH, Germany, 2009

[81] FRICKER, S. A.; GLINZ, M.: Comparison of Requirements Hand-Off, Analysis, and Negotiation: Case Study. In: *2010 IEEE 18th International Conference on Requirements Engineering (RE)* IEEE, 2010, pp. 167–176

[82] FRICKER, S. A.; GORSCHEK, T.; BYMAN, C.; SCHMIDLE, A.: Handshaking with Implementation Proposals: Negotiating Requirements Understanding. In: *IEEE Software* 27 (2010), No. 2, pp. 72–80

[83] FRICKER, S. A.; GORSCHEK, T.; GLINZ, M.: Goal-Oriented Requirements Communication in New Product Development. In: *2008 Second International Workshop on Software Product Management* IEEE, 2008, pp. 27–34

[84] FRICKER, S. A.; GRAU, R.; ZWINGLI, A.: Requirements Engineering: Best Practice. In: *Requirements Engineering for Digital Health.* Springer, 2015, pp. 25–46

[85] FRICKER, S. A.; GRÜNBACHER, P.: Negotiation Constellations – Method Selection Framework for Requirements Negotiation. In: *International Working Conference on Requirements Engineering: Foundation for Software Quality* Springer, 2008, pp. 37–51

[86] FRICKER, S. A.; SCHNEIDER, K.; FOTROUSI, F.; THUEMMLER, C.: Workshop Videos for Requirements Communication. In: *Requirements Engineering* 21 (2016), No. 4, pp. 521–552

[87] FRÜHAUF, K.; LUDEWIG, J.; SANDMAYR, H.: *Software-Prüfung: Eine Anleitung zum Test und zur Inspektion.* vdf Hochschulverlag AG, 2007

[88]   GALL, M.; BRUEGGE, B.; BERENBACH, B: Towards a Framework for Real Time Require-
       ments Elicitation. In: *2006 1st International Workshop on Multimedia Requirements Engineer-
       ing* IEEE, 2006, pp. 17–23

[89]   GEORGITIS, N.; PEACH, K.; RODRIGUEZ, S.: *ARSC Video Production Guidelines.* `http:`
       `//www.arsc-audio.org/pdf/videoproductionguidelines.pdf`

[90]   GLAUER, L.: *Specification of GUI Interactions as Videos*, Leibniz Universität Hannover,
       Bachelor thesis, 2017

[91]   GLINZ, M.: A Glossary of Requirements Engineering Terminology. In: *Standard Glossary
       of the Certified Professional for Requirements Engineering (CPRE) Studies and Exam, Version*
       1.7 (2017)

[92]   GLINZ, M.; FRICKER, S. A.:   On Shared Understanding in Software Engineering: An
       Essay. In: *Computer Science – Research and Development* 30 (2014), No. 3-4, pp. 363–376

[93]   GORSCHEK, T.; GARRE, P.; LARSSON, S.; WOHLIN, C.: A Model for Technology Transfer
       in Practice. In: *IEEE Software* 23 (2006), No. 6, pp. 88–95

[94]   GOTTESDIENER, E.: *Requirements by Collaboration: Workshops for Defining Needs*. Addison-
       Wesley Professional, 2002

[95]   GOTTESDIENER, E.; GORMAN, M.: *Discover to Deliver: Agile Product Planning and Analysis*.
       EBG Consulting, 2014

[96]   GULLIKSEN, J.; LANTZ, A.: Design Versus Design – From the Shaping of Products to the
       Creation of User Experiences. In: *International Journal of Human-Computer Interaction* 15
       (2003), No. 1, pp. 5–20

[97]   GUO, P. J.; KIM, J.; RUBIN, R.: How Video Production Affects Student Engagement: An
       Empirical Study of MOOC Videos. In: *Proceedings of the 1st ACM Conference on Learning
       @ Scale Conference* ACM, 2014, pp. 41–50

[98]   HAGEDORN, J.; HAILPERN, J.; KARAHALIOS, K. G.:   VCode and VData: Illustrating a
       New Framework for Supporting the Video Annotation Workflow. In: *Proceedings of the
       Working Conference on Advanced Visual Interfaces*, 2008, pp. 317–321

[99]   HALL, T.; BEECHAM, S.; RAINER, A.: Requirements Problems in Twelve Software Com-
       panies: An Empirical Analysis. In: *IEE Proceedings-Software* 149 (2002), No. 5, pp. 153–160

[100] HAMEL, G.; PRAHALAD, C. K.: Strategic Intent. In: *Harvard Business Review* 83 (2005),
       No. 7, pp. 148–161

[101] HANJALIC, A.; KOFLER, C.; LARSON, M.: Intent and its Discontents: The User at the Wheel of the Online Video Search Engine. In: *Proceedings of the 20th ACM International Conference on Multimedia* ACM, 2012, pp. 1239–1248

[102] HARRISON, B. L.; BAECKER, R. M.: Designing Video Annotation and Analysis Systems. In: *Graphics Interface* Vol. 92, 1992, pp. 157–166

[103] HAUMER, P.; POHL, K.; WEIDENHAUPT, K.: Requirements Elicitation and Validation with Real World Scenes. In: *IEEE Transactions on Software Engineering* 24 (1998), No. 12, pp. 1036–1054

[104] HAUSMANN, C.: *Design and Implementation of a Framework for Integrating Individual Tools for Multimedia Requirements Elicitation and Validation*, Leibniz Universität Hannover, Bachelor thesis, 2019

[105] HEATH, C.; HINDMARSH, J.; LUFF, P.: *Video in Qualitative Research: Analysing Social Interaction in Everyday Life*. Sage, 2010

[106] HOFFMANN, A.; BITTNER, E. A. C.; LEIMEISTER, J. M.: The Emergence of Mutual and Shared Understanding in the System Development Process. In: *International Working Conference on Requirements Engineering: Foundation for Software Quality* Springer, 2013, pp. 174–189

[107] HOLM, S.: A Simple Sequentially Rejective Multiple Test Procedure. In: *Scandinavian Journal of Statistics* (1979), pp. 65–70

[108] HOSMER, D. W.; LEMESHOW, S.: *Applied Logistic Regression*. Wiley New York, 2000

[109] HÖST, M.; REGNELL, B.; WOHLIN, C.: Using Students as Subjects – A Comparative Study of Students and Professionals in Lead-Time Impact Assessment. In: *Empirical Software Engineering* 5 (2000), No. 3, pp. 201–214

[110] HYVÖNEN, J.: Creating Shared Understanding with Lego Serious Play. In: *Proceedings of the Seminar on Data- and Value-Driven Software Engineering with Deep Customer Insight* Vol. 58314308, 2014, pp. 36–42

[111] IMTIAZ, S.; BANO, M.; IKRAM, N.; NIAZI, M.: A Tertiary Study: Experiences of Conducting Systematic Literature Reviews in Software Engineering. In: *Proceedings of the 17th International Conference on Evaluation and Assessment in Software Engineering* ACM, 2013, pp. 177–182

[112] *ISO/IEC FDIS 25010:2010: Systems and Software Engineering – Systems and Software Product Quality Requirements and Evaluation (SQuaRE) – System and Software Quality Models*. 2010

[113] *ISO/IEC/IEEE 29148:2011: Systems and Software Engineering – Life Cycle Processes – Requirements Engineering.* 2011

[114] ITU-R Study Group 6: *BT500-14 (10/2019) – Methodology for the Subjective Assessment of the Quality of Television Pictures.* https://www.itu.int/rec/R-REC-BT.500-14-201910-I/en. Version: 1.0, 2019

[115] ITU-T Study Group 12: *ITU-T P.911 (12/1998) – Subjective Audiovisual Quality Assessment Methods for Multimedia Applications.* http://handle.itu.int/11.1002/1000/4538. Version: 1.0, 1998

[116] ITU-T Study Group 12: *ITU-T P.910 (04/2008) – Subjective Video Quality Assessment Methods for Multimedia Applications.* http://handle.itu.int/11.1002/1000/9317. Version: 3.0, 2008

[117] ITU-T Study Group 12: *ITU-T P.913 (03/2016) – Methods for the Subjective Assessment of Video Quality, Audio Quality and Audiovisual Quality of Internet Video and Distribution Quality Television in any Environment.* http://handle.itu.int/11.1002/1000/127. Version: 2.0, 2016

[118] Jirotka, M.; Luff, P.: Supporting Requirements with Video-Based Analysis. In: *IEEE Software* 23 (2006), No. 3, pp. 42–44

[119] Kaiya, H. ; Saeki, M. ; Ochimizu, K. : Design of a Hyper Media Tool to Support Requirements Elicitation Meetings. In: *7th International Workshop on Computer-Aided Software Engineering*, 1995, pp. 250–259

[120] Kamsties, E.; Hörmann, K.; Schlich, M.: Requirements Engineering in Small and Medium Enterprises. In: *Requirements Engineering* 3 (1998), No. 2, pp. 84–90

[121] Kanumuri, S.; Cosman, P. C.; Reibman, A. R.; Vaishampayan, V. A.: Modeling Packet-Loss Visibility in MPEG-2 Video. In: *IEEE Transactions on Multimedia* 8 (2006), No. 2, pp. 341–355

[122] Kanumuri, S.; Subramanian, S. G.; Cosman, P. C.; Reibman, A. R.: Predicting H.264 Packet Loss Visibility Using a Generalized Linear Model. In: *IEEE International Conference on Image Processing* IEEE, 2006, pp. 2245–2248

[123] Karras, O.: *Tool-Supported Analysis of Requirements Workshop Videos*, Leibniz Universität Hannover, Master thesis, 2015

[124] Karras, O.: Software Professionals' Attitudes towards Video as a Medium in Requirements Engineering. In: *International Conference on Product-Focused Software Process Improvement* Springer, 2018, pp. 150–158

[125] KARRAS, O.: *Survey Data Set Part 1 – Attitudes Towards Videos as a Documentation Option for Communication in Requirements Engineering.* http://dx.doi.org/10.5281/zenodo.3245770. Version: 1.1, 2018

[126] KARRAS, O.: *Communicating Stakeholders' Needs – Vision Videos to Disclose, Discuss, and Align Mental Models for Shared Understanding.* http://blog.ieeesoftware.org/2019/10/communicating-stakeholders-needs-with.html. , 2019

[127] KARRAS, O.: *Survey Data Set Part 2 – Attitudes Towards Videos as a Documentation Option for Communication in Requirements Engineering.* http://dx.doi.org/10.5281/zenodo.4064741. Version: 1.0, 2020

[128] KARRAS, O.: *Vision Video – Interaction Process of the Purchase of a Product by a Customer in a Webshop.* http://dx.doi.org/10.5281/zenodo.3696798. Version: 1.0, 2020

[129] KARRAS, O.; HAMADEH, A.; SCHNEIDER, K.: Enriching Requirements Specifications with Videos – The Use of Videos to Support Requirements Communication. In: *Softwaretechnik-Trends* 38 (2017), No. 1, pp. 51–52

[130] KARRAS, O.; KIESLING, S.; SCHNEIDER, K.: Supporting Requirements Elicitation by Tool-Supported Video Analysis. In: *2016 IEEE 24th International Requirements Engineering Conference (RE)* IEEE, 2016, pp. 146–155

[131] KARRAS, O.; KLÜNDER, J.; SCHNEIDER, K.: Tool-Supported Experiments for Continuously Collecting Data of Subjective Video Quality Assessments During Video Playback. In: *Softwaretechnik-Trends* 40 (2019), No. 1, pp. 17–18

[132] KARRAS, O.; KLÜNDER, J.; SCHNEIDER, K.: Enrichment of Requirements Specifications with Videos: Enhancing the Comprehensibility of Textual Requirements. In: *Proceedings of Videos in Digital Libraries – What's in it for Libraries, Scientists, and Publishers? (TPDL),* Zenodo, 2016

[133] KARRAS, O.; POLST, S.; SPÄTH, K.: Using Vision Videos in a Virtual Focus Group: Experiences and Recommendations. In: *Softwaretechnik-Trends* 41 (2021), No. 1.

[134] KARRAS, O.; RISCH, A.; SCHNEIDER, K.: Interrelating Use Cases and Associated Requirements by Links: An Eye Tracking Study on the Impact of Different Linking Variants on the Reading Behavior. In: *Proceedings of the 22nd International Conference on Evaluation and Assessment in Software Engineering 2018,* ACM, 2018, pp. 2–12

[135] KARRAS, O.; RISCH, A.; SCHNEIDER, K.: Linking Use Cases and Associated Requirements: On the Impact of Linking Variants on Reading Behavior. In: *Software Engineering and Software Management 2019,* Gesellschaft für Informatik e.V., 2019, pp. 95–96

[136] KARRAS, O.; SCHNEIDER, K.: Software Professionals are Not Directors: What Constitutes a Good Video? In: *2018 1st International Workshop on Learning from other Disciplines for Requirements Engineering (D4RE)* IEEE, 2018, pp. 18–21

[137] KARRAS, O.; SCHNEIDER, K.: An Interdisciplinary Guideline for the Production of Videos and Vision Videos by Software Professionals, Software Engineering Group, Leibniz Universität Hannover. Version: 1.0, 2020. `https://arxiv.org/abs/2001.06675`. – Technical Report

[138] KARRAS, O.; SCHNEIDER, K.; FRICKER, S. A.: *Experiment Data – 952 Assessments of 8 Vision Videos Regarding Overall Video Quality and 15 Individual Quality Characteristics.* `http://dx.doi.org/10.5281/zenodo.3549436`. Version: 1.0, 2019

[139] KARRAS, O.; SCHNEIDER, K.; FRICKER, S. A.: Representing Software Project Vision by Means of Video: A Quality Model for Vision Videos. In: *Journal of Systems and Software* 162 (2020)

[140] KARRAS, O.; UNGER-WINDELER, C.; GLAUER, L.; SCHNEIDER, K.: Video as a By-Product of Digital Prototyping: Capturing the Dynamic Aspect of Interaction. In: *2017 IEEE 25th International Requirements Engineering Conference Workshops (REW)* IEEE, 2017, pp. 118–124

[141] KEENEY, S.; MCKENNA, H.; HASSON, F.: *The Delphi Technique in Nursing and Health Research.* John Wiley & Sons, 2011

[142] KESSLER, E. H.; CHAKRABARTI, A. K.: Innovation Speed: A Conceptual Model of Context, Antecedents, and Outcomes. In: *Academy of Management Review* 21 (1996), No. 4, pp. 1143–1191

[143] KIESLING, S.: *Verbesserung des Requirements Engineering mit Hilfe von Videos und Informationsflüssen.* Logos Verlag Berlin GmbH, 2018

[144] KIESLING, S.; KARRAS, O.; SCHNEIDER, K.: ReqVidA – Requirements Video Analyzer. In: *Softwaretechnik-Trends* 36 (2015), No. 3

[145] KITCHENHAM, B.; BRERETON, P.: A Systematic Review of Systematic Review Process Research in Software Engineering. In: *Information and Software Technology* 55 (2013), No. 12, pp. 2049–2075

[146] KITCHENHAM, B. A.; BRERETON, P.; TURNER, M.; NIAZI, M. K.; LINKMAN, S.; PRETORIUS, R.; BUDGEN, D.: Refining the Systematic Literature Review Process – Two Participant-Observer Case Studies. In: *Empirical Software Engineering* 15 (2010), No. 6, pp. 618–653

[147] KITCHENHAM, B. A.; PFLEEGER, S. L.: Personal Opinion Surveys. In: *Guide to Advanced Empirical Software Engineering*. Springer, 2008, pp. 63–92

[148] KITCHENHAM, B. A.; S., C.: Guidelines for Performing Systematic Literature Reviews in Software Engineering, Software Engineering Group, School of Computer Science and Mathematics, Keele University. 2.3. 2007. – Technical Report

[149] KITTLAUS, H.-B.; FRICKER, S. A.: *Software Product Management: The ISPMA-Compliant Study Guide and Handbook*. Springer, 2017

[150] KLÜNDER, J.; KARRAS, O.; KORTUM, F.; CASSELT, M.; SCHNEIDER, K.: Different Views on Project Success: When Communication Is Not the Same. In: *Product-Focused Software Process Improvement*, Springer, 2017, pp. 497–507

[151] KNAUSS, E.; DAMIAN, D.; CLELAND-HUANG, J.; HELMS, R.: Patterns of Continuous Requirements Clarification. In: *Requirements Engineering* 20 (2015), No. 4, pp. 383–403

[152] KOFLER, C.; BHATTACHARYA, S.; LARSON, M.; CHEN, T.; HANJALIC, A.; CHANG, S.-F.: Uploader Intent for Online Video: Typology, Inference, and Applications. In: *IEEE Transactions on Multimedia* 17 (2015), No. 8

[153] KOFLER, C.; LARSON, M.; HANJALIC, A.: Intent-Aware Video Search Result Optimization. In: *IEEE Transactions on Multimedia* 16 (2014), No. 5

[154] KORKALA, M.; MAURER, F.: Waste Identification as the Means for Improving Communication in Globally Distributed Agile Software Development. In: *Journal of Systems and Software* 95 (2014), pp. 122–140

[155] LANDIS, J. R.; KOCH, G. G.: The Measurement of Observer Agreement for Categorical Data. In: *Biometrics* (1977), pp. 159–174

[156] LESSMANN, H.: *Durchführung einer Umfrage-Studie zur Nutzung von Code-Reviews in der Praxis*, Leibniz Universität Hannover, Master thesis, 2017

[157] LETHBRIDGE, T. C.; SINGER, J.; FORWARD, A.: How Software Engineers Use Documentation: The State of the Practice. In: *IEEE Software* 20 (2003), No. 6, pp. 35–39

[158] LISKIN, O.: How Artifacts Support and Impede Requirements Communication. In: *International Working Conference on Requirements Engineering: Foundation for Software Quality* Springer, 2015, pp. 132–147

[159] LISKIN, O.; SCHNEIDER, K.: Improving Project Communication with Virtual Team Boards. In: *2012 IEEE Seventh International Conference on Global Software Engineering Workshops* IEEE, 2012, pp. 35–36

[160] LUBIN, J.; FIBUSH, D.: *Sarnoff JND Vision Model*. 1997

[161] LYNN, G. S.; AKGÜN, A. E.:   Project Visioning: Its Components and Impact on New Product Success. In: *Journal of Product Innovation Management* 18 (2001), No. 6, pp. 374–387

[162] LYNN, G. S.; SKOV, R. B.; ABEL, K. D.: Practices that Support Team Learning and their Impact on Speed to Market and New Product Success. In: *Journal of Product Innovation Management: AN INTERNATIONAL PUBLICATION OF THE PRODUCT DEVELOPMENT & MANAGEMENT ASSOCIATION* 16 (1999), No. 5, pp. 439–454

[163] LYVER, D.: *Basics of the Video Production Diary*. Focal Press, 2013

[164] MACKAY, W. E.; FAYARD, A. L.:   Video Brainstorming and Prototyping: Techniques for Participatory Design. In: *CHI'99 Extended Abstracts on Human Factors in Computing Systems* ACM, 1999, pp. 118–119

[165] MACKAY, W. E.; RATZER, A. V.; JANECEK, P.:   Video Artifacts for Design: Bridging the Gap Between Abstraction and Detail. In: *Proceedings of the 3rd Conference on Designing Interactive Systems: Processes, Practices, Methods, and Techniques* ACM, 2000, pp. 72–82

[166] MAHOOD, Q.; VAN EERD, D.; IRVIN, E.:   Searching for Grey Literature for Systematic Reviews: Challenges and Benefits. In: *Research Synthesis Methods* 5 (2014), No. 3, pp. 221–234

[167] MANCINI, C.; ROGERS, Y.; BANDARA, A. K.; COE, T.; JEDRZEJCZYK, L.; JOINSON, A. N.; PRICE, B. A.; THOMAS, K.; NUSEIBEH, B.:   ContraVision: Exploring Users' Reactions to Futuristic Technology. In: *Proceedings of the SIGCHI Conference on Human Factors in Computing Systems*, 2010, pp. 153–162

[168] MANN, H. B.; WHITNEY, D. R.:   On a Test of Whether One of Two Random Variables is Stochastically Larger than the Other. In: *The Annals of Mathematical Statistics* (1947), pp. 50–60

[169] MANNIO, M.; NIKULA, U.:   Requirements Elicitation Using a Combination of Prototypes and Scenarios. In: *4th Workshop on Requirements Engineering (WER)* Citeseer, 2001, pp. 283–296

[170] MCGRATH, M. E.: *Product Strategy for High-Technology Companies: Accelerating your Business to Web Speed*. McGraw-Hill, 2001

[171] MERGENTHALER, C.: *Mechanisms for Interactive Viewing of Vision Videos in Requirements Engineering*, Leibniz Universität Hannover, Master thesis, 2019

[172] MICH, L.; FRANCH, M.; NOVI INVERARDI, P. L.: Market Research for Requirements Analysis Using Linguistic Tools. In: *Requirements Engineering* 9 (2004), No. 1, pp. 40–56

[173] MØLLER, L.; TOLLESTRUP, C.: *Creating Shared Understanding in Product Development Teams: How to 'Build the Beginning'.* Springer Science & Business Media, 2012

[174] MOLLÉRI, J. S.; PETERSEN, K.; MENDES, E.: An Empirically Evaluated Checklist for Surveys in Software Engineering. In: *Information and Software Technology* 119 (2020)

[175] MOODY, D. L.: Theoretical and Practical Issues in Evaluating the Quality of Conceptual Models: Current State and Future Directions. In: *Data & Knowledge Engineering* 55 (2005), No. 3, pp. 243–276

[176] MOORE, G. A.: *Crossing the Chasm: Marketing and Selling High-Tech Products to Mainstream Customers.* Harper Business Essentials, 1991

[177] MURPHY, M.; BLACK, N.; LAMPING, D.; MCKEE, C.; SANDERSON, C.; ASKHAM, J.; MARTEAU, T.: Consensus Development Methods, and Their Use in Clinical Guideline Development. In: *Health Technology Assessment* 2 (1998), No. 3

[178] MUSBURGER, R. B.: *Single-Camera Video Production.* Focal Press, 2012

[179] NAGELKERKE, N. J.: A Note on a General Definition of the Coefficient of Determination. In: *Biometrika* 78 (1991), No. 3, pp. 691–692

[180] NIKULA, U.; SAJANIEMI, J.; KÄLVIÄINEN, H.: *A State-of-the-Practice Survey on Requirements Engineering in Small-and Medium-sized Enterprises.* Lappeenranta University of Technology Lappeenranta, Finland, 2000

[181] NORMAN, D. A.: *The Design of Everyday Things.* Basic Books, 2013

[182] NUSEIBEH, B.; EASTERBROOK, S.: Requirements Engineering: A Roadmap. In: *Proceedings of the Conference on the Future of Software Engineering* ACM, 2000, pp. 35–46

[183] NWORIE, J.: Using the Delphi Technique in Educational Technology Research. In: *TechTrends* 55 (2011), No. 5

[184] OCHODEK, M.; KOPCZYŃSKA, S.: Perceived Importance of Agile Requirements Engineering Practices – A Survey. In: *Journal of Systems and Software* 143 (2018), pp. 29 – 43

[185] OWENS, J.; MILLERSON, G.: *Video Production Handbook.* Focal Press, 2011

[186] PEARSON, K.: X. On the Criterion that a Given System of Deviations from the Probable in the Case of a Correlated System of Variables is such that it can be Reasonably Supposed to

Have Arisen from Random Sampling. In: *The London, Edinburgh, and Dublin Philosophical Magazine and Journal of Science* 50 (1900), No. 302, pp. 157–175

[187] PENG, C.-Y. J.; LEE, K. L.; INGERSOLL, G. M.: An Introduction to Logistic Regression Analysis and Reporting. In: *The Journal of Educational Research* 96 (2002), No. 1, pp. 3–14

[188] PEREIRA, F.: A Triple User Characterization Model for Video Adaptation and Quality of Experience Evaluation. In: *2005 IEEE 7th Workshop on Multimedia Signal Processing* IEEE, 2005, pp. 1–4

[189] PERNSTÅL, J.; GORSCHEK, T.; FELDT, R.; FLORÉN, D.: Requirements Communication and Balancing in Large-Scale Software-Intensive Product Development. In: *Information and Software Technology* 67 (2015), pp. 44–64

[190] PETERSEN, K.; VAKKALANKA, S.; KUZNIARZ, L.: Guidelines for Conducting Systematic Mapping Studies in Software Engineering: An Update. In: *Information and Software Technology* 64 (2015), pp. 1–18

[191] PHAM, R.; HOLZMANN, H.; SCHNEIDER, K.; BRÜGGEMANN, C.: Tailoring Video Recording to Support Efficient GUI Testing and Debugging. In: *Software Quality Journal* 22 (2014), No. 2, pp. 273–292

[192] PHAM, R.; MEYER, S.; KITZMANN, I.; SCHNEIDER, K.: Interactive Multimedia Storyboard for Facilitating Stakeholder Interaction: Supporting Continuous Improvement in IT-Ecosystems. In: *2012 8th International Conference on the Quality of Information and Communications Technology* IEEE, 2012, pp. 120–123

[193] PIIRAINEN, K.; KOLFSCHOTEN, G.; LUKOSCH, S.: Unraveling Challenges in Collaborative Design: A Literature Study. In: *International Conference on Collaboration and Technology* Springer, 2009, pp. 247–261

[194] PINSON, M. H.; WOLF, S.: A New Standardized Method for Objectively Measuring Video Quality. In: *IEEE Transactions on Broadcasting* 50 (2004), No. 3, pp. 312–322

[195] POHL, K.: *Requirements Engineering: Fundamentals, Principles, and Techniques.* Springer Publishing Company, Incorporated, 2010

[196] POHL, K.; RUPP, C.: *Requirements Engineering Fundamentals: A Study Guide for the Certified Professional for Requirements Engineering Exam-Foundation Level-IREB Compliant.* Rocky Nook, Inc., 2016

[197] POLIT, D. F.; BECK, C. T.; OWEN, S. V.: Is the CVI an Acceptable Indicator of Content Validity? Appraisal and Recommendations. In: *Research in Nursing & Health* 30 (2007), No. 4, pp. 459–467

[198] RABISER, R.; SEYFF, N.; GRÜNBACHER, P.; MAIDEN, N.: Capturing Multimedia Requirements Descriptions with Mobile RE Tools. In: *2006 1st International Workshop on Multimedia Requirements Engineering (MERE'06 – RE'06 Workshop)* IEEE, 2006

[199] REASON, J.: *Human Error.* Cambridge University Press, 1990

[200] REASON, J.: Human Error: Models and Management. In: *BMJ* 320 (2000), No. 7237, pp. 768–770

[201] RIEGLER, M.; CALVET, L.; CALVET, A.; HALVORSEN, P.; GRIWODZ, C.: Exploitation of Producer Intent in Relation to Bandwidth and QoE for Online Video Streaming Services. In: *25th ACM Workshop on Network and Operating Systems Support for Digital Audio and Video* ACM, 2015, pp. 7–12

[202] ROBERTSON, S.; ROBERTSON, J.: *Mastering the Requirements Process: Getting Requirements Right.* Addison-Wesley, 2012

[203] ROBSON, C.; MCCARTAN, K.: *Real World Research.* John Wiley & Sons, 2016

[204] RODDEN, T. A.; FISCHER, J. E.; PANTIDI, N.; BACHOUR, K.; MORAN, S.: At Home with Agents: Exploring Attitudes towards Future Smart Energy Infrastructures. In: *Proceedings of the SIGCHI Conference on Human Factors in Computing Systems*, 2013, pp. 1173–1182

[205] ROHDE, A.: *Verification of Recommendations for the Production and Use of Vision Videos based on Subjective Video Quality Assessments*, Leibniz Universität Hannover, Bachelor thesis, 2020

[206] ROUIBAH, K.; AL-RAFEE, S.: Requirement Engineering Elicitation Methods: A Kuwaiti Empirical Study about Familiarity, Usage, and Perceived Value. In: *Information Management & Computer Security* (2009)

[207] RUNESON, P.; HÖST, M.: Guidelines for Conducting and Reporting Case Study Research in Software Engineering. In: *Empirical Software Engineering* 14 (2009), No. 2, pp. 131

[208] RUPP, C. et al.: *Requirements-Engineering und -Management: Aus der Praxis von klassisch bis agil.* Carl Hanser Verlag GmbH Co KG, 2014

[209] RUPP, C.; DOVICA, J.; BEZOLD, M.; WIENER, M.; FRYER, B.: Pimp my Spec: Tuning von Spezifikationen durch Videos. In: *Softwaretechnik-Trends* 39 (2018), No. 1, pp. 15–16

[210] RYAN, S.; O'CONNOR, R. V.: Acquiring and Sharing Tacit Knowledge in Software Development Teams: An Empirical Study. In: *Information and Software Technology* 55 (2013), No. 9, pp. 1614–1624

[211] SALDAÑA, J.: *The Coding Manual for Qualitative Researchers*. Sage, 2015

[212] SANDREY, M. A.; BULGER, S. M.: The Delphi Method: An Approach for Facilitating Evidence Based Practice in Athletic Training. In: *Athletic Training Education Journal* 3 (2008), No. 4, pp. 135–142

[213] SCHNEIDER, K.: Rationale as a By-Product. In: *Rationale Management in Software Engineering*. Springer, 2006, pp. 91–109

[214] SCHNEIDER, K.: Generating Fast Feedback in Requirements Elicitation. In: *International Working Conference on Requirements Engineering: Foundation for Software Quality* Springer, 2007, pp. 160–174

[215] SCHNEIDER, K.: Focusing Spontaneous Feedback to Support System Evolution. In: *2011 19th IEEE International Requirements Engineering Conference (RE)* IEEE, 2011, pp. 165–174

[216] SCHNEIDER, K.; BERTOLLI, L. M.: Video Variants for CrowdRE: How to Create Linear Videos, Vision Videos, and Interactive Videos. In: *2019 IEEE 27th International Requirements Engineering Conference Workshops (REW)* IEEE, 2019, pp. 186–192

[217] SCHNEIDER, K.; BUSCH, M.; KARRAS, O.; SCHRAPEL, M.; ROHS, M.: Refining Vision Videos. In: *International Working Conference on Requirements Engineering: Foundation for Software Quality* Springer, 2019, pp. 135–150

[218] SCHNEIDER, K.; KARRAS, O.; FINGER, A.; ZIBELL, B.: Reframing Societal Discourse as Requirements Negotiation: Vision Statement. In: *2017 IEEE 25th International Requirements Engineering Conference Workshops (REW)* IEEE, 2017, pp. 188–193

[219] SCHÖN, D. A.: *The Reflective Practitioner: How Professionals Think in Action*. Routledge, 2017

[220] SEGAL, J.: When Software Engineers met Research Scientists: A Case Study. In: *Empirical Software Engineering* 10 (2005), No. 4, pp. 517–536

[221] SESHADRINATHAN, K.; BOVIK, A. C.: Motion Tuned Spatio-Temporal Quality Assessment of Natural Videos. In: *IEEE Transactions on Image Processing* 19 (2010), No. 2, pp. 335–350

[222] SHAHID, M.; ROSSHOLM, A.; LÖVSTRÖM, B.; ZEPERNICK, H.-J.: No-Reference Image and Video Quality Assessment: A Classification and Review of Recent Approaches. In: *EURASIP Journal on Image and Video Processing* 2014 (2014), No. 1

[223] SHAN, Y.; LIU, L.; PENG, F.: MEGORE: Multimedia Enhanced Goal-Oriented Requirement Elicitation Experience in China. In: *2008 3rd International Workshop on Multimedia and Enjoyable Requirements Engineering – Beyond MERE Descriptions and with More Fun and Games* IEEE, 2008, pp. 37–41

[224] SHANNON, C. E.; WEAVER, W.: The Mathematical Theory of Communication, University of Illinois Press, 1949

[225] SHAPIRO, S. S.; WILK, M. B.: An Analysis of Variance Test for Normality. In: *Biometrika* 52 (1965), No. 3/4, pp. 591–611

[226] SINEK, S.: *Start with Why: How Great Leaders Inspire Everyone to Take Action.* Penguin, 2009

[227] SJØBERG, D. I. K.; ANDA, B.; ARISHOLM, E.; DYBÅ, T.; JØRGENSEN, M.; KARAHASANOVIC, A.; KOREN, E. F.; VOKÁC, M.: Conducting Realistic Experiments in Software Engineering. In: *Proceedings International Symposium on Empirical Software Engineering* IEEE, 2002, pp. 17–26

[228] SLATER, S. F.; NARVER, J. C.: Market Orientation and the Learning Organization. In: *Journal of Marketing* 59 (1995), No. 3, pp. 63–74

[229] SMOOTS, G. C.; GARSTENAUER, A.; BLACKBURN, T.: Measuring System Usability During Requirement Engineering: Requirements Engineering. In: *2016 International Conference on Information Systems Engineering (ICISE)* IEEE, 2016, pp. 68–72

[230] SNYDER, C.: *Paper Prototyping: The Fast and Easy Way to Design and Refine User Interfaces.* Morgan Kaufmann, 2003

[231] SONG, X. M.; MONTOYA-WEISS, M. M.: Critical Development Activities for Really New Versus Incremental Products. In: *Journal of Product Innovation Management* 15 (1998), No. 2, pp. 124–135

[232] SPEARMAN, C.: The Proof and Measurement of Association Between Two Things. In: *The American Journal of Psychology* 100 (1987), No. 3/4, pp. 441–471

[233] STACHOWIAK, H.: *Allgemeine Modelltheorie.* Springer-Verlag, 1973

[234] STANGL, H.; CREIGHTON, O.: Continuous Demonstration. In: *2011 4th International Workshop on Multimedia and Enjoyable Requirements Engineering* IEEE, 2011, pp. 38–41

[235] STANGL, H. F.: *Script: A Framework for Scenario-Driven Prototyping,* Technische Universität München, PhD thesis, 2012

[236] STAPEL, K.: *Informationsflusstheorie der Softwareentwicklung.* Verlag Dr. Hut, 2012

[237] STUDENT: The Probable Error of a Mean. In: *Biometrika* (1908), pp. 1–25

[238] SUTCLIFFE, A.; SAWYER, P.: Requirements Elicitation: Towards the Unknown Unknowns. In: *2013 21st IEEE International Requirements Engineering Conference (RE)* IEEE, 2013, pp. 92–104

[239] SWELLER, J.; AYRES, P.; KALYUGA, S.: *Cognitive Load Theory*. Vol. 1. 2011

[240] TESSAROLO, P.: Is Integration Enough for Fast Product Development? An Empirical Investigation of the Contextual Effects of Product Vision. In: *Journal of Product Innovation Management* 24 (2007), No. 1, pp. 69–82

[241] TONGCO, M. D. C.: Purposive Sampling as a Tool for Informant Selection. In: *Ethnobotany Research and Applications* 5 (2007), pp. 147–158

[242] UNIVERSITY OF LEEDS: *Video Guidelines and Quality Assurance.* http://comms.leeds.ac.uk/video/video-guidelines/

[243] VAN DEN BRANDEN LAMBRECHT, C. J.; VERSCHEURE, O.: Perceptual Quality Measure Using a Spatio-Temporal Model of the Human Visual System. In: *Digital Video Compression: Algorithms and Technologies 1996* Vol. 2668 International Society for Optics and Photonics, 1996, pp. 450–462

[244] VAN SOLINGEN, R.; BERGHOUT, E.: *The Goal/Question/Metric Method: A Practical Guide for Quality Improvement of Software Development.* McGraw-Hill, 1999

[245] VERSCHEURE, O.; FROSSARD, P.; HAMDI, M.: User-Oriented QoS Analysis in MPEG-2 Video Delivery. In: *Real-Time Imaging* 5 (1999), No. 5, pp. 305–314

[246] VISTISEN, P.; POULSEN, S. B.: Return of the Vision Video: Can Corporate Vision Videos Serve as Setting for Participation? In: *7th Nordic Design Research Conference*, 2017

[247] VRANJEŠ, M.; RIMAC-DRLJE, S.; GRGIĆ, K.: Review of Objective Video Quality Metrics and Performance Comparison using Different Databases. In: *Signal Processing: Image Communication* 28 (2013), No. 1, pp. 1–19

[248] WAGNER, S.; FERNÁNDEZ, D. M.; FELDERER, M.; VETRÒ, A.; KALINOWSKI, M.; WIERINGA, R.; PFAHL, D.; CONTE, T.; CHRISTIANSSON, M.-T.; GREER, D. et al.: Status Quo in Requirements Engineering: A Theory and a Global Family of Surveys. In: *ACM Transactions on Software Engineering and Methodology (TOSEM)* 28 (2019), No. 2

[249] WANG, Z.; LU, L.; BOVIK, A. C.: Video Quality Assessment based on Structural Distortion Measurement. In: *Signal Processing: Image Communication* 19 (2004), No. 2, pp. 121–132

[250] WHITEHEAD, J.: Collaboration in Software Engineering: A Roadmap. In: *Future of Software Engineering (FOSE'07)* IEEE, 2007, pp. 214–225

[251] WIEGERS, K.; BEATTY, J.: *Software Requirements*. Pearson Education, 2013

[252] WINKLER, S.; MOHANDAS, P.: The Evolution of Video Quality Measurement: From PSNR to Hybrid Metrics. In: *IEEE Transactions on Broadcasting* 54 (2008), No. 3, pp. 660–668

[253] WINKLER, S.: Perceptual Distortion Metric for Digital Color Video. In: *Human Vision and Electronic Imaging IV* Vol. 3644 International Society for Optics and Photonics, 1999, pp. 175–185

[254] WINKLER, S.: Video Quality and Beyond. In: *2007 15th European Signal Processing Conference* IEEE, 2007, pp. 150–153

[255] WINKLER, S.: Video Quality Measurement Standards – Current Status and Trends. In: *2009 7th International Conference on Information, Communications and Signal Processing (ICICS)* IEEE, 2009, pp. 1–5

[256] WNUK, K.; GORSCHEK, T.; CALLELE, D.; KARLSSON, E.-A.; ÅHLIN, E.; REGNELL, B.: Supporting Scope Tracking and Visualization for Very Large-Scale Requirements Engineering-Utilizing FSC+, Decision Patterns, and Atomic Decision Visualizations. In: *IEEE Transactions on Software Engineering* 42 (2015), No. 1, pp. 47–74

[257] WOHLIN, C.; RUNESON, P.; HÖST, M.; OHLSSON, M. C.; REGNELL, B.; WESSLÉN, A.: *Experimentation in Software Engineering*. Springer Science & Business Media, 2012

[258] XU, H.; CREIGHTON, O.; BOULILA, N.; BRUEGGE, B.: From Pixels to Bytes: Evolutionary Scenario Based Design with Video. In: *Proceedings of the ACM SIGSOFT 20th International Symposium on the Foundations of Software Engineering* ACM, 2012, pp. 1–4

[259] XU, H.; CREIGHTON, O.; BOULILA, N.; DEMMEL, R.: User Model and System Model: The Yin and Yang in User-Centered Software Development. In: *Proceedings of the 2013 ACM International Symposium on New Ideas, New Paradigms, and Reflections on Programming & Software* ACM, 2013, pp. 91–100

[260] YU, X.; PETTER, S.: Understanding Agile Software Development Practices Using Shared Mental Models Theory. In: *Information and Software Technology* 56 (2014), No. 8, pp. 911–921

[261] YUSOFF, M. S. B.: ABC of Content Validation and Content Validity Index Calculation. In: *Education in Medicine Journal* 11 (2019), No. 2

[262] ZACHOS, K.; MAIDEN, N.: ART-SCENE: Enhancing Scenario Walkthroughs with Multi-Media Scenarios. In: *2004 IEEE 12th International Requirements Engineering Conference (RE)* IEEE, 2004, pp. 360–361

[263] ZHOU, X.; JIN, Y.; ZHANG, H.; LI, S.; HUANG, X.: A Map of Threats to Validity of Systematic Literature Reviews in Software Engineering. In: *2016 23rd Asia-Pacific Software Engineering Conference* IEEE, 2016, pp. 153–160

[264] ZOWGHI, D.; COULIN, C.: Requirements Elicitation: A Survey of Techniques, Approaches, and Tools. In: *Engineering and Managing Software Requirements*. Springer, 2005, pp. 19–46

Curriculum Vitae

Oliver Karras
born on October 27, 1987 in Celle, Germany

Professional Experience

since 04/2021	**Data Scientist** at *Data Science & Digital Libraries Research Group, Leibniz Information Centre for Science and Technology – TIB*, Germany
01/2016 – 03/2021	**Research Associate** at *Software Engineering Group, Leibniz Universität Hannover*, Germany
10/2011 – 12/2015	**Student Associate** at *Software Engineering Group, Leibniz Universität Hannover*, Germany
07/2007 – 03/2008	**Staff Service Soldier** at *Aufklärungslehrkompanie 90 Basic Military Service*, Germany

Professional Activities

since 11/2019	**Deputy Speaker** of *Fachgruppe Requirements Engineering, Gesellschaft für Informatik*
12/04/2021 – 15/04/2021	Organizing Committee: **Social Media and Publicity Co-Chair** *International Working Conference on Requirements Engineering: Foundation for Software Quality 2021*
12/04/2021 – 15/04/2021	Program Committee Member: **Posters and Tools** *International Working Conference on Requirements Engineering: Foundation for Software Quality 2021*
31/08/2020 – 04/09/2020	Organizing Committee: **Student Volunteer Co-Chair** *28th IEEE International Requirements Engineering Conference 2020*
31/08/2020 – 04/09/2020	Program Committee Member: **Posters and Tool Demos** *28th IEEE International Requirements Engineering Conference 2020*
24/03/2020 – 27/03/2020	Program Committee Member: **Posters and Tools** *26th International Working Conference on Requirements Engineering: Foundation for Software Quality 2020*
27/11/2019 – 29/11/2019	Program Committee Member: **Full Research Papers** *20th International Conference on Product-Focused Software Process Improvement 2019*

Education

01/2016 – 03/2021	**Doctor of Science: Computer Science,** Leibniz Universität Hannover, Germany
10/2013 – 12/2015	**Master of Science: Computer Science,** *Leibniz Universität Hannover*, Germany
04/2010 – 09/2013	**Bachelor of Science: Computer Science,** *Leibniz Universität Hannover*, Germany
04/2008 – 03/2010	**Bachelor of Science: Computer Science,** *Christian-Albrechts-Universität zu Kiel*, Germany
09/2000 – 06/2007	**School Education with General University Entrance Qualification,** *Kaiserin-Auguste-Viktoria Gymnasium*, Germany

List of Scientific Publications

1. Jil Klünder, Melanie Busch, Natalie Dehn, **Oliver Karras**: *Towards Shaping the Software Lifecycle with Methods and Practices*, IEEE/ACM International Conference on Software and System Processes, ACM, 2021.

2. Jil Klünder, Dzejlana Karajic, Paolo Tell, **Oliver Karras**, Christian Münkel, Jürgen Münch, Stephen G. MacDonell, Regina Hebig, Marco Kuhrmann: *Determining Context Factors for Hybrid Development Methods with Trained Models*, Software Engineering 2021, Gesellschaft für Informatik e.V. 2021.

3. **Oliver Karras**: *Geteilte Projektvision mittels Vision Videos: Ein Medium für proaktiven Informationsaustausch*, Gesellschaft für Informatik, GI Radar 278: Vision Videos im Requirements Engineering, 2021.

4. **Oliver Karras**, Svenja Polst, Kathleen Späth: *Using Vision Videos in a Virtual Focus Group: Experiences and Recommendations*, Softwaretechnik-Trends, 41 (1), 2021.

5. Anne Heß, Marcus Trapp, **Oliver Karras**, Norbert Seyff: *Welcome Message from the D4RE 2020 Workshop Chairs*, 4th International Workshop on Learning from Other Disciplines for Requirements Engineering, 2020.

6. Jil Klünder, Julian Horstmann, **Oliver Karras**: *Identifying the Mood of a Software Development Team by Analyzing Text-Based Communication in Chats with Machine Learning*, Proceedings of the 8th International Working Conference on Human-Centered Software Engineering, 2020.

7. Fabian Kortum, Jil Klünder, **Oliver Karras**, Wasja Brunotte, Kurt Schneider: *Which Information Help Agile Teams the Most? An Experience Report on the Problems and Needs*, 46th Euromicro Conference on Software Engineering and Advanced Applications, 2020.

8. Jil Klünder, **Oliver Karras**, Kurt Schneider: *Affecting Mood, Motivation and Productivity in Requirements Engineering Meetings and Beyond: A Research Vision*, IEEE 28th International Requirements Engineering Conference Workshops, IEEE 2020.

9. Jil Klünder, Dzejlana Karajic, Paolo Tell, **Oliver Karras**, Christian Münkel, Jürgen Münch, Stephen G. MacDonell, Regina Hebig, Marco Kuhrmann: *Determining Context Factors for Hybrid Development Methods with Trained Models*, IEEE/ACM International Conference on Software and System Processes, ACM 2020.

10. Melanie Busch, **Oliver Karras**, Kurt Schneider, Maike Ahrens: *Vision Meets Visualization: Are Animated Videos an Alternative?*, International Working Conference on Requirements Engineering: Foundation for Software Quality, Springer 2020.

11. Anne Heß, Marcus Trapp, **Oliver Karras**, Norbert Seyff: *Let's get "InspiRE-D" for RE by Other Disciplines – A Creativity-Based Approach*, Joint Proceedings of REFSQ-2020 Workshops, Doctoral Symposium, Live Studies, and Poster Track, 2020.

12. **Oliver Karras**, Kurt Schneider, Samuel A. Fricker: *Representing Software Project Vision by Means of Video: A Quality Model for Vision Videos*, Journal of Systems and Software, 162, 2020.

13. **Oliver Karras**, Kurt Schneider: *An Interdisciplinary Guideline for the Production of Videos and Vision Videos by Software Professionals*, Technical Report (1.0), Leibniz Universität Hannover, Software Engineering Group, 2020.

14. **Oliver Karras**, Jil Klünder, Kurt Schneider: *Tool-Supported Experiments for Continuously Collecting Data of Subjective Video Quality Assessments During Video Playback*, Softwaretechnik-Trends, 40 (1), 2020.

15. Gerald Heller, Hartmut Schmitt, Carsten Schlipf, **Oliver Karras**, Anne Heß: *Potentiale und Herausforderungen in der Zusammenarbeit zwischen RE und UX*, Softwaretechnik-Trends, 40 (1), 2020.

16. Fabian Kortum, **Oliver Karras**, Jil Klünder, Kurt Schneider: *Towards a Better Understanding of Team-Driven Dynamics in Agile Software Projects - A Characterization and Visualization Support in JIRA*, International Conference on Product-Focused Software Process Improvement, Springer 2019.

17. **Oliver Karras**: *Communicating Stakeholders' Needs – Vision Videos to Disclose, Discuss, and Align Mental Models for Shared Understanding*, IEEE Software Blog 2019.

18. Larissa Chazette, **Oliver Karras**, Kurt Schneider: *Do End-Users Want Explanations? Analyzing the Role of Explainability as an Emerging Aspect of Non-Functional Requirements*, IEEE 27th International Requirements Engineering Conference, IEEE 2019.

19. Anne Heß, Marcus Trapp, **Oliver Karras**, Norbert Seyff, Kim Lauenroth: *Welcome to the 3rd International Workshop on Learning from Other Disciplines for Requirements Engineering*, IEEE 27th International Requirements Engineering Conference Workshops, IEEE 2019.

20. Gerald Heller, Carsten Schlipf, **Oliver Karras**, Hartmut Schmitt, Anne Heß: *Wie interagieren UX-Professionals mit ihrem Umfeld und ihren Kollegen?*, Mensch und Computer 2019 – Usability Professionals, Gesellschaft für Informatik e.V. und German UPA e.V. 2019.

21. Anne Heß, Marcus Trapp, Kim Lauenroth, Norbert Seyff, **Oliver Karras**: *Welcome to the 2nd International Workshop on Learning from Other Disciplines for Requirements Engineering*, Joint Proceedings of REFSQ-2019 Workshops, Doctoral Symposium, Live Studies Track, and Poster Track, 2019.

22. Kurt Schneider, Melanie Busch, **Oliver Karras**, Maximilian Schrapel, Michael Rohs: *Refining Vision Videos*, International Working Conference on Requirements Engineering: Foundation for Software Quality, Springer 2019.

23. **Oliver Karras**, Alexandra Risch, Kurt Schneider: *Linking Use Cases and Associated Requirements: On the Impact of Linking Variants on Reading Behavior*, Software Engineering and

Software Management 2019, Gesellschaft für Informatik e.V. 2019.

24. **Oliver Karras**: *Software Professionals' Attitudes Towards Video as a Medium in Requirements Engineering*, International Conference on Product-Focused Software Process Improvement, Springer 2018.

25. Jil Klünder, **Oliver Karras**, Nils Prenner, Kurt Schneider: *Modeling and Analyzing Information Flow in Development Teams as a Pipe System*, MODELS 2018 Workshops, 2018.

26. **Oliver Karras**, Kurt Schneider: *Software Professionals are Not Directors: What Constitutes a Good Video?*, 1st International Workshop on Learning from other Disciplines for Requirements Engineering, IEEE 2018.

27. **Oliver Karras**, Alexandra Risch, Kurt Schneider: *Interrelating Use Cases and Associated Requirements by Links: An Eye Tracking Study on the Impact of Different Linking Variants on the Reading Behavior*, 22nd International Conference on Evaluation and Assessment in Software Engineering, ACM 2018.

28. Zahra Shakeri Hossein Abad, **Oliver Karras**, Kurt Schneider, Ken Barker, Mike Bauer: *Task Interruption in Software Development Projects: What Makes some Interruptions More Disruptive than Others?*, 22nd International Conference on Evaluation and Assessment in Software Engineering, ACM 2018.

29. **Oliver Karras**, Ahmad Hamadeh, Kurt Schneider: *Enriching Requirements Specifications with Videos – The Use of Videos to Support Requirements Communication*, Softwaretechnik-Trends, 38 (1), 2018.

30. Fabien Patrick Viertel, **Oliver Karras**, Kurt Schneider: *Vulnerability Recognition by Execution Trace Differentiation*, Softwaretechnik-Trends, 37 (3), 2017.

31. Jil Klünder, **Oliver Karras**, Fabian Kortum, Mathias Casselt, Kurt Schneider: *Different Views on Project Success: When Communication Is Not the Same*, International Conference on Product-Focused Software Process Improvement, Springer 2017.

32. **Oliver Karras**, Jil Klünder, Kurt Schneider: *Is Task Board Customization Beneficial?*, International Conference on Product-Focused Software Process Improvement, Springer 2017.

33. Kurt Schneider, **Oliver Karras**, Anne Finger, Barbara Zibell: *Reframing Societal Discourse as Requirements Negotiation: Vision Statement*, IEEE 25th International Requirements Engineering Conference Workshops, IEEE 2017.

34. **Oliver Karras**, Carolin Unger-Windeler, Lennart Glauer, Kurt Schneider: *Video as a By-Product of Digital Prototyping: Capturing the Dynamic Aspect of Interaction*, IEEE 25th International Requirements Engineering Conference Workshops, IEEE 2017.

35. Zahra Shakeri Hossein Abad, **Oliver Karras**, Parisa Ghazi, Martin Glinz, Guenther Ruhe, Kurt Schneider: *What Works Better? A Study of Classifying Requirements*, IEEE 25th International Requirements Engineering Conference, IEEE 2017.

36. **Oliver Karras**, Jil Klünder, Kurt Schneider: *Indicating Potential Risks for Project Success Based on Requirements Fulfillment*, Softwaretechnik-Trends, 37 (2), 2017.

37. Jil Klünder, **Oliver Karras**, Fabian Kortum, Kurt Schneider: *Forecasting Communication Behavior in Student Software Projects*, Proceedings of the 12th International Conference on Predictive Models and Data Analytics in Software Engineering, ACM 2016.

38. **Oliver Karras**, Jil Klünder, Kurt Schneider: *Enrichment of Requirements Specifications with Videos – Enhancing the Comprehensibility of Textual Requirements*, Proceedings of the Workshop: Videos in Digital Libraries – What's in it for Libraries, Scientists, and Publishers?, Zenodo 2016.

39. **Oliver Karras**, Stephan Kiesling, Kurt Schneider: *Supporting Requirements Elicitation by Tool-Supported Video Analysis*, IEEE 24th International Requirements Engineering Conference, IEEE 2016.

40. **Oliver Karras**: *Tool-Supported Analysis of Requirements Workshop Videos*, Master Thesis, Leibniz Universität Hannover, Software Engineering Group, 2015.

41. Stephan Kiesling, **Oliver Karras**, Kurt Schneider: *ReqVidA – Requirements Video Analyzer*, Softwaretechnik-Trends, 36 (3), 2015.

42. Henning Pohl, Markus Hettig, **Oliver Karras**, Hatice Ötztürk, Michael Rohs: *CapCouch: Home Control with a Posture-Sensing Couch*, Adjunct Proceedings of the ACM International Joint Conference on Pervasive and Ubiquitous Computing and ACM International Symposium on Wearable Computers, ACM 2015.

43. **Oliver Karras**: *Supporting User Story Management with a Mobile Application*, Bachelor Thesis, Leibniz Universität Hannover, Software Engineering Group, 2013.